EVEN AT THE DOOR

EVEN
AT
THE
DOOR

by
G. EDWARD REID
Best-selling Author of *It's Your Money, Isn't It?*

The author assumes responsibility for the accuracy of material quoted in this book. In all cases the emphasis has been supplied by the author to highlight special significance in quoted material.

Unless otherwise noted all Bible texts quoted are from The New King James Version. Copyright © 1979, 1980, 1982, Thomas Nelson, Inc., Publishers.

Texts credited to NEB are from *The New English Bible.* © The Delegates of the Oxford University Press and the Syndics of the Cambridge University Press 1961, 1970. Reprinted by permission.

Verses marked TLB are taken from *The Living Bible*, copyright © 1971 by Tyndale House Publishers, Wheaton, Ill. Used by permission.

This book was
Edited by Lincoln E. Steed
Designed by Byron Steele
Cover photo: © COMSTOCK, 1994
Typeset: Times 11/13

Printed by Review and Herald Graphics,
55 West Oak Ridge Drive,
Hagerstown, MD 21740

PRINTED IN U.S.A.

03 02 01 00   10 9 8 7 6 5 4 3

ISBN 0-8280-0895-7

Foreword

Why are so many church members saying, "We never hear sermons anymore about the second coming of Christ"?

Why, when we are quite literally on the threshold of eternity, are so few excitedly shouting the good news?

Will the judgments of God have to start falling on a sinful earth before we really get serious about where we are in time and the nearness of Christ's coming?

Troubled by these questions I spent much time re-studying the Bible's great time prophecies and everything I could find in the writings of Ellen White regarding the end of time, the second coming of Christ, and related topics. What I found amazed me! If the Bible and the Spirit of Prophecy are to be believed, we are literally on the threshold of eternity. And very soon Jesus, who has delayed His coming in mercy toward the Laodicean church, is about to say, "Ready or not, here I come!"

I have shared this material at churches, camp meetings, spiritual retreats, and in private conversations, and many others seem to have the same convictions.

We are told that when it is too late, many will come to us and say, "You knew these things were coming; why didn't you tell us?" I believe that some Adventists feel reluctant to share the second coming of Christ with others because of lack of knowledge or confidence. My hope is that this book will give a renewed sense of urgency and confidence in the promise of Jesus, "I will come again!"

My study has led me to believe that we could well be living in the last decade of Earth's history. But this book is not an attempt to set the day and hour of Christ's coming. It is only a sincere attempt to tell you that it is near—very near!

If you are an "Adventist" I believe that you will find this book to be good news. It is my prayer that you will have the fires of your "first love" rekindled and that you will transfer your affections permanently from this world to the next.

Contents

CHAPTER 1

An End-Time Generation

With the year 2000 looming up and almost staring us in the face, many are wondering out loud if perhaps there may be some eschatological significance in that date.

Will the end of this century mean anything more to mankind than the dawning of another millennium? Visit your local Christian bookstore and you will get the impression that it is. One can easily find more than fifty books with words in the titles like "end," "1994," "1996," "2000," "Armageddon," "messiah," "rapture," "tribulation," and "last days." It is quite apparent that the evangelical world is expecting the end of the world in this decade—or at least the ushering in of the long awaited millennial reign of Christ.

Ever since Jesus left this earth when the cloud received Him out of the sight of the disciples, men have been wondering and speculating about His return. Jesus did not want us to forget about His coming. The New Testament alone mentions the Second Coming more than 300 times. To many Christians the Second Coming is the "Blessed Hope." This hope is what gives them courage to carry on in the face of trials and tribulations.

After talking about all manner of signs and the gospel going to all the world in Matthew 24, Jesus says, "Now learn this parable from the fig tree; when its branch has already become tender and puts forth leaves, you know that summer is near. So you also, when you see all these things, know that it is near, at the very doors. Assuredly, I say to you, this generation will by no means pass away till all these things are fulfilled. Heaven and earth will pass away, but My words will by no means pass away." (Matthew 24:32-35, NKJV)

When commenting on these verses Ellen White states, "At the close of the great papal persecution, Christ declared, the sun should be darkened, and the moon should not give her light. Next, the stars should fall from heaven. And He says, 'Learn a parable of the fig tree; When his branch is yet tender, and putteth forth leaves, ye know that summer is nigh: so likewise ye, when ye shall see all these things, know that He is near, even at the door.' (Matthew 24:32, 33, margin)

"Christ has given signs of His coming He declares that we may know when He is near, even at the doors. He says of those who see these signs, 'This generation shall not pass, till all these things be fulfilled.' These signs have appeared. <u>Now we know of a surety that the Lord's coming is at hand</u>. 'Heaven and earth shall pass away,' He says, 'but My words shall not pass away.'" *(The Desire of Ages,* p. 632)

I believe that the evidence is overwhelming that we are the generation that will see the actual, literal, second coming of Christ in the clouds of heaven. Yes, of course, for the Christian the second coming is in a sense never more than a lifetime away because the moment you die the next conscious thought is at the resurrection and the coming of Jesus. But the actual, literal return of Jesus will happen someday, and I believe the evidence is overwhelming that it will be in our generation. And while it could even occur in this decade, before the year 2000, this book is not being written to set a date for the Second Coming. Its purpose is only to point out clearly that the coming is near—at the very door.

Yes, Ellen White warned us to beware of exact time predictions. "There are those who claim to know <u>the very day and hour</u> of our Lord's appearing," she wrote. "Very earnest are they in mapping out the future. But the Lord has warned them off the ground they occupy. The <u>exact time</u> of the second coming of the Son of man is God's mystery." *(The Desire of Ages,* pp. 632, 633) But she balances this warning with a very pointed requirement. "Though no man knoweth the *day* nor the *hour* of His coming, we are instructed and required to know when it is near. We are further taught that to disregard His warning, and refuse or neglect to know when His advent is near, will be as fatal for us as it was for those who lived in the days of Noah not to know when the flood was coming." *(The Great Controversy,* pp. 370, 371, italics in original)

I believe the evidence is clear that:

• The appointed time is almost here;
• We can know for a certainty where we are in time; (See *Testimonies,* vol. 4, p. 592.)

- We are near the second coming of Christ and the conclusion of "the time of the end" that began in 1798;
- We are not waiting for Jesus—He is waiting for us to claim the promise of the Holy Spirit's power to perfect our characters and to empower us to take the gospel to all the world;
- Any generation since 1844—the last fixed date in the Bible's great time prophecies—could have witnessed the second coming of Christ if it had been really in earnest about fulfilling the great gospel commission;
- Jesus could have come before now—perhaps as early as around 1890, but the Second Coming has been delayed because of God's mercy; There is a time beyond which Jesus cannot and will not wait. There is a set time for the Second Coming that only the Father knows. And Jesus will not wait longer than the set time; and
- All of the Bible's time prophecies with ending dates have run their course. The next great eschatological event will be the close of the investigative judgment and the second coming of Christ.

All of the above points are given particular force because of the so-called "six thousand year theory" as an overall umbrella time prophecy. This position is defensible from Scripture and is also supported strongly by the Spirit of Prophecy, as well as the testimony of Bible scholars from the early church fathers on. Martin Luther, William Miller, J. N. Andrews, S. N. Haskell, J. N. Loughborough (the Adventist pioneer/historian), and many others took the 6,000 years as fact.

Though God is eternal, He deals with man within the parameters of time. Biblical chronology and prophecy present a time period of approximately 7,000 years from the creation of the earth to the earth made new. The 6,000 years for the great controversy struggle is to be followed by a 1,000-year "sabbath" while the earth lies desolate during the millennium.

It really concerns me when some Adventists state that they believe Christ will return someday. "It could be tonight," they say, "or it could be 100 years from now." From my perspective neither of these statements is true. Jesus could not literally come tonight because there are certain events that must happen first, i.e., the mercy judgments, the Sunday law, the death decree, and the seven last plagues. On the other hand, it will not be a hundred years from now, as we will see.

We can have a sense of meaning, purpose, and fulfillment in our lives by recognizing that we are a part of God's plan. Salvation history and the story of the great controversy is still being written, and **we are writing the conclusion—the final chapter!**

How sad, then, that we spend so much of our time arguing among ourselves about such things as how the tithe should be used, whether or not women should be ordained, or how much jewelry God will allow. These questions, as important as they are, should have been settled years ago. It seems to me that the wise will be seeking to understand the prophecies, sharing their understanding with others, and preparing themselves for Jesus' return.

By studying the prophecies of Daniel and Revelation, we can see the big picture come into focus. Ellen White over and over again encouraged the study of these great books.

"We are standing on the threshold of great and solemn events. Many of the prophecies are about to be fulfilled in quick succession. . . As we near the close of this world's history, the prophecies relating to the last days especially demand our study." *(Testimonies to Ministers, p. 116)*

"The perils of the last days are upon us, and in our work we are to warn the people of the danger they are in. Let not the solemn scenes which prophecy has revealed be left untouched. If our people were half awake, if they realized the nearness of the events portrayed in the Revelation, a reformation would be wrought in our churches, and many more would believe the message. We have no time to lose; God calls upon us to watch for souls as they that must give an account." *(Ibid.,* p. 118)

"The attention of the people should be called to the momentous event which is so near at hand. The signs of the times should be kept fresh before their minds. The prophetic visions of Daniel and John foretell a period of moral darkness and declension; but at the time of the end, the time in which we are now living, the vision was to speak and not lie. When the signs predicted begin to come to pass, the waiting, watching ones are bidden to look up, and lift up their heads and rejoice because their redemption draweth nigh." *(Testimonies for the Church,* vol. 5, pp. 9, 10)

Living 2,000 years before the time of Christ, Abraham saw the promises "afar off." In fact it was 4,000 years away!

Daniel, living about 500 years before Christ, saw that the prophecies outlined in his book would be understood at the time of the end.

"The apostle Paul warned the church not to look for the coming of Christ in his day. 'That day shall not come,' he says, 'except there come a falling away first, and that man of sin be revealed.' II Thessalonians 2:3. Not until after the great apostasy, and the long period of the reign of the 'man of sin,' can we look for the advent of our Lord. The 'man of sin,' which is also styled the 'mystery of iniquity,' 'the son of perdition,' and 'that wicked,' represents the papacy, which as foretold in prophecy, was to maintain its supremacy for 1260 years. This period ended in 1798. The coming of Christ could not take place before that time. Paul covers with his caution the whole of the Christian dispensation down to the year 1798. It is this side of that time that the message of Christ's second coming is to be proclaimed." *(The Great Controversy,* p. 356)

We are now living 150 years since Christ began the final phase of His ministry! All the Bible's major time prophecies have run their course. In fact no time prophecy with a fixed date extends beyond 1844.

The increase of knowledge spoken of in Daniel 12:4 primarily refers to an increase of prophetic knowledge or spiritual things, yet it seems to follow that when there is a spiritual awakening there is also an accompanying increase of general and technical knowledge. It is a matter of historical record that the great Protestant Reformation triggered the Renaissance and the Industrial Revolution. In like manner, following the great awakening of the last century there was a tremendous explosion of technical knowledge as well. This is particularly true when we look at communication and travel.

The increase of knowledge is very striking when we look at the big picture. Roughly speaking there has been 6,000 years of time since creation to the present—sixty centuries. For the first fifty-nine centuries if a man wanted to travel faster or farther than he could walk, he rode on the backs of animals or was towed by them. It has only been in this present sixtieth century of time that we have gone from horseback to the moon!

Airplanes date only from 1903! A few years ago our family spent vacation time at Kitty Hawk, North Carolina. While there we visited the Wright Brothers Museum. There we saw a copy of the telegram Wilbur Wright sent to his mother back in Kansas on December 17, 1903. It went something like this: "Success at last. We will be home for Christmas." They had flown 100 feet!

Automobiles were first mass produced in 1909. Millions of adults can still remember life without television. And yet today, we have computers, video players and recorders, satellite antennas, cellular telephones, microwave ovens, and. . .

Without a doubt we are living in the time of the end.

CHAPTER 2

The Days of Noah

The Scriptures record in the words of Christ, "But as the days of Noah were, so also will the coming of the Son of Man be. For as in the days before the flood, they were eating and drinking, marrying and giving in marriage, until the day that Noah entered the ark, and did not know until the flood came and took them all away, so also will the coming of the Son of man be." (Matthew 24:37-39) Does this passage mean that the people weren't warned of a coming flood or does it mean they didn't believe that it would come? They had plenty of warning, but they chose to ignore and ridicule the message and the messenger.

"The time of Noah prefigures the present age. Christ tells us that as it was in the time of Noah, so shall it be in the days that immediately precede his appearing in the clouds of heaven. Human nature in our day, uninfluenced by the Spirit of God, is the same as in the age of Noah. And Satan is not asleep; he is as active and vigilant now as he was then. While the voice of God is making itself heard through His servants in warning and entreaties, he is mustering his forces. He engages his host with gigantic energies to make, through his sophistry, cruelties, and oppression, the words of warning of none effect. The people are tested, and the great mass will be found on the side of the great deceiver, and will be overwhelmed in swift and irretrievable destruction. But those that heed the warnings of God, and in their lives bring forth fruits meet for repentance, shall 'dwell in the secret place of the Most High;' they 'shall abide under the shadow of the Almighty.' For with them is the promise: 'With long life will I satisfy him, and show him my salvation.'" *(Signs of the Times,* April 1, 1886)

The Scriptures declare, "By faith Noah, being divinely warned of things not yet seen, moved with godly fear, prepared an ark for the saving of his household, by which he condemned the world and became heir of the righteousness which is according to faith." (Hebrews 11:7)

Noah's message was simple and straight to the point. "The Lord has told me that because of the wickedness on the earth that He will give us 120 years to repent and turn things around. If we don't repent He will destroy the world by a flood of waters. In the meantime, I have been asked by Him to build a special boat to save those who love and obey Him."

"It was Noah's consistent faith and works combined that condemned the world. <u>He not only preached the present truth for that time, but he acted every sermon.</u> Had he never lifted up his voice in warning, his works, his holy character among the corrupt and ungodly would have been condemning sermons to the unbelieving and dissolute of that age. He bore himself with a Christlike patience and meekness under the provoking insults, taunts, and mockery. His voice was often heard in prayer to God for His power and help that he might do all the commandments of God. This was a condemning power to the unbelieving." *(This Day With God,* p. 235)

Not only his preaching but his example in building the ark, testified of his sincerity and condemned the world. "Every blow struck upon the ark was preaching to the people. Noah directed, he preached, he worked, while the people looked on in amazement, and regarded him as a fanatic." *(The Spirit of Prophecy,* vol. 1, p. 70) (See Appendix, Chapter 2 for a powerful statement on a Noah-like obedience.)

The world laughed at Noah's warning. "But Noah found grace in the eyes of the Lord. . . Noah was a just man and perfect in his generations, and Noah walked with God. (Gen. 6:8, 9) Yes, amid the corruption of that degenerate age, <u>Noah was a pleasure to his Creator."</u> *(Selected Messages,* vol. 1, p. 90) This statement begs the question of us. Do we believe that Jesus is coming soon and that the world as we now know it will be destroyed? If so, can others see this by our current activities and lifestyle? And will we remain faithful even if laughed at and ignored?

We must remember that at the time Noah was preaching the world was only about 1,600 years old and, of course, had not seen any natural disaster such as we are familiar with today. There had never been floods, tornados, earthquakes, hurricanes and such to destroy the beauty of the earth. The fixed laws of nature had kept everything on a very even keel.

Ellen White described the reception of Noah's preaching in a series of articles in the *Signs of the Times* around the turn of the century. The following are representative:

"At that time the world showed scarcely the first signs of decay. Everything in nature was beautiful and lovely. The lofty trees, the towering mountains, the signs that God had hung in the heavens, appeared so great and grand to the people that they refused to believe that the earth was to be destroyed." *(Signs of the Times,* April 10, 1901)

"The antediluvians were warned, but the record states that they knew not until the flood came and took them all away. 'We can not believe your message,' they said to Noah. 'Everything about us is so firm, so enduring. Look at the beautiful earth. It knows nothing of decay, neither will it for thousands of years.'" *(Ibid.)*

After hearing the words of Noah the people consulted their scientists and philosophers. These "wise" men told them, "'You need not be alarmed. Such an event as the destruction of the world by the God who made it, and the punishment of the beings he has created, will never take place. Be at peace; fear not. Noah is crazy; he is the wildest fanatic.' So the people did not humble their hearts before God, but continued their disobedience and wickedness, the same as though God had not spoken to them through his servant." *(Ibid.,* April 1, 1886)

As far as human wisdom could see, the event predicted by Noah was not likely to occur. Rain had never fallen; a mist or dew had watered the earth. The brooks and rivers safely flowed along their channels, emptying into the sea.

Through the years as Noah preached, as time passed without any apparent change in nature, men who had at first trembled with fear began to be reassured and went to even greater lengths in wickedness. And so, "in Noah's day, the inhabitants of the old world laughed to scorn what they termed the superstitious fears and forebodings of the preacher of righteousness. He was denounced as a visionary character, a fanatic, an alarmist. 'As it was in the days of Noah, so shall it be also in the days of the Son of Man.' Men will reject the solemn message of warning in our day as they did in Noah's time. They will refer to those false teachers who have predicted the event and set the definite time, and will say that they have no more faith in our warning than in theirs. This is the attitude of the world today. Unbelief is widespread, and the preaching of Christ's coming is mocked at and derided. This makes it all the more essential that those who believe present truth should show their faith by their works. They should be sanctified through the truth which they profess to believe; for they are savors of life unto life, or of death unto death." *(Ibid.,* Oct. 8, 1902)

After 120 years of preaching and building "Everything was now ready for the closing of the ark, which could not be done by Noah from within. The scoffing multitude behold an angel descending from heaven, clothed with brightness like the lightning. He closes that massive outer door, and then takes his course upward to heaven again. Seven days were the family of Noah in the ark before the rain began to descend. During this time they were arranging for their long stay while the waters should be upon the earth. And these were days of blasphemous merriment by the unbelieving masses. Because the prophecy of Noah was not fulfilled immediately after he entered the ark, they thought that he was deceived, and that it was impossible for the world to be destroyed by a flood. Notwithstanding the solemn scenes which they had witnessed, the beasts leaving the mountains and forests and going into the ark, and the angel of God, clothed with brightness and terrible in majesty, descending from Heaven and closing the door, they hardened their hearts and continued to revel and sport over the signal manifestations of divine power." *(Ibid.,* March 6, 1879)

When God sends a message, if the messenger checks out according to God's Word, we should, according to Noah's experience, accept the message even though it may not "make sense" to us by logic and reason. "But the days before the flood steal silently on as a thief in the night. Noah is now making his last effort in warnings, entreaty, and appeal to the rejecters of God's message. With tearful eye, trembling lip, and quivering voice he makes his last entreaty for them to believe and secure a refuge in the ark. But they turn from him with impatience and contempt that he should be so egotistical as to suppose his family are the only ones right in the vast population of the earth. They have no patience with his warnings, with his strange work of building an immense boat on dry ground. Noah, they said, was insane." *(Manuscript Releases,* vol. 10, p. 374) "They laughed and mocked at his words, and said, Does he not speak in parables? But their unbelief did not prevent the flood, and they finally drank the waters that covered the earth. We do not want to be like them." *(Ibid.,* vol. 3, p. 90)

Time is running out for this old world. All about us are signs that

Jesus gave as indications that the end is near. Search the Scriptures for yourself and compare them with current events as I have done in this book and decide for yourself what course you will pursue. The times in which we live are very serious. This is not a laughing matter. What could be more important than making sure that you and your family are prepared to follow God's leading?

Some folks have interpreted Matthew 24:37-39 where it says, "They did not know until the flood came and took them all away" to mean that the Second Coming will come suddenly, unexpectedly, and no one will be prepared. I believe that this explanation of the text is wrong because only the wicked were "taken all away." The saved, Noah and his family, were safe within the ark—traveling to the new world. In fact, by the time the Seven Last Plagues have fallen, everyone on earth will realize that the end of the world is here. The big surprise will be the close of probation—when the door of mercy is shut. When the angel shut the door of the ark it was forever too late to get on board—even though it didn't start raining for seven days.

Daniel says, "Many shall be purified, made white, and refined, but the wicked shall do wickedly; and none of the wicked shall understand, but the wise shall understand." (Daniel 12:10) Paul echoes the same sentiments in 1 Thessalonians 5:1-4, "But concerning the times and the seasons, brethren, you have no need that I should write to you. For you yourselves know perfectly that the day of the Lord so comes as a thief in the night. For when they say, 'Peace and safety!' then sudden destruction comes upon them, as labor pains upon a pregnant woman. And they shall not escape. But you, brethren, are not in darkness, so that this Day should overtake you as a thief."

As I emphasize throughout this book, we serve a God of order. At the appointed time the flood came. At the appointed time the Exodus occurred. At the appointed time Jesus performed His earthly ministry. And at the appointed time Christ will return the second time! "As it was in the days of Noah so also shall it be in the coming of the Son of Man." Did the people know when to expect the flood? Was there some kind of a time-line? Or was it just a coincidence that Noah preached 120 years and that Methuselah died the year of the flood. I believe there was a precise timetable for the flood just like all the other major epochs of time as we will discuss in Chapter 9.

"Referring to the wickedness of the antediluvians, God said: 'My

Spirit shall not abide in man for ever, for he is flesh, but his *days* shall be a hundred and twenty *years.'* (Genesis 6:3, italics supplied)

"The time mentioned here conveys a *prophecy* about a future probationary period. During this time Noah would preach and endeavor to persuade that sinful generation to accept God's offer of mercy while probation lingered. Already in Gen. 6, therefore, we find a <u>prophecy about a sharply delimited amount of future time</u>. And in this *first time prophecy* of Scripture the terms 'days' and 'years' are linked directly together." (William H. Shea, "Selected Studies on Prophetic Interpretation," *Daniel and Revelation Committee Series,* vol. l, p. 67)

There are many parallels between the flood and the Second Coming of Christ. One is that both are preceded by a period of probation. In the case of the flood that period was exactly 120 years—a sharply delimited amount of future time. Ellen White calls this period a time of probation. I will list several short comments from her pen.

"For one hundred twenty years He (God) sent them warnings through His servant Noah. But they used the <u>probation</u> so graciously granted them in ridiculing Noah." *(Seventh-day Adventist Bible Commentary,* vol. 1, p. 1090)

"For one hundred and twenty years the antediluvians were <u>on probation,</u> free to choose to obey the voice of God and find refuge in the ark, or to refuse to hear His voice, and be destroyed. They chose to disobey and were destroyed." *(Review and Herald,* Sept. 15, 1904)

It is interesting to note that Noah had to remain faithful all this period of time too. He was basically standing alone and all the while being mocked and ridiculed. How was he able to stand up under all this? "Noah had faith in God. His position was a trying one; he had to fight the good fight of faith at every step. <u>One hundred and twenty years of probation was granted to the inhabitants of the world,</u> and Noah was to live through that generation. . . Nearly the whole world was against Noah." *(Signs of the Times,* April 18, 1895)

By looking at the following statements I am led to believe that Noah announced from the beginning to the people that God would destroy the world in one hundred and twenty years. From that point on it was a countdown to the year of destruction. The very name of Methuselah carried a message. It meant, "When he dies, it will be sent." (I will enlarge on this "coincidence" later on in the book.) In the last year before the flood Methuselah died and the countdown was reading months or weeks—not years! Consider the following time-limiting statements:

"The Lord sent the message by Noah that at the end of one hundred and twenty years He would send a flood of waters upon the impenitent inhabitants of the earth." (*Manuscript Releases*, vol. 10, p. 369)

"The testimony of Noah, in regard to the judgments that were to fall upon the antediluvian world, was not received by the people as the message of God. The servant of God gave to the transgressors of the law of Jehovah, a warning which announced that in one hundred and twenty years the world would be destroyed by a flood. His warning was scoffed at, ridiculed, and rejected." *(Review and Herald,* Sept. 25, 1888)

God did not tell Noah, "When you get the ark finished I will send the flood." Rather He told him that the flood would come in 120 years, so he should have the ark completed by then. There was a limited time in which to work.

As the 120 years ran out God sent enhanced warnings to the people. The ark was finished. The provisions were put on board. The animals and birds came in without any guidance from man.

"The Spirit of God continued to strive with rebellious man until the time specified had nearly expired, when Noah and his family entered the ark, and the hand of God closed its door. Mercy had stepped from the golden throne, no longer to intercede for the guilty sinner." *(Signs of the Times,* April 1, 1886)

"The period of their probation was drawing near its close. The unbelieving, scoffing inhabitants of the world were to have a special sign of God's divine power. Noah had faithfully followed the instructions God had given to him. The ark was finished exactly as God had directed. He had laid in store immense quantities of food for man and beast. And after this was accomplished, God commanded the faithful Noah, 'Come thou, and all thy house, into the ark, for thee have I seen righteous before me.' Angels were sent to collect from the forest and field the beasts which God had created. Angels went before these animals and they followed, two by two, male and female, and clean beasts by sevens. These beasts, from the most ferocious, down to the most gentle and harmless, peacefully and solemnly marched into the ark. The sky seemed clouded with birds of every description. They came flying to the ark, two and two, male and female, and the clean birds by sevens. The world looked on in wonder—some with fear, but they had become so hardened by rebellion that this most signal manifestation of God's power had but a momentary influence upon them. For seven days these animals were coming into the ark, and Noah was arranging them in the places prepared for them." *(The Spirit of Prophecy,* vol. 1, p. 71)

In spite of all these obvious miracles the people who had been hardening their heart for 120 years continued to reject the words of Noah.

The Bible tells us that after Noah and his family entered the ark and the door was shut, it did not begin to rain until after seven days. This was a real time of trial and test for Noah, for although he was safe inside the predicted flood was not forthcoming. But God had said the flood was coming, and Noah rested in His word.

Patriarchs and Prophets gives a very graphic description of the eighth day. "But upon the eighth day, dark clouds overspread the heavens. There followed the muttering of thunder and the flash of lightning. Soon large drops of rain began to fall. The world had never witnessed anything like this, and the hearts of men were struck with fear. All were secretly inquiring, 'Can it be that Noah was in the right, and that the world is doomed to destruction?' Darker and darker grew the heavens, and faster came the falling rain. The beasts were roaming about in the wildest terror, and their discordant cries seemed to moan out their own destiny and the fate of many. Then 'the fountains of the great deep were broken up, and the windows of heaven were opened.' Water appeared to come from the clouds in mighty cataracts. Rivers broke away from their boundaries, and overflowed the valleys. Jets of water burst from the earth with indescribable force, throwing massive rocks hundreds of feet into the air, and these, in falling, buried themselves deep in the ground." *(Patriarchs and Prophets,* p. 99)

One can only imagine the terror of the lost. The rain lasted for forty days and forty nights. Each day as the people got up they listened to the weather report and heard the dreadful words, "It is still raining." It happened like this for forty days! Early on the homes in the valleys were flooded so the people fled to their "high place" temples but soon they, too, were swept away by the raging waters. Ellen White describes the last few days of human life outside the ark in these words: "Everywhere could be seen human beings fleeing in search of a refuge. The time had come when they would have been only too glad to accept an invitation to enter the ark. Filled with anguish they cried, 'O for a place of safety!'

Some shrieked to Noah, pleading for admission into the ark. But amid the furious blast of the tempest their voices were unheard. Some clung to the ark till they were washed away by the dashing waves. God had shut in those who believed His word, and no others could enter.

"Parents with their children sought the highest branches of the trees yet standing; but no sooner had they reached this refuge than the wind flung tree and people into the foaming, seething water. Terrified animals and terrified human beings climbed the highest mountains, only to be swept together into the angry flood.

"Where was now the ark and those at whom the people had jeered and mocked? Preserved by the power of God, the immense boat was riding safely upon the waters, and Noah and his family were safe inside." *(Signs of the Times,* April 10, 1901)

Now what can we learn from all of this? Several things. First, the Lord does not bring judgments on the earth without first warning mankind through His servants, the prophets. Second, God will do what He predicted right on time. And third, Peter tells us that scoffers in the last days willfully forget the flood—and Noah's countdown—and will also reject God's countdown to the Second Coming. I don't know when it will end because we are told it will be cut short. But I do have my eyes open. I do recognize that world conditions all around us are fulfilling the words of Jesus.

"When Noah proclaimed the solemn message, yet an hundred and twenty years the judgments of God in a flood of water should destroy the world and its inhabitants, <u>men would not receive it, so it is at the present time</u>. Those who warn the transgressors of the law to repent and turn to their allegiance for the Lawgiver is coming to punish the disobedient, will plead and entreat and warn the majority in vain. <u>Peter describes the attitude of the world in reference to the last message</u>: 'There shall come in the last days scoffers, walking after their own lusts and saying, where is the promise of His coming? for since the fathers fell asleep all things continue as they were from the beginning of the creation. For this they willingly are ignorant of, that by the word of God the heavens were of old, and the earth standing out of the water and in the water; whereby the world that then was, being overflowed with water, perished; but the heavens and the earth, which are now, by the same word are kept in store, reserved unto fire against the day of judgment and perdition of ungodly men. <u>But beloved, be not ignorant of this one thing, that one day is with</u>

the Lord as a thousand years, and a thousand years as one day. The Lord is not slack concerning His promise, as some men count slackness; but is longsuffering to us-ward, not willing that any should perish, but that all should come to repentance. But the day of the Lord will come as a thief in the night; in the which the heavens shall pass away with a great noise, and the elements shall melt with fervent heat, the earth also and the works that are therein shall be burned up.'" (*Signs of the Times*, Jan. 3, 1878)

Our work is definitely laid out for us. "As Noah warned the people of the coming flood, so God desires His people today to give the warning message of Christ's soon coming. There is no time to lose. Christ's coming is near at hand, and instead of spending our lives in inactivity, instead of investing our means in the things of this world, we should use our talents to the glory of God." (*Signs of the Times*, April 17, 1881)

At the time of the flood only eight were saved—essentially the whole world perished. At the time of the destruction of Sodom only three were saved, but both groups had a warning. We must not follow the majority in spiritual things. If we do, we will be lost. We must listen to the voice of God. We must read the clear instructions for survival in His Holy Word. It will tell us when the time of our deliverance is near.

CHAPTER 3

Fighting Fire With Fire

The beast of Revelation 13 with horns like a lamb that later speaks like a dragon represents Protestant America. Adventists recognize that "the Protestants of the United States will be foremost in stretching their hands across the gulf to grasp the hand of spiritualism; they will reach over the abyss to clasp hands with the Roman power; and under the influence of this threefold union, this country will follow in the steps of Rome in trampling on the rights of conscience." *(The Great Controversy,* p. 588)

This is occurring at the present time. While it may appear that Protestant groups are losing members, the fact is that the evangelical wing of Protestantism is growing both in numbers and in strength.

The Christian Coalition was started by Pat Robertson of the *700 Club* and the Christian Broadcasting Network and Regent University following his unsuccessful campaign to be the Republican candidate for the 1988 U.S. Presidential election. Pat considers his failure to achieve political office not a defeat as in losing a war but rather a setback as in losing only a particular battle. "The war has just begun," he states.

Robertson is no hayseed or dummy. He is a graduate (magna cum laude) from Washington and Lee University and holds graduate degrees—Juris Doctor from Yale University Law School and Master of Divinity from New York University. He evidently felt that with his education and name recognition as host of the *700 Club* winning the presidency would be a relatively easy task. What he learned is that to win in the U.S. political arena one needs a grassroots organization. That he is now building with such rapidity that the membership is doubling every year!

A good example of the growing influence of the Christian Coalition is that at the 1992 Republican National Convention in Houston, Texas, forty-three of forty-six delegates from the state of Iowa were members of the Christian Coalition!

The Christian Coalition is headquartered in Virginia Beach, Virginia, in connection with Regent University. This is also the location for the headquarters for the Christian Broadcasting Network (CBN). The CBN studios are said to be the most sophisticated and state of the art in the world. In 1992 profits made from one of Robertson's cable television transactions resulted in a gift of over $100 million to Regent University.

Why was Regent University established? Let the promotional material from the school speak for itself. "Christian leadership to change the world! This is the bold vision that launched Regent University and that beckons us to enter a challenging new era of research, training and teaching—an era that will change the way America and the nations of the world think. . . At Regent, leaders are being challenged and commissioned to claim and occupy our nation's courtrooms, classrooms, businesses, churches, media and the arts." *(Regent University Impact, 1992)*

Dr. Herb Titus, a cum laude graduate of the Harvard School of Law and the founding dean of the College of Law and Government at Regent University, states, regarding the Law School, "The Lord gave me a vision for a school to prepare people for influencing the political life of this nation." *(Ibid.)*

On the first weekend after Labor Day in 1992 and 1993, I had the opportunity to attend the **Road to Victory Conference and Strategy Briefing of the Christian Coalition.** The meetings were held in 1992 at Founders Inn on the Regent University campus and in 1993 at the Washington, D.C., Hilton, which boast the largest ballroom in the city. The theme for the 1993 conference was "The Tide Is Turning."

Emotions run high when the audience consists of individuals who are both political activists and religious zealots. The high profile speakers took every advantage of the "electricity" generated from the 2,200 people in attendance. Some speakers were introduced by as many as three others who in turn were introduced by others. Each of these "introducers" made mini-speeches of their own.

According to the *Wall Street Journal,* the Christian Coalition is a growing force in American politics that has doubled its membership each year over the last three years to a dues-paying membership that now totals over 450,000 people. The article states, "Its potential seems high. The coalition defines its audience broadly as churchgoing families with children. Its core of national members, who pay $15 annual dues, forms only part of the coalition's computerized data base of 750,000 activists who have been helpful in local political campaigns or have signed petitions. Those sympathizers can be activated by computer-generated mailings or mass phone drives. In addition, the coalition has what amounts to a national precinct organization, thanks to its computer listing of 35,000 churches it can contact to disseminate its messages." *(The Wall Street Journal,* Sept. 7, 1993)

The official program of the 1993 convention described itself this way: "The Christian Coalition has quickly gained a reputation as one of the most effective grassroots citizen organizations in the nation. This growing alliance of evangelicals, Catholics, Greek orthodox, Russian orthodox, and other people of faith seeks to enact public policy that is friendly to the family." (See Chapter 3, Appendix, for more of the Coalition's self-descripton and goals.)

So that is the self-perspective from the Christian Coalition. Now let me share with you some of my observations from the 1993 Christian Coalition conference.

There were two obvious differences in the 1993 convention as compared to 1992. The first was the planned inclusion of Blacks, Jews, and a large number of Roman Catholic laymen and clergy. The second was the stated broadening of the Coalition's emphasis beyond the dual theme of opposition to homosexuality and abortion. As a result of these two changes the overall theme in the 1993 convention was quite simple: We are facing a moral crisis in America, and it is going to take all of the good guys working together to solve the problem.

I had thought that it would take either a financial crisis, which obviously is coming soon, or another major natural disaster to trigger the full force of this group. From my perspective either of these phenomena will offer a "mandate" to get America back to God with all that goal entails. However, the moral crisis in America seems to be providing more than adequate motivation for Christian political activism.

The convention began with an invocation by Roman Catholic Father Hopkins, a young priest, who was introduced as being personally ordained by Pope John Paul II three years earlier. He is now active in the Christian Coalition endeavors.

In his introductory remarks Dr. Ralph Reed, Jr., executive director of the Christian Coalition, stated: "We are not poor, uneducated, and easy to command as stated by the Washington *Post*. We are mainstream America.

"The pro-family movement has limited its effectiveness by concentrating disproportionately on issues such as abortion and homosexuality. These are vital moral issues, and must remain an important part of the message. To win at the ballot box and in the court of public opinion, however, the pro-family movement must speak to the concerns of average voters in the area of taxes, crime, government waste, health care, and financial security."

Haley Barbour, chairman of the Republican National Committee, in his brief remarks at the convention said, "President Clinton has made it plain—the difference between Democrats and Republicans. I am proud of the Christian Coalition. Thanks to the Christian Coalition we have a Republican Senator from Georgia (Paul Coverdale) who defeated the Democratic incumbent, Wyche Fowler. Paul Coverdale told me, 'I would not be a U.S. Senator today if it were not for the support of the Christian Coalition.'"

Pat Robertson stated, "We are working shoulder to shoulder with Roman Catholics and other people of faith. People say that we are the right wing. I am to the right of the Washington *Post*, I am to the right of the ACLU. I am to the right of Planned Parenthood. Eighty-two percent of white Americans agree with us. Eighty-one percent of black Americans agree with us. We are the mainstream. The group that is in this room has the power to turn the tide in America. We do not need the Bubba from Arkansas and the aging Woodstock generation. The Christian Coaliton will oppose any policy or person that would seek to destroy this nation. To political leaders let me say, 'If you advocate the agenda of the radical left you will not be re-elected.'"

Newt Gingrich, Republican from Georgia and the House minority whip, was introduced as a friend of the family and the Christian Coalition. Gingrich proclaimed, "Two persons in this century stand above all the rest, Martin Luther King, Jr., and Pat Robertson." He went on to say, "We don't want to oppose Bill and Hillary—we want to replace them. We (Christians) are a pre-governing majority. We are the only hope this planet has. We will lead the American civilization into the 21st century with peace and prosperity."

Senator Phil Gramm from Texas gave a rousing speech in which he said, "I view my work here in Washington as doing the Lord's work in the devil's city. I want every American family to have the same right that Bill and Hillary have—to send their children to a private school. We need to focus on 1994. (It was stated at the convention that all 435 seats in the House of Representatives, 32 Senate seats, and 36 State governorships will be at stake in the 1994 elections.) Give me a Republican majority in the Senate and you won't have to wait until 1996. We will shut down the Clinton tax and spend program. We owe this country a lot, and we can pay this debt by working together in 1994 and 1996."

Gary Bauer of the Family Research Council and senior vice president of *Focus on the Family* stated, "Before this decade is over our values will prevail."

The presence of Jewish speakers was very noticeable at the conference. The first, Rabbi Jack Abramoff, present to introduce Don Feder, staff writer for the Boston *Globe,* made a short speech himself, saying: "There are hundreds of thousands of conservative Jews who support the conservative agenda of the Christian Coalition."

Don Feder in his primary speech stated, "I have a timely Jewish message to the Christian Coalition: Ladies and Gentlemen, if you are the religious right, then so am I. Your agenda makes moral sense and common sense. We must protest the effort to protect perversion as a civil right. The Talmud refers to the fetus as the handiwork of the Living God. Family values started with Abraham and were codified by Almighty God at Sinai. Please force your values on me. They are my values, too. Clinton's Cabinet are the Neo-Pagans. All laws are based on morality because ultimately all laws are based on someone's concept of right and wrong."

Feder went on to say that "Christians and Jews are the seed bearers of western civilization. We must work together to bring God into society. Our cause transcends denominational divisions. None of us will survive if our adversaries prevail."

Rabbi Daniel Lapin, senior rabbi of the Pacific Jewish Center in Venice, California, and founder of Toward Tradition, a venue for Christians and Jews cooperating on national issues from a traditional Judeo-Christian standpoint, gave a very stirring presentation. Rabbi Lapin started Toward Tradition in 1991 as a coalition of Christians and Jews, who felt more united by a common Judeo-Christian ethic than they felt separated by differing theologies. In his closing appeal he said, "America is the victim of a thirty year collision with secularism. Now is not the time to debate theology. America is in the emergency room. We need to work together to save America."

There were two Black speakers at the 1993 conference. Kay James of the Family Research Counsel made the point that "The liberal media can't tell blacks anymore that they are not wanted in the Christian Right." The other Black speaker was Roy Innis, national chairman of the Congress of Racial Equality (CORE). He was an active participant in the New York City School Board elections in which Black community activists, the Roman Catholic Arch-diocese and the Christian Coalition cooperated to elect many "pro family" school board members. He commented that, "We (Blacks) need you, and you (Christian Coalition) need us."

A strong Roman Catholic emphasis concluded the conference. Keith Fournier, formerly associated with the Franciscan University of Stubenville, Ohio, and the "charismatic, evangelical, Roman Catholic attorney," who now heads up the American Center for Law and Justice under Pat Robertson, boasted of the diverse backgrounds of those now giving leadership to the Christian Coalition. He stated, "We have eighteen attorneys in the ACLJ, five Roman Catholics, five Jews and eight Evangelicals." His most remarkable statement was "Many think of the United States as a post-Christian nation, but I prefer to look at the United States as a pre-Christian nation." He said, "In World War II the Allies had a common cause. And so, what joins us in common is Jesus Christ and common goals."

Father Michael Scanlon, president of the Franciscan University of Stubenville, Ohio, was featured several times at the conference. He is a Harvard Law School graduate and a Roman Catholic priest. While talking about Protestants and Catholics working together he remarked, "I spoke recently at Wheaton College, and James Dobson gave the commencement address at Stubenville." He concluded his remarks by saying, "It is important that the Christian Coalition state openly that they want Catholics involved, so that prejudice and suspicions can be dealt with."

The featured speaker for the closing banquet was Jesuit trained Roman Catholic Bill Bennett. Bennett, as the former Secretary of Education and Drug Czar is no stranger to American politics. Following the invocation given by a Roman Catholic priest during which nearly half of the platform participants made the sign of the cross, Bennett remarked to Ralph Reed, the executive director of the Christian Coalition, "Ralph, if this ratio of Catholics continues to grow, we will soon outnumber you." Then, following comments about the Christian struggle with the liberal, immoral, present government leadership, Bennett declared, "What we need now is the political equivalent to the Council of Trent." As you may recall, the Council of Trent was called by the Catholic Church in order to assess the damage caused by the Protestant Reformation and to plan the church's strategy to deal with Protestantism. He went on to state that, "Religion is a domain we ignore at our peril."

With such statements in mind such as "We will be in power before the end of this decade," and "We need to influence legislation in this country," and "Our cause transcends denominational divisions" I began to match them with those of Ellen White in *The Great Controversy.*

For example: "In order for the United States to form an image to the beast, the religious power must so control the civil government that the authority of the state will also be employed by the church to accomplish her own ends." (p. 443)

"When the leading churches of the United States, uniting upon such points of doctrine as are held by them in common, shall influence the state to enforce their decrees and to sustain their institutions, then Protestant America will have formed an image of the Roman hierarchy, and the infliction of civil penalties upon dissenters will inevitably result." (p. 445)

"Romanism is now regarded by Protestants with far greater favor than in former years . . . The time was when Protestants placed a high value upon the liberty of conscience which had been so dearly purchased. They taught their children to abhor popery and held that to seek harmony with Rome would be disloyalty to God. But how widely different are the sentiments now expressed." (p. 563)

"In the movements now in progress in the United States to secure for the institutions and usages of the church the support of the state, Protestants are following in the steps of papists. Nay, more, they are opening the door for the papacy to regain in Protestant America the supremacy which she has lost in the Old World. And that which gives greater significance to this movement is the fact that the principle object contemplated is the enforcement of Sunday observance—a custom which originated with Rome, and which she claims as the sign of her authority." (p. 573)

"Let the principle once be established in the United States that the church may employ or control the power of the state; that religious observances may be enforced by secular laws; in short, that the authority of church and state is to dominate the conscience, and the triumph of Rome in this country is assured . . . The Protestant world will learn what the purposes of Rome really are, only when it is too late to escape the snare." (p. 581)

Have you ever wondered how the Christian Coalition voter guides work? They simply tell how an elected leader has voted on issues supported by the Christian Coalition. If they are not supportive, they will be targeted for defeat at the next election. Remember, we were told that this process of intimidation would be used at the end. "Even in free America, rulers and legislators, in order to secure public favor, (to stay on the right side in the voter guide!) will yield to the popular demand for a law enforcing Sunday observance." (p. 592)

Draw your own conclusions! I believe we are seeing the beginnings of the final events.

Hearing the speeches of the Christian Coalition leaders, you feel a kinship with their concerns. What red-blooded Christian is not saddened by the declining moral values in America? They have correctly diagnosed the problem, but they have prescribed a cure that is worse than the disease. I am referring to the fact that the Christian Coalition constantly decries the "wall of separation between church and state," and seeks to correct the evil of society by "influencing legislation."

Keith Fournier, the Roman Catholic executive director of the American Center for Law and Justice, the "religious liberty" arm of the Christian Coalition, has stated, "The wall of separation between church and state that was erected by secular humanists and other enemies of religious freedom has to come down. That wall is more of a threat to society than the Berlin wall ever was." He went on to say, "Those opposing our views are the new fascists."

The president of the Christian Coalition, Pat Robertson, proclaimed in his banquet speech that closed the 1992 Christian Coalition Conference and Strategy Briefing, "God told me in December, 1991, that He was going to bless the Christian Coalition beyond our wildest expectations. Before the year 2000, the Christian Coalition will be the most powerful organization in the United States of America. We will soon have over 1.7 million Christian activists. All counties and voting precincts in America will have an active Christian Coalition chapter. <u>People will be calling from Washington (D.C.) to ask, 'What is the position of the Christian Coalition, so we will know how to vote?'"</u>

Any thinking American is shockingly aware of the serious decline in moral values in this country. But the idea of Christians taking over the government to "legislate" Christian values will, prophecy predicts, turn out to be worse than the problem. I believe those in the Christian Coalition are sincere in their efforts to reform America. Evidently, they don't recognize where their steps are tending. "Though they (Protestants) blind their own eyes to the fact, they are now adopting a course which will lead to the persecution of those who conscientiously refuse to do what the rest of the Christian world are doing, and acknowledge the claims of the papal sabbath." *(The Great Controversy,* p. 592)

An additional problem for me is that I don't like to be forced to make a decision between two alternatives as if they are the only ones available. For example, in a very simple way, "Which do you like better, your mother or your father?" The fact is that I like them both the same, thank you. But more to the point "Are you a left wing liberal or a right wing conservative?" Don't let anyone make you think you must adopt a radical position—period!

What will be the result of the church getting involved in politics? Listen to this inspired prediction. "When the Protestant churches shall unite with the secular power to sustain a false religion, for opposing which their ancestors endured the fiercest persecution; when the state shall use its power to enforce the decrees and sustain the institutions of the church—then will Protestant America have formed an image to the papacy, and there will be a national apostasy which will end only in national ruin." *(Signs of the Times,* March 22, 1910)

"When the churches of our land, uniting upon such points of faith as are held by them in common, shall influence the State to enforce their decrees and sustain their institutions, then will Protestant America have formed an image of the Roman hierarchy. Then the true church will be assailed by persecution, as were God's ancient people. Almost every century furnishes examples of what bigotry and malice can do under a plea of serving God by protecting the rights of Church and State. . .

EATD-2

Persecution always follows religious favoritism on the part of secular governments." *(The Spirit of Prophecy,* vol. 4, p. 278)

"The mingling of church craft and state craft is represented by the iron and the clay. This union is weakening all the power of churches. This investing the church with the power of the state will bring evil results. Men have almost passed the point of God's forbearance. They have invested their strength in politics, and have united with the papacy. But the time will come when God will punish those who have made void His law, and their evil work will recoil upon themselves." *(Manuscript Releases,* vol. 1, p. 51)

Some folks are inclined to say that the Christian Coalition movement is just a flash in the pan and will go the way of the Moral Majority. But, on the contrary, this organization has announced that it will hang in there "until we win it all." Have there been any victories? Indeed there have been. The following are examples:

Following the 1992 Presidential elections, when the dust settled, the candidate the Christian Coalition backed lost in the presidential election, but they gained seats in both the Senate and the House of Representatives. On the day after the election one Senate seat was still not decided. The Democratic incumbent, Wyche Fowler from Georgia, did not receive sufficient votes to win re-election outright in a field of challengers for his Senate seat, so he was forced into a runoff election with his closest competitor, Republican Paul Coverdale. Recognizing the importance of this runoff both President Clinton and Vice President Gore went to Georgia and campaigned for Fowler. The Christian Coalition, in turn, worked for Coverdale. Guess who won? Yes, the Christian-Coalition-supported Coverdale.

Another example comes from the state of Texas. When Senator Benson, the Democrat from Texas, was asked by Bill Clinton to join his cabinet as Secretary of the Treasury, that left a Senate seat open in Texas. Did another Democrat fill his vacated spot? No! Guess who won? The Christian-Coalition-supported Republican, Kay Bailey Hutchinson.

The list could go on, but I will share just one more with you. When Bill Clinton resigned as governor of the state of Arkansas to become president, by law the lieutenant governor became governor until the next election. That left the position of lieutenant governor open. President Clinton had supported his Democratic friend, Nate Coulter, in the special election. But the Christian Coalition supported the Republican challenger, ordained Baptist minister Mike Huckabee. Guess who won! You guessed it—the Baptist minister!

These political successes tell me that the Christian Coalition is no flash in the pan. But, of course, there is more. In addition to the Catholic and Jewish leaders mentioned above, there are many other well known and respected religious leaders who support the aims and philosophy of the Christian Coalition. To name a few:

Bill Gothard—Institute in Basic Life Principles, with 70,000 pastors trained and many thousands more lay alumni on his contact list;

James Dobson—who produced, endorsed, and placed his picture on "The Tennessee Citizen 1992 Voters Guide," and more and more is involved in politics on his radio show *Focus on the Family* that is aired on more than 2,000 U.S. radio stations every day. Dobson dedicated his new 400,000 square foot multimillion dollar facility on September 25, 1993, in Colorado Springs. The new facility employs 1,300 and the ministry has a budget of $350,000 per day; and

Charles Stanley—leader of "In Touch Ministries" from the 10,000 plus member First Baptist Church in Atlanta. In addition to the radio and TV ministry, this organization produces a monthly paper and boasts one of the largest tape ministries in the world.

Other supporters of the Christian Coalition include:

D. James Kennedy, Coral Ridge Ministries of Ft. Lauderdale, Florida;

Ruth Osborne, The Salvation Army;

Ed Young, President of the Southern Baptist Convention; and

Adrian Rogers, past president of the Southern Baptist Convention.

Even Larry Burkett, founder and director of Christian Financial Concepts, spoke to the 1993 Christian Coalition meeting and in his latest book, *Whatever Happened to the American Dream?* encourages Christians to get involved in the movement to bring America back to God.

The list could go on to include others like Rush Limbaugh who help from the background. Suffice it to say that the Christian Coalition is well funded and supported by a wide range of individuals and organizations. I believe Ellen White saw not only the great evil of our day but also the secular and political attempts of religionists to deal with it when she wrote that "The agencies of evil are combining their forces and consolidating. They are strengthening for the last great crisis. Great changes are soon to take place in our world, and the final movements will be rapid ones." *(Testimonies for the Church,* vol. 9, p. 11)

CHAPTER 4

History Repeats

Bible scholars from Reformation times to the present have identified the "little horn power" of Daniel 7 and the first beast of Revelation 13 as the Papacy—the Roman Catholic system. "The third angel's warning is, 'If any man worship the beast and his image, and receive his mark in his forehead, or in his hand, the same shall drink of the wine of the wrath of God.' 'The beast' mentioned in this message, whose worship is enforced by the two-horned beast, is the first, or leopard-like beast of Revelation 13,—the Papacy. The 'image to the beast' represents that form of apostate Protestantism which will be developed when the Protestant churches shall seek the aid of the civil power for the enforcement of their dogmas." *(The Great Controversy,* p. 445)

When we talk about the great controversy between Christ and Satan we are not just talking about a book by that name. The primary focus is on the warfare between good and evil—the conflict between the good forces of heaven and the evil forces of the devil. "Through paganism, and then through the Papacy, Satan exerted his power for many centuries in an effort to blot from the earth God's faithful witnesses. Pagans and Papists were actuated by the same dragon spirit. They differed only in that the Papacy, making a pretense of serving God, was the more dangerous and cruel foe. Through the agency of Romanism, Satan took the world captive. The professed church of God was swept into the ranks of this delusion, and for more than a thousand years the professed people of God suffered under the dragon's ire." *(Signs of the Times,* Nov. 1, 1899)

The crime, cruelty, and savagery carried on by the Catholic Church toward the Protestant "heretics" during the Reformation times is probably not known to one in ten thousand people alive today. Ellen White states, "In the thirteenth century was established that most terrible of all the engines of the papacy, the Inquisition. The prince of darkness wrought with the leaders of the papal hierarchy. In their secret councils, Satan and his angels presided, while unseen in the midst stood an angel of God, taking the fearful record of their iniquitous decrees, and writing the history of deeds too horrible to appear to human eyes. 'Babylon the great' was 'drunken with the blood of the saints.' The mangled forms of millions of martyrs cried to God for vengeance upon that apostate power." (*The Spirit of Prophecy,* vol. 4, p. 63)

In the same chapter, speaking of the papal atrocities of the sixteenth century she states, "Christians were forced to choose, either to yield their integrity and accept the papal ceremonies and worship, or to wear away their lives in dungeon cells, or suffer death by the rack, the fagot, or the headsman's ax." (*Ibid.,* p. 57) There is absolutely no question that these statements are true because of the documented evidence we have in such books as D'Aubigne's *History of the Reformation,* Foxx's *Book of Martyrs,* and Morland's *The History of the Evangelical Churches of the Valleys of Piemont,* all of which I have in my personal library. Samuel Morland, a Protestant attorney from Geneva, personally investigated the bloody massacre of Protestants by Catholic soldiers in April of 1655. His findings were printed in London in 1658. In chapter VI of his book, pages 326 to 384, fifty-eight pages of small print, he gives what he calls "a brief and most authentick Narrative of some part of those extraordinary cruelties which were exercised against the poor Protestants of the Valleys of Piemont, during the heat of the late massacre, in the year of our Lord 1655, in the month of April." (See Chapter 4, Appendix.)

These accounts of Morland (like those of the other historians) are gruesome. Author Malachi Martin states in his book, *The Keys of This Blood,* that the present pope plans to regain the power that the Papacy lost two hundred years ago and again rule the world with a strong hand. John Paul II has served notice that he intends "to take up and effectively exercise once more the international role that had been central to the tradition of Rome, and to the very mandate Catholics maintain was conferred by Christ upon Peter and upon each of his successors." (p. 22)

Marie Durand was imprisoned for thirty-eight years for no other reason than she was a Huguenot (a French Protestant). Marie was fifteen years old when she crossed the deep moat that led to her prison cell in the massive tower of the ancient fortress that still stands. The walls are eighteen feet thick. They have no windows, and narrow slits in the massive masonry permit little light but much wind and cold to enter. In the middle of the floor of the circular room is an opening covered with heavy iron grating through which guards could pass food.

Marie Durand was confined in this tower from 1730 until 1768. On any day of those thirty-eight years she could have had her freedom by saying two words, "I recant." Can you imagine the temptation to say them? Why waste your youth behind these grim walls? Outside you will see sunshine, hear the happy laughter of children, find the love of friends and the comforts of home. No doubt she visualized herself in a courtship and marriage and as a happy mother caring for a helpless baby and being rewarded by its sweet smiles. But she resisted all seductions to purchase liberty at the price of compromise. Into the masonry of her prison cell she scratched the word "Resist."

One of Marie's letters preserved in the Paris Protestant Library contains the following sentences: "I am in this awful prison thirty-three years. . . We must not be Judases by betraying our own consciences. . . Your humble servant, Marie Durand."

What was it really like to be a Protestant Christian during the Middle Ages—the time Malachi Martin says his church wants to return to? Listen. Here is a word picture.

"In the days of Rome's supremacy there were instruments of torture to compel assent to her doctrines. There was the stake for those who would not concede to her claims. There were massacres on a scale that will never be known until revealed in the judgment. Dignitaries of the church studied, under Satan their master, to invent means to cause the greatest possible torture and not end the life of the victim. In many cases the infernal process was repeated to the utmost limit of human endurance, until nature gave up the struggle, and the sufferer hailed death as a sweet release." (*The Great Controversy,* p. 569)

"To stand in defense of truth and righteousness when the majority forsake us, to fight the battles of the Lord when champions are few—this will be our test. At this time we must gather warmth from the coldness of others, courage from their cowardice, and loyalty from their treason." (*Testimonies,* vol. 5, p. 136)

But hasn't the church changed? Is it really fair to judge the church by what happened hundreds of years ago? Listen to these insights. "The Roman church now presents a fair front to the world, covering with apologies her record of horrible cruelties. She has clothed herself in Christlike garments; but she is unchanged. Every principle of the papacy that existed in past ages exists today. The doctrines devised in the darkest ages are still held. Let none deceive themselves. The papacy that Protestants are now so ready to honor is the same that ruled the world in the days of the Reformation, when men of God stood up, at the peril of their lives, to expose her iniquity. She possesses the same pride and arrogant assumption that lorded it over kings and princes, and claimed the prerogatives of God. Her spirit is no less cruel and despotic now than when she crushed out human liberty and slew the saints of the Most High.

"The papacy is just what prophecy declared that she would be, the apostasy of the latter times. II Thessalonians 2:3, 4. It is a part of her policy to assume the character which will best accomplish her purpose; but beneath the variable appearance of the chameleon she conceals the invariable venom of the serpent." (*The Great Controversy,* p. 571)

Papal authority and infallibility is an issue that has led Protestants to protest and Catholics to persecute. Note the following sequence of statements that underscore this topic. Ellen White states in *The Great Controversy,* "The papal church will never relinquish her claim to infallibility. All that she has done in her persecution of those who reject her dogmas she holds to be right; and would she not repeat the same acts, should the opportunity be presented? Let the restraints now imposed by secular governments be removed and Rome be reinstated in her former power, and there would speedily be a revival of her tyranny and persecution." (p. 564)

Does the papacy still claim papal authority? Read the following news note from the "World Scene" section of *Christianity Today,* Nov. 8, 1993. It was titled **"Pope Fires Warning Shot."** "In an encyclical six years in the making Pope John Paul II reaffirms moral truth and calls upon church leaders to resist the tide of relativism that has swept through the church in the nearly three decades since the Second Vatican Council.

"The release of *Veritatis Splendor* in October (1993) is a shot across the bow of Catholic clergy and teachers who have challenged the Vatican's authority on issues ranging from abortion to homosexual activity.

"Though the encyclical had been expected to be a diatribe against homosexuality, abortion, and contraception, the final document contains little about such subjects, reserving most of its space and energy for an argument in favor of truth, against moral relativism, and for papal authority." (p. 58)

It is a sad commentary indeed to read of the frequent molestation charges against priests, bishops, and cardinals. One could overlook the weakness of individuals. However, upon investigation of the church teachings, it is easy to see why such a high percentage of priests are either alcoholic or homosexual or both. The unbiblical teaching of the celibacy of the priesthood denies any Catholic church worker the right to marry and carry on a normal family life. Accordingly, these men who are starving for intimate relationships develop them with other men's wives, other men, and even children whom they are supposed to teach, guide, and protect. And why so many alcoholic priests? The same reason— unbiblical church teaching. The use of fermented wine in mass is one reason. Now imagine if you can confessing your sins to a priest who might happen to be an alcoholic homosexual.

Ellen White comments on the confessional in this manner: "He who kneels before fallen man, and opens in confession the secret thoughts and imaginations of his heart, is debasing his manhood and degrading every noble instinct of his soul. In unfolding the sins of his life to a priest,—an erring, sinful mortal, and too often corrupted with wine and licentiousness,—his standard of character is lowered, and he is defiled in consequence." (*The Great Controversy*, p. 567)

The growing influence of the Catholic Church was noted even in the past century. "The Roman Church is far-reaching in her plans and modes of operation. She is employing every device to extend her influence and increase her power in preparation for a fierce and determined conflict to regain control of the world, to re-establish persecution, and to undo all that Protestantism has done. Catholicism is gaining ground upon every side. See the increasing number of her churches and chapels in Protestant countries. Look at the popularity of her colleges and seminaries in America, so widely patronized by Protestants." (*The Great Controversy*, pp. 565, 566)

Dave Hunt asks, "Why do world leaders want to get into bed with the Vatican? The heads of state in today's world all recognize that the Pope wields a power which in many ways is even greater than their own. It is not only Catholicism's 900 million subjects and enormous wealth that causes the world's most powerful governments to cultivate friendly relations with the Roman Catholic Church; it is because Vatican City's citizens are found in great numbers in nearly every country. They constitute an international network that reaches into the inside circles of the world's power centers." (*Global Peace and the Rise of Antichrist*, p. 116)

Malachi Martin, former Jesuit priest and professor at the Vatican Pontifical Biblical Institute, when speaking of the vastness of Pope John Paul II's empire, states (in the past tense), "True, his Church had something in excess of 907 million nominal adherents—about 18 percent of the present world population. He had 483,488 priests and about 3,000 increasingly rambunctious bishops serving some 211,156 parishes, which formed the world's 1,920 dioceses and 513 archdioceses. His institutional organization included an infrastructure of schools, universities, research institutes, medical and social science centers, hospitals, convents, churches, cathedrals, chapels, monasteries, religious centers, embassies, legations, archives, libraries, museums, newspapers, magazines, publishing houses, radio and television stations. True, too, he controlled his own Vatican Bank, with its team of international advisers who administered an extensive portfolio of the Holy See's holdings and investments in virtually every sector of the world's commercial and industrial activity. . .

"Most of the 116 full-fledged embassies on Vatican Hill are, in the internationally recognized formula, accredited to the 'Holy See.' In practical terms, Karol Wojtyla, as Pope John Paul II, is that Holy See." (Martin, *The Keys of This Blood,* p. 111)

The vast Vatican empire has a full diplomatic corps. "Like any secular diplomatic corps, this personal papal network is divided into ranks of some complexity. In this case, the rankings go by such names as Apostolic Delegate, Nuncio, Pro-Nuncio, Internuncio, Charge' d'Affaires, Apostolic Delegate and Envoy, and so on through a diplomatic system as intricate and complete as the most sophisticated of its secular counterparts. Thus, each rank is designed to cover a particular type of mission. And each rank, each title and each mission functions as a working, living part of a global system of government and influence whose center is the Vatican and whose embodiment is the Pope himself in his international designation as the 'Holy See.'

"What captures the unwavering attention of the secular leaders of the world in this remarkable network of the Roman Catholic Church is precisely the fact that it places at the personal disposal of the Pope a supranational, supracontinental, supra-trade-bloc structure that is so built and oriented that if tomorrow or next week, by a sudden miracle, a one-world government were established, the Church would not have to undergo any essential structural change in order to retain its dominant position and to further its global aims." (*Ibid.*, pp. 142, 143)

When it comes to the accumulation of wealth, art, and splendor, the Roman Catholic Church is unsurpassed. Dave Hunt recalls a recent visit to Jerusalem and Rome. "Recently, after spending some time in Israel we flew directly from there to Rome. As we passed along the colonnade skirting the vast open square in front of the cathedral, I realized that the image I had retained in my mind from a past visit did not do justice to the vast dimensions and classic beauty of this place. Jerusalem's Temple Mount was dwarfed by Roman Catholicism's New Jerusalem. Here was the headquarters of the church which, claiming to have replaced the seed of Abraham and to be the new kingdom of God on earth, refused to give the State of Israel official recognition.

"Entering the basilica I found myself comparing it with the Muslim shrine we had just visited. In surprise I realized there was no comparison. Half-a-dozen Domes of the Rock could fit inside St. Peter's immense interior! And as for beauty, the countless statues by such masters as Michelangelo, the endless dazzling mosaic depictions of biblical stories, the huge sunlit stained-glass windows—left one gasping in awe. Gazing around me in stunned awe at the incomparable wealth that was beyond calculation, I understood something of what the apostle John expressed when he was given a vision of the power and wealth of this church: 'When I saw her, I wondered with great admiration.' (Revelation 17:6)." (Dave Hunt, *Global Peace and the Rise of Antichrist*, pp. 113, 114)

Ellen White adds, "Many Protestants suppose that the Catholic religion is unattractive and that its worship is a dull, meaningless round of ceremony. Here they mistake. While Romanism is based upon deception, it is not a coarse and clumsy imposture. The religious service of the Roman Church is a most impressive ceremonial. Its gorgeous display and solemn rites fascinate the senses of the people and silence the voice of reason and of conscience. . . . A religion of externals is attractive to the unrenewed heart. <u>The pomp and ceremony of the Catholic worship has a seductive, bewitching power, by which many are deceived; and they come to look upon the Roman Church as the very gate of heaven.</u> None but those who have planted their feet firmly upon the foundation of truth, and whose hearts are renewed by the Spirit of God, are proof against her influence. Thousands who have not an experimental knowledge of Christ will be led to accept the forms of godliness without the power. Such a religion is just what the multitudes desire." (*The Great Controversy*, pp. 566, 567)

One of the unique characteristics about the Adventist Church is the uniformity of belief and practice around the world. We share fundamental teachings and a teacher from one area can serve in another without having to learn a new belief system. The situation is somewhat different in the Catholic system. Though there is a basic works oriented belief system, there is a strange mixture of Christianity and heathenism. In other words, wherever the Catholic Church exists, it is typically found to include in the religious practice of the region relics of heathenism. I have personally observed this in New Guinea and Guatemala. In Guatemala, for example, heathen witch doctors carry on prayers and religious services right inside the Catholic cathedral! In the service I attended I saw only one "priest" but three "witch doctors" present. And the witch doctors had the most floor space in the church. There they were with smoking canisters being waved over burning candles and piles of corn and grain accepting money to bless gardens and keep the evil spirits away. As reported in a recent edition of the *National Geographic* magazine, in Belize the heathen religious leaders even offer chicken sacrifices in the Catholic Church!

Dave Hunt observes, "No other church has even come close to committing the spiritual 'fornication' of which she has been guilty. Since Catholicism as it developed beginning with Constantine was paganism disguised as Christianity, it has consistently accommodated itself to the pagan religions of those peoples which it 'Christianized.' In Haiti, for example, every Voodoo ceremony begins with Catholic prayers. There is a saying that Haiti is 85 percent Catholic and 110 percent Voudun. The frightening spirit cult of Santeria exploding across America is also a blend of African paganism and 'Christianity' carried on in the name of Catholic saints who front for demons. Visit the cemeteries in Rio de Janeiro on any religious holiday and you will find the Catholic faithful there petitioning the spirits of their ancestors along with the Catholic Saints." (Hunt, *Global Peace and the Rise of Antichrist*, p. 128)

Why have I taken an entire chapter to point out the errors, heathenism, plans and activities of the Roman Catholic Church? Simply because most Protestants have forgotten the Reformation and the corruption in the papal system that led to it. They are even now becoming involved in joint activities in preparation for total unity.

In his discussion of the subject Hunt goes on to say, "While we may appear to be spending too much time on pointing out the heresies innate within Catholicism, we must be careful and thorough in our identification of the false religious system that will seduce not only the world of the last days but multiplied millions who consider themselves to be Christians. It is especially important in view of the increasing acceptance of and joint evangelism with Catholics by Protestant leaders, including some evangelicals who once considered Rome to represent the Antichrist system." (*Ibid.*, p. 128)

The serious danger for true God-fearing Christians is that unless they are made aware, they will not be prepared for the sweeping changes soon to take place in this world and will with the majority of others "wonder after the beast."

"Romanism is now regarded by Protestants with far greater favor than in former years. In those countries where Catholicism is not in the ascendancy, and the papists are taking a conciliatory course in order to gain influence, there is an increasing indifference concerning the doctrines that separate the reformed churches from the papal hierarchy; the opinion is gaining ground that, after all, we do not differ so widely upon vital points as has been supposed, and that a little concession on our part will bring us into a better understanding with Rome. The time was when Protestants placed a high value upon the liberty of conscience which had been so dearly purchased. (Remember the millions of Protestant martyrs.) They taught their children to abhor popery and held that to seek harmony with Rome would be disloyalty to God. But how widely different are the sentiments now expressed!" (*The Great Controversy*, p. 563)

The defenders of the papacy declare that the church has been maligned and that Protestants are "Catholic bashers" and that those who oppose the growing dominance of the Catholic system are either prejudiced or bigoted or both. Remember that the homosexual community claim that those who oppose their lifestyle are bigots, too.

"There are many who are disposed to attribute any fear of Roman Catholicism in the United States to bigotry or childishness. Such see nothing in the character and attitude of Romanism that is hostile to our free institutions, or find nothing portentous in its growth . . . But Romanism as a system is no more in harmony with the gospel of Christ now than at any former period in her history. The Protestant churches are in great darkness, or they would discern the signs of the times." (*Ibid.,* pp. 564, 565)

What I am sharing with you in this chapter may be new to some readers. It shouldn't be. But if it is, please accept this as a wake-up call. The end is near, and the forces of evil are preparing for the last great conflict.

"It is not without reason that the claim has been put forth in Protestant countries that Catholicism differs less widely from Protestantism than in former times. There has been a change; but the change is not in the papacy. Catholicism indeed resembles much of the Protestantism that now exists, because Protestantism has so greatly degenerated since the days of the Reformers.

"As the Protestant churches have been seeking the favor of the world, false charity has blinded their eyes. They do not see but that it is right to believe good of all evil, and as the inevitable result they will finally believe evil of all good. Instead of standing in defense of the faith once delivered to the saints, they are now, as it were, apologizing to Rome for the uncharitable opinion of her, begging pardon for their bigotry.

"A large class, even of those who look upon Romanism with no favor, apprehend little danger from her power and influence." (*Ibid.,* pp. 571, 572)

We need to be aware that the papacy is a most dangerous foe to civil and religious liberty.

CHAPTER 5

The Deadly Wound Is Healing

The apostle John, author of the Revelation, states, "Then I stood on the sand of the sea. And I saw a beast rising up out of the sea, having seven heads and ten horns, and on his horns ten crowns, and on his heads a blasphemous name. Now the beast which I saw was like a leopard, his feet were like the feet of a bear, and his mouth like the mouth of a lion. And the dragon gave him his power, his throne, and great authority. I saw one of his heads as if it had been mortally wounded, and his deadly wound was healed. And all the world marveled and followed the beast." (Revelation 13:1-3) In just three verses John summarises the prophetic picture Daniel 7 painted of world empires. Much of what Daniel had predicted about Babylon, Medo/Persia, Greece, and Pagan Rome had become a matter of history. John is now predicting the rise of Papal Rome.

What does Ellen White say about the future of the papacy? "God's word has given warning of the impending danger; let this be unheeded, and the Protestant world will learn what the purposes of Rome really are, only when it is too late to escape the snare. She is silently growing into power. Her doctrines are exerting their influence in legislative halls, in the churches, and in the hearts of men. She is piling up her lofty and massive structures in the secret recesses of which her former persecutions will be repeated. Stealthily and unsuspectedly she is strengthening her forces to further her own ends when the time shall come for her to strike. All that she desires is vantage ground, and this is already being given her. We shall soon see and shall feel what the purpose of the Roman element is. Whoever shall believe and obey the word of God will thereby incur reproach and persecution." (*The Great Controversy,* p. 581)

47

A little note that appeared in the "Washington Whispers" section of *U. S. News & World Report,* Aug. 13, 1990, was significant. **"Rome calling,"** it began. "Pope John Paul II discusses world affairs on the telephone with George Bush and Mikhail Gorbachev at least once a week, according to Prof. Malachi Martin, a Roman Catholic theologian and Vatican insider. In a new book, *The Keys of This Blood, . . .* by Simon & Schuster, Martin describes how during the crisis over Lithuania's declaration of independence the Polish-born Pontiff and the embattled Kremlin leader had intense conversations, sometimes several times a day. The Pope advised Gorbachev against violence; in return, he counseled Baltic and Ukrainian Catholics against 'pushing Gorbachev into a corner.' As for his talks with Bush, Martin says the Pope offers the President informed analyses prepared by the Vatican's intelligence network about developments in Eastern Europe and his personal assessments of the new leaders there as well as in the Soviet Union." Many Adventists purchased this book as soon it was available. Very few read all 698 pages, but many read enough to see that the Catholic self-perception was not much different than the Adventist perception of the aims of the papacy.

That the book *is* significant can easily be demonstrated by a few basic questions.

- Is Malachi Martin a Catholic?
- Was he trained as a Jesuit?
- Did he at one time teach at the Vatican's Pontifical Biblical Institute and therefore have occasion to spend a great deal of time in the Vatican?
- Does he know the facts about the background of the present pope?
- Are his statements regarding the downfall of Poland essentially correct?
- Is Martin's knowledge about the history of Communism in Russia basically correct?
- Was he correct in stating that at the time of the writing of *The Keys of This Blood* the world's superpowers were the United States (the Capitalist West) and the Soviet Union (Gorbachev) and the unique religio/political power (the Papacy with nearly 1 billion supporters)?
- Would the fact that two of these three powers conspired and united to bring about the downfall of the third (see *Time,* Feb. 24, 1992,

cover story, "Holy Alliance") lend some credibility to the book even though it certainly happened faster and with less bloodshed than the author, or any commentator, could have anticipated?

No doubt you answered "Yes" to all or the majority of the above questions. Remember Martin does not claim to be a prophet. Let's not expect more from him than he gives. As a life-time Roman Catholic, trained as a Jesuit, having lived and worked in the Vatican for a number of years, he is only giving his personal insights regarding the power and plans of the Papacy. The startling fact is how closely his insights harmonize with those expressed by Ellen White in *The Great Controversy*—particularly Chapters 35, 36.

Simply stated Martin believes that the Roman Catholic System—the Pope—will be the dominant power by the year 2000. For his belief to be anywhere near accurate things had to happen fast. They have! The fact that Gorbachev is no longer in the picture is used by some to downplay the message of the book. I tend to think that the downfall of Communism underscores the premise of the book! The bottom line is that the book is simply one person's educated guess about the role of the papacy in the future. And he does give us insight into general Catholic thought.

Now I would like to go back to a statement quoted from Ellen White above, "She (the Papacy) is silently growing into power." Is this true? Can we see anything in current events that would support this? The answers is "yes" to both questions.

Why is it that so many world leaders seek the recognition and support of the Vatican? For example, "Jewish leaders from around the world met with Pope John Paul II and other Vatican officials early this month (Dec., 1990). They acknowledged approvingly his personal endorsement of a statement urging the Catholic Church to repent for past anti-Semitism. However, they expressed frustration and disappointment at the Holy See's continual refusal to grant diplomatic recognition to the state of Israel." (*National & International Religion Report,* Dec. 17, 1990)

The historic step of full diplomatic relations between Israel and the Vatican has finally been taken. It made the front page of the Washington *Post.* (December 30, 1993) Israel's primary interest in the historic accord was recognition as a nation with a right to exist and a place to exist. Apparently the Israelies had been seeking this agreement for many years but not until the Vatican's interests were met did she give approval for the accord. What did the Vatican want and get? They wanted to be part of the Middle East peace talks; the Pope wants to visit Israel in 1994; they wanted a say in the future of Jerusalem; they wanted Israel to guarantee a number of rights to the Vatican including: freedom of worship, running of its own schools, communications media, charities, hospitals and welfare agencies in the Holy Land; the Vatican wanted to avoid paying property taxes on extensive property in Israel. Evidently, all of these requests by the Vatican will be granted by Israel in exchange for the recognition of having full diplomatic relations with the Vatican.

The bombshell that really exposed the Vatican's current involvement in international politics was the February 24, 1992, issue of *Time* magazine. The cover story, "Holy Alliance," subtitled "How Reagan and the Pope Conspired to Assist Poland's Solidarity Movement and Hasten the Demise of Communism." The title is self-explanatory. The facts in the article are a matter of history and, I might add, fulfilled prophecy. (See Chapter 5, Appendix, for excerpts from the *Time* article.)

A major upshot of the "Holy Alliance" was that shipyard worker Lech Walesa became president of Poland, the most populous of the former Soviet satellites in Eastern Europe. He was certainly used to advance the aims of the Vatican. And what happens in a country where the Vatican is in charge? *The Wall Street Journal* has this to say on that: "Now that Poland has freedom again, the Polish church has begun to seek what it sees as just reward for its troubles: a place in a new constitution for the teaching of Catholicism. . . . They won their first objective, the classroom, last fall. In a deal never debated in public, the government allowed the church to ease religious instruction into the state's schools. Teachers and students fussed when the priests arrived, but soon settled down. The bishops then moved on to the next item on their list: abortion.

"Under the Communists, who couldn't perfect the pill or supply the condom, doctors aborted 500,000 pregnancies a year. The bishops simply wanted it banned." (*The Wall Street Journal,* May 31, 1991) As you are, no doubt, aware the Polish government has since banned abortion and taken the country from the most liberal to the most restrictive abortion laws.

After essentially taking over in Poland as I have described above the Vatican has its eyes on the rest of Europe as well. As reported in the public press the Pope called all the bishops of Eastern and Western Europe together for a two-week meeting at the Vatican in November of 1991 to lay out a strategy for "shaping the religious values" of the region. One source stated, "O Holy Day—Beginning November 28, 135 bishops from Eastern and Western Europe will meet in Vatican City in their first gathering ever to discuss the spiritual fate of Europe." (*U.S. News & World Report,* Nov. 25, 1991)

The National & International Religion Report of December 30, 1991, noted, "Nearly 140 European Catholic bishops spent two weeks at a special Vatican synod on evangelization in post-Communist Europe. Pope John Paul II had summoned the bishops and non-Catholic church leaders to help forge a strategy to ensure that the new Europe is shaped by religious values. But Russian and other Orthodox leaders boycotted the synod, charging that the Catholic Church is too aggressive in eastern Europe (I wonder where they ever got that idea?) and insensitive to Orthodox concerns. Some Protestant leaders complained that they were not included in discussions and had virtually no input into the synod's summary document."

The Associated Press coverage on the opening date of the meeting had this headline, **"Orthodox to Sit Out Meeting, Slam Catholic 'Power Grab'** VATICAN CITY—In a sign of dissent following the collapse of Communism, four Orthodox Church leaders have announced they will boycott a Catholic bishops' synod on Europe that opens today.

"Pope John Paul II called the two-week gathering to chart a course for Europe's 300 million Catholics. About 200 bishops, Vatican officials, scholars, representatives of non-Catholic faiths, and others will take part.

"Several Orthodox leaders have charged that the Vatican's activism in former Communist nations amounts to an attempt to steal followers and expand its power."

In its ever expanding power play the Vatican is now putting pressure on Cuba to open up to Catholicism. The news is: "Pope John Paul II last week urged Fidel Castro's Cuba to open its government to Catholics, who reportedly account for about 41% of the country's population of 10.5 million (though less than 2% of the people are baptized, according to Washington, D.C.-based Puebla Institute). Such a move will contribute to dialogue and to the welfare of society, he told Cuba's new ambassador to the Vatican at a ceremonial meeting. He also lectured the envoy on the need for governments to respect human rights, (the same thing he told the Polish government). . . In response, a high-ranking government official denounced the church along with the CIA on the floor of the National Assembly, and he accused both of promoting counter-revolution. Nevertheless, many analysts believe the Catholic Church will end up playing a crucial role in the peaceful transition to democracy." (*National & International Religion Report,* March 9, 1992)

The Roman Catholic Church is flexing its muscles all over the world. However, the area of most concern to students of Bible prophecy, particularly Revelation 13, involves the Papacy and the United States. Let's take a look at some of the more obvious developments here.

I was a sophomore in college on Nov. 22, 1963, the day President John F. Kennedy was assasinated. How well I remember the national trauma. That was 30 years ago. Things were different then. "For starters, the social divisions in the country were differently arrayed in many respects than they are now. Kennedy's Catholicism was a dominant issue in his campaign. Catholic Americans in 1960 lived almost in a nation apart. The descendants of Irish, German, Italian and Polish immigrants were still concentrated in industrial cities. They ate fish on Friday and attended mass every Sunday, shunned birth control and boasted of large families and sent their children to schools run by celibate priests and nuns. In this Catholic America, John Fitzgerald Kennedy was an aristocrat, grandson of the mayor of Boston, son of one of the richest Catholics in America.

"Kennedy's support from Catholics made him a front-runner in polls before he declared. On the campaign trail, he was cheered by nuns and Catholic school children and greeted by heavily Catholic crowds that waited hours to throng him, like one in Waterbury, Conn. till 3 o'clock in the morning. But suspicions among Protestants remained. Kennedy had to win primaries in mostly Protestant Wisconsin and almost entirely Protestant West Virginia before the big-city bosses—almost all of them Catholic—would back him. In the fall, popular Protestant minister Norman Vincent Peale questioned the loyalty of Catholics. In Houston, Kennedy faced down 300 Protestant ministers and assured them he would resign the presidency if he found any conflict between his public duties and religious faith.

"But religion was still a critical issue. Bare majorities of Protestants and voters over fifty said they were willing to vote for a Catholic. Religious fears as well as enthusiasm swelled 1960 voter turnout to the highest levels since 1908, 64% of those eligible, compared with 55% in 1992. Kennedy won 78% of Catholics' votes but only 38% of Protestants'.

"For many Catholics, Kennedy's victory was a symbol of their full acceptance. For all Americans, it narrowed the rift between Catholic and Protestant." (*U.S. News & World Report,* Nov. 15, 1993, pp. 39, 40)

Based on my own study and the modus operandi of the Papacy, I believe that "Plan A" was to take over the Executive Office of the United States. Failing that, "Plan B" was to dominate the U.S. Congress and the U.S. Supreme Court. "Plan A" was thwarted by Kennedy's assassination. However, the "Holy Alliance" article certainly shows that there has been a continuing and strong Catholic influence over the White House. "Plan B" on the other hand seems to have succeeded.

Remember President Kennedy's statements that he was an American first and a Roman Catholic second. One has to understand Roman Catholic theology in order to recognize that his statement was pure political rhetoric. For the Roman Catholic, with his works-oriented theology, church membership and one's allegiance to the church means everything. To a Catholic excommunication is a fate worse than death itself. Once you are excommunicated there is no hope of heaven or eternal life whatsoever. You can never be "prayed out" of purgatory or hell no matter how much money your relatives pay the priest. You can't receive last rites or be buried in a church cemetery. You are simply lost.

Contemporary proof that Kennedy's statement was political rhetoric comes by way of Cardinal John O'Connor, archbishop of New York, arguably the most influential religious figure in the United States today.

"There is little about the seventy-year-old former rear admiral and chief of Navy chaplains that evokes indifference. He is beloved as a devoted man of God and he is reviled as a demagogue; he is respected for unflinching fidelity to church teachings and he is faulted for dogmatic inflexibility; he is admired as a champion of the rights of the unborn and he is feared as a dangerous fanatic who would impose his view of morality upon all.

"As leader of the 2.2 million-member New York archdiocese, O'Connor is probably the best-known Roman Catholic in America after the Pope. His influence in church matters is bolstered by his close ties to the Vatican. 'He has the Pope's ear as no other American bishop,' says Richard McBrien, chairman of the theology department at the University of Notre Dame.

"It is O'Connor's penchant for 'plain talk' on the most delicate issues that frequently gets him into the headlines and occasionally into trouble. He has repeatedly used his pulpit at St. Patrick's Cathedral and his easy access to the media to condemn abortion and to admonish fellow Catholics, especially politicians, who refuse to abide by the church's teachings on the subject. He created a stir earlier in the year when he declared in a newspaper column that 'bishops may decide' that Catholic politicians who take a pro-choice stand 'must be warned . . . that they risk excommunication.'"

"O'Connor makes no excuses for the positions he takes, even if they sometimes seem harsh or unyielding. 'I must preach what the church preaches, teach what the church teaches,' he said at the end of a service disrupted by AIDS activists. The church, after all, is not a democracy, he notes, nor is it seeking a comfortable position in the cultural mainstream." (*U.S. News & World Report,* Dec. 31, 1990/Jan. 7, 1991)

But wait, there is more. "Pennsylvania's eighteen Catholic bishops called on Catholic legislators to uphold teachings of the church on abortion. Calling abortion an 'unspeakable crime,' they declared that 'one cannot be a Catholic in good standing while publicly rejecting and advocating the abandonment of its teaching.' Their pastoral letter, which did not specify what action the church might take against erring lawmakers, will wield political clout in a state that is 33% Catholic, observers said. Chris Niebryzdowski, president of the state's National Organization for Women, criticized the bishop's plea, agreeing that it will carry weight because of Catholics' unwillingness to risk being cast out of their church." (*National & International Religion Report,* April 23, 1990)

Do we need more evidence? Author Dave Hunt who has studied the topic in depth states, "Are these millions of Roman Catholics of every nationality loyal? While some may criticize their clergy, deep down in his soul every Catholic still believes that the Church holds keys to heaven and that without her favor only hell waits. Thus the power that Rome holds over its subjects is far greater than that of any secular government over its citizens. When the time comes to make a choice concerning where one's real loyalty lies, there is little doubt of the outcome for the Catholic of whatever citizenship." (Dave Hunt, *Global Peace and the Rise of Antichrist,* p. 116)

And a few years ago Ellen White wrote these words: "The Roman Catholic Church, with all its ramifications throughout the world, forms one vast organization under the control, and designed to serve the interests, of the papal see. Its millions of communicants, in every country on the globe, are instructed to hold themselves as bound in allegiance to the pope. Whatever their nationality or their government, they are to regard the authority of the church as above all other. Though they may take the oath pledging their loyalty to the state, yet back of this lies the vow of obedience to Rome, absolving them from every pledge inimical to her interests." (*The Great Controversy,* p. 580)

So John Fitzgerald Kennedy opened the door. And just look at what has happened since. All three branches of the U.S. government now have strong Catholic influence. Actually, four areas—I must not forget the Department of State. There is always the ambassador.

On January 23, 1984, *Newsweek* magazine carried the story of the appointment by Ronald Reagan of William Wilson to be the U.S. Ambassador to the Holy See. The story began with these words: "More than 200 years ago, John Adams predicted that the United States would never send a representative to the Holy See or permit 'an ecclesiastical tyrant' from the papal diplomatic corps to sully American soil. Adams was a good Protestant but a poor prophet: last week the White House and the Vatican announced they had established full diplomatic relations, thus consummating a courtship the papacy has been quietly pushing for a century." The article closes with these words: "For the pope, diplomatic recognition provides full access to a superpower in his quest for world peace."

The *Time* magazine report of the same date gave this perspective: "Given the historic nature of the step, there was remarkably little fanfare. The word came first from Rome. A few hours later, the State Department made it official. After a lapse of 117 years, the U.S. was establishing full diplomatic relations with the Vatican.

"Ronald Reagan chose William Wilson, who has been the presidential representative to the Vatican since 1981, to serve as the new ambassador. Wilson, 69, is a California real estate developer and charter member of Reagan's kitchen cabinet of personal advisers. Archbishop Pio Laghi, 61, the apostolic delegate in Washington, will become Wilson's counterpart, the papal pro-nuncio. One of the Holy See's ablest diplomats, he previously served in Argentina, where he assisted the Vatican's mediation of the Beagle Channel dispute between Argentina and Chile.

"No Pope in modern times has taken such a direct interest in wielding diplomatic influence as John Paul II. Now that the U.S. has become the 107th nation with which it has diplomatic relations, the Vatican may move to establish ties with the world's other superpower." (*Time,* Jan. 23, 1984)

So after more than a century of pressing, the Catholic Church now has full diplomatic relations with the world's only remaining superpower. Since 1984 the U.S. has maintained that relationship, and Southern Baptist Bill Clinton has continued the arrangement in spite of many voices appealing to him to sever the contact. The April 26, 1993, issue of *Christianity Today* in its "World Scene" department gave this coverage: "President Clinton's decision to appoint Boston Mayor Raymond Flynn to be the next ambassador to the Vatican drew sharp criticism from Evangelical and church/state separation groups that had urged an end to official diplomatic relations with the Holy See.

" 'Such a decision by any President is bad, but coming from a Baptist President, it is even worse,' said Richard Land, executive director of the Southern Baptist Convention Christian Life Commission, citing the 'cherished Baptist heritage' of the separation of church and state. In February, the CLC, the National Association of Evangelicals, Church of the Brethren, Seventh-day Adventist Church, and Presbyterian Church (USA) joined in a letter calling on Clinton to break diplomatic ties to the Vatican. The National Council of Churches also opposed the appointment.

"Also condemning Clinton's decision was Barry Lynn, executive director of Americans United for Separation of Church and State, who said the continued 'official relationship between the United States government and the hierarchy of the Roman Catholic church' violates the First Amendment. Noting that Flynn, like his three predecessors, is a Catholic, Lynn raised concerns that the United States is establishing 'a defacto religious test for this office.'

"Flynn, a prolife Democrat, says he hopes to be a bridge between the White House and Pope John Paul II on the concerns they share on 'social and economic justice.'"

When, back in 1984, President Reagan established full diplomatic relations with the Holy See and the exchange of ambassadors was accomplished the Catholic community expressed its pleasure with the arrangement.

"Catholic reaction to the appointment has been positive but quiet. 'It is not a religious issue but a public policy question, which happily has now been addressed and settled in that context,' said a spokesman for the U.S. Catholic Conference (USCC). It does not confer a 'special blessing' on Catholicism, he said, but recognizes the power, influence, and prestige of the current pope.

"Catholics are pleased as well about the tone of the opposing groups, which the USCC spokesman described as 'restrained, courteous, and friendly—a tribute to ecumenical progress.'

"In 1951, unified, vigorous Protestant opposition blocked Truman's appointment of an ambassador to the Vatican. Today, Christians are less easily stirred to action on the issue. There is general agreement that the right President chose the right time to change a situation that had remained unresolved and uncomfortable for more than a century." (*Christianity Today,* Feb. 17, 1984)

Why all the fuss about diplomatic relations with the Vatican you may ask? Besides the very obvious to the student of Bible prophecy—we are dealing with the little horn power of Daniel 7, and beast power of Revelation 13 and the great whore of Revelation 17. The deadly wound has all but healed.

The *Adventist Review,* April 22, 1993, carried an article by B. B. Beach in which he gave five problems with the diplomatic relations issue. I will cite three:

"In January 1984 the United States and the Roman Catholic Church announced the establishment of diplomatic relations between them. This radical change in longstanding national policy was accomplished without public discussion or hearings, and without substantive debate in either House. The Seventh-day Adventist Church objects for the following reasons.

"**Separation of Church and State.** Diplomatic ties with the Holy See run counter to the fundamental U.S. tradition of separation of church and state. Not only do diplomatic relations with the Papacy entangle the United States with the problems, views, and claims of a church, but they involve that church in the political affairs of the United States. Church political ambition runs counter to the American national spirit and heritage.

"**A Form of Religious Discrimination.** These diplomatic relations are discriminatory. They represent a violation of the American principle of pluralism and equality of all religions before the law. The diplomatic tie in question favors one church because of its size and influence, and because historically it has claimed civil authority. Granting the Roman Catholic Church special recognition and direct access to the State Department and the White House is discriminatory toward other churches, especially world churches and world ecclesiastical councils.

"The Pope and Curia Comprise the Holy See. It is impossible to differentiate between the pope as head of the Roman Catholic Church and as head of the Vatican City State. In fact, diplomatic relations are *not* with Vatican City but with the *Holy See*. The pope and the Curia together comprise the Holy See. Any interpretation that separates the Holy See and the Roman Catholic Church is misleading. The Roman Catholic Church itself makes this clear by the dual role assigned to nuncios as ambassadors to the government and as papal representatives to the Catholic bishops of the same country." (*Adventist Review,* April 22, 1993)

No doubt about it the deadly wound is healing. This book is not just to validate the timeliness of our prophetic interpretation, but to point out that current world events, particularly those with political/religio overtones, are the predicted harbingers of the end. And the papacy is a major player in this scenario.

CHAPTER 6

And the World Wonders

In August of 1993 when Pope John Paul II's plane landed in Denver on his third visit to the United States, President Bill Clinton was there to meet him—just like President Reagan flew to Florida the last time he came. It is noteworthy to recognize that the pope always makes the secular leaders come to see him instead of asking for an appointment to see them. In reporting on the Denver meeting *U.S News* reported, "They stood together, in the summer rains of Denver, the pope and the president, embodying what Victor Hugo described in 1830 as 'these two halves of God': the civic and the spiritual, the temporal and the eternal. Each man, in his own way, radiates a special aura and symbolizes a set of enduring values. No matter how low a president sinks in his polls, he remains head of state, as well as head of government, a living monument to the nation's strength and survival. The pope, by contrast, represents faith, not force; moral purity instead of power. Both elements are necessary for a whole and balanced society." Then a very significant statement follows in the article, "Both Reagan and Bush won the Catholic vote (as Republicans) before Clinton (as a Democrat) reversed the trend last year." (*U.S. News & World Report,* Aug. 23, 1993)

That last sentence was very significant. The last three U.S. presidents have been supported by the Catholic vote. The same issue of *U.S. News* that reported the meeting of President Clinton and the pope in Denver contained the announcement that he was nominating General John Shalikashvili to be the new chairman of the Joint Chiefs of Staff to replace retiring General Colin Powell. Of all those qualified to fill the position, the president chose a Polish Catholic immigrant with the same basic roots as the pope to head up the largest and most powerful army in the world!

Much more could be said about the Roman Catholic presence and influence in the Executive Branch of the government both in the past and present. I'll share just one further reference to the Catholic influence on U.S. presidents from the Boston *Herald* of February 5, 1990: "Six years after Boston's Cardinal Bernard Law first met George Bush at a Washington charity dinner, Law has emerged as one of the president's closest friends and advisers outside the White House. . .

"The president trusts the cardinal's judgment. . . . Law gives his opinion right away, and the president listens. . .

"The prelate also has a strong relationship with White House Chief of Staff John Sununu, speaking with him at least once a week and often two or three times weekly, according to a Bush aide. . . 'Bush talks to Law as much as he does to any other outside adviser,' said Wead, who defined 'outside adviser' as someone not on the White House payroll.

"It is a relationship that lugs at the vaguely defined borders separating church and state. . .

"Law has been credited, along with other religious leaders, with helping to convince Bush to set a national day of prayer for the hostages . . .

"'Sununu is an active practicing Catholic and has been an important catalyst between Law and Bush,' a senior Bush aide said."

Congress today—the combined House of Representatives and Senate—has more Roman Catholics in it than any other religion by far. With 138 out of the total of 534 members, the Catholics have a 26% voting block. Here again the potential for papal influence is very strong.

During the Reagan/Bush years in the White House the judicial branch of government also began its shift to a strong Catholic presence. This may have been due to the "Holy Alliance." Court watchers observed a very unusual set of circumstances. As you are aware, when the president nominates someone for a position on the Supreme Court, that person must then be confirmed by the Senate before he/she actually is seated on the high court bench. Most of the time the nominee is confirmed. In fact, in the entire history of the U.S. Supreme Court up until the presidency of Ronald Reagan, only two Supreme Court nominees had failed to be confirmed. Then all at once two Reagan nominees in succession were denied confirmation.

When Reagan nominated Judge Robert Bork, a conservative but not a professing Christian, the Senate denied confirmation. They "borked" him. He then nominated Judge Ginsberg, a Jew, who had a good ten-year record as a judge. He was denied confirmation, ostensibly because he had at one time experimented with marijuana while in college. Then when the president wanted a "sure thing," he nominated Judge Anthony Kennedy, a Catholic, and he was confirmed with a unanimous vote.

Then later when President Bush nominated Clarence Thomas to fill a vacancy on the court the most unusual and unfortunate confirmation hearing of all time occurred—much of it on national television and radio. Judge Clarence Thomas was probably not guilty of the trumped up charges leveled at him by the Democrats through Anita Hill. However, these facts remain: Clarence Thomas was not supported by the NAACP. He received the lowest rating ever given by the American Bar Association for a Supreme Court nominee. He reportedly used marijuana while in college. He went straight from law school to an administrative position with a government agency from which he was later appointed to a federal judgeship. In other words, he had no experience as a trial attorney. He had only been a judge for about two years with few written opinions. And all of this was topped off by the allegations of Anita Hill.

Yet in spite of all this, Clarence Thomas was confirmed! Why? I believe the simple answer is that he had a strong Catholic influence in his background. His first words through the national media spoken at Kennebunkport, Maine, when introduced by President Bush at his summer home were, "I want to thank the sisters (Roman Catholic nuns who taught him in school) for believing in me." Virginia governor, L. Douglas Wilder, is quoted in the *Journal of the American Bar Association* as saying, "He (Clarence Thomas) has indicated he's a very devout Catholic, and that is the issue before us. The question is how much allegiance is there to the Pope?" (September, 1991) Thomas claims he is an Episcopalian today.

In addition Clarence Thomas was supported by the Christian Coalition and featured in their publication, *Christian American.* D. James Kennedy of Coral Ridge Ministries sent out a large "mass mailing" in which he solicited funds for a full-page ad in *USA Today* seeking support for Thomas.

So how is the court leaning? *U.S. News & World Report* ran an article in its June 18, 1990, issue entitled "The Court's New Catechism," subtitled "The Reagan Appointees on the Supreme Court Are Redrawing the Lines Between Church and State." Relatively new Chief Justice

William Rehnquist has stated, "The 'wall of separation between church and state' is a metaphor based on bad history, a metaphor which has proven useless as a guide to judging. It should be frankly and explicitly abandoned." Judge Kennedy is described as a persistent advocate of weakening the separation between church and state, who has accused liberals on the Supreme Court of "an unjustified hostility toward religion." And, of course, Justice Scalia, in the much publicized "Smith Decision" stated in essence that as a nation we can not afford the luxury of striking down laws simply because they limit someone's religious practices. Justice O'Connor is frequently a swing vote on religious questions.

Another interesting activity that has been reported is that "Four members of the U.S. Supreme Court knelt in prayer at St. Matthew's Cathedral in Washington, D.C., on the Sunday before the high court opened its new term, and they listened to a sermon by Detroit's Catholic Archbishop Adam J. Maida. Chief Justice William Rehnquist, along with Justices Sandra Day O'Connor, Antonin Scalia, and William Kennedy, participated in the traditional Red Mass, held each year to invoke God's blessing on the legal system." (*National & International Religion Report,* Oct. 21, 1991) This was before the confirmation of Judge Thomas, so he, too, may join them in this service in the future.

One final report on the current U.S. Supreme Court. The Washington *Post* reported in its Tuesday, July 6, 1993, issue a summary of the voting patterns of the Supreme Court. That article pointed out that in the 1992-93 term that Chief Justice Rehnquist and the Catholic justices, Kennedy, Scalia, and Thomas (Catholic background) voted together in the majority in over 90% of the cases before the Court.

The 365,000-member American Bar Association has been a very powerful organization over the years. Recently, the ABA took an official pro-choice position on abortion. Within six months of that decision because of pressure from pro-life forces led by the Catholic Church the ABA modified its position to one of "neutrality." It was also reported that, "Yielding to pressure from Catholics, the AFL-CIO (the largest and most powerful labor union in the U.S.) also will be abortion neutral, a decision that disappointed some unionists who hoped an official pro-choice stand would attract women and minorities into the struggling labor movement. Lane Kirkland, president of the 14.2 million member federation, announced that his group's executive council felt abortion 'was a matter of deep conscience, conviction, and religion.' Cardinal John O'Connor of New York gave signals earlier this year that he and other pro-life clerics might lobby labor union members to withhold dues if the AFL-CIO adopted a pro-choice position." (*National & International Religion Report,* Aug. 27, 1990)

There is also a new strange kind of cooperation between Catholics and Protestants. It is the common enemy syndrome. In *Newsweek,* Nov. 8, 1993, the magazine showed a photograph of Cardinal O'Connor standing in front of St. Patrick's Cathedral. The article was titled "Allies in a Cultural War." A subtitle asked the question "Can Catholics and Evangelicals Use Their Common Ground to Become Political Partners?"

The article stated in part, "Until a month ago, the closest Pat Robertson had come to the Roman Catholic Church was sharing his digs at Yale Law School with a graduate of the University of Notre Dame. That was in the 1950s, long before Robertson had his 'born again' conversion, became a Southern Baptist minister, and learned to pray in tongues. But now Robertson's Christian Coalition (See Chapter 3)— heretofore a political engine for evangelical Protestants—is openly courting conservative Catholics. At its September meeting in Washington, D.C., the coalition bestowed its first Catholic Layman of the Year award on Rep. Henry Hyde of Illinois, held a workshop on Catholic-evangelical cooperation, and—holy heterodoxy!—closed its meeting with a Sunday Mass as well as a Protestant service.

"Is a political alliance between evangelicals and Catholics possible? Historically, the two groups have viewed each other as religious enemies. Theologically as well as geographically, evangelicals and Catholics still sit in very different pews. But according to University of Virginia sociologist James Davison Hunter, doctrinal differences among religious Americans are less important than cultural antagonisms between secular liberals and serious believers of all faiths. In today's culture wars, Hunter argues, conservative in both religious camps have discovered certain common concerns: opposition to abortion, support for parental choice in education, and a shared sense of persecution in public life.

"Robertson's Christian Coalition hopes to exploit this cultural convergence among believers. His movement managed a significant breakthrough last May when New York's Cardinal John O'Connor agreed to let the coalition distribute 100,000 voter guides in Catholic churches. (In addition as reported in *National & International Religion Report,*

May 17, 1993, "Cardinal John O'Connor, archbishop of New York, shared church mailing lists with Pat Robertson's Christian Coalition, and the groups established phone banks to urge parents to vote." This was in connection with the New York City school board elections.) In Atlanta last week, a spokesman for Catholic Archbishop John Donoghue reported that the church shares 'many common goals' with the Christian Coalition.

"Overt support from Catholics could make an enormous difference to the Christian Coalition. One fourth of the American electorate identify themselves as evangelicals, another fourth as Catholics. 'We expect to top out with 1 million Protestant members,' says Ralph Reed, the coalition's executive director. 'With Catholics, we can double that.' To that end, Robertson recently appointed Marlene Elwell, his Midwest campaign director in 1988, as liaison to U.S. Catholics. 'Frankly,' Robertson writes in the current issue of his magazine, *Christian American,* 'I feel I have a lot more in common with this Pope than with liberal Protestants.'"

The world's most well known and respected Protestant evangelist, Billy Graham, who has had recent visits with the pope while in Europe for evangelism, held a crusade in Three Rivers Stadium in Pittsburgh on June 2-6, 1993. The fact that "Pittsburgh has more bridges than any other U.S. city was an analogy not wasted on the organizers. The crusade had the support of 1,030 churches in sixty five denominations, and enjoyed generous cooperation from the Catholic Church (Six members of the seventy-seven-person executive committee were Catholic.). . . Graham said he was impressed with the unity of the city's religious leaders, and spent one morning meeting with eight (Catholic) bishops and executives from various denominations." (*National and International Religion Report,* June 14, 1993)

For years the ecumenical movement consisted largely of various Protestant groups getting together for mutual benefit. The Catholics stayed on the fringes or in the background preferring to think and speak of Protestants as "separated brethren" who should be encouraged to "come home to the mother church." Now things have changed. The Catholics are actively seeking unity with Protestants. They say that we are all the children of a great divorce, referring to the Protestant Reformation. The point is that though our parents quarrelled, we don't have to, and we should therefore get together for evangelism and world

church unity under the pope.

The *Adventist News Review* of November 17-30, 1993, reported **"HIGH-LEVEL DISCUSSIONS OF WCC-ROMAN CATHOLIC RELATIONS:** The president of the Pontifical Council for Promotin Christian Unity, Cardinal Edward Idris Cassidy, met with officers an senior staff of the World Council of Churches in Geneva on 6 Novembe Accompanying Cassidy were PCPCU secretary Bishop Pierre Dupro and Msgr. John Radano.

"The WCC was represented by the moderator and one of the vi moderators of the Central Committee, Archbishop Aram Keshishian a Ephorus Soritua Nababan, General Secretary Konard Raiser, Dep General Secretary Wesley Ariarajah, church and ecumenical relati executive secretary George Lemopoulos and Sr Monica Coone Roman Catholic responsible for relations with Catholic mission socie in the WCC programme Unit on Life, Education, and Mission.

"High on the agenda of the meeting—the first formal one betv the WCC officers and the PCPCU—was strengthening relations betv the WCC and the Roman Catholic Church.

"Particular attention was given to cooperation in the framewo the WCC-Vatican Joint Working Group, ongoing work in the Faitl Order Commission, and collaboration in reflection on mission ar social and ethical issues.

"It was stressed that the ecumenical commitment of the R Catholic Church at local, national, and regional levels through na councils of churches and regional ecumenical organizations offer ecumenical possibilities which should be deepened together."

Though Martin Luther, after whom the world's various Lu bodies take their name, was one of the major Protestant refo Lutherans are now more serious than ever regarding improven relations with the Roman Catholic Church. "In September, the Lu World Federation (LWF), an organization of 114 Lutheran l released a statement on its recent meeting with the Vatican.

"In it, the LWF notes a 'decisive improvement in Lutheran-Catholic relations' since its first talks with the Vatican in 196 also notes a resurgence among both groups of 'theologically d attitudes, which endanger ecumenical progress.' However, in clo LWF reaffirms its 'belief that ecumenism is not optional, but ess the church.'" (*Christianity Today,* Nov. 9, 1992)

EATD-3

Roman Catholic attorney Keith Fournier wrote a book published in 1990 entitled *Evangelical Catholics,* subtitled "A Call for Christian Cooperation to Penetrate the Darkness With the Light of the Gospel." At the time he wrote the book he was General Counsel and Dean of Evangelism at Franciscan University of Steubenville, Ohio. He is now working for Pat Robertson's Christian Coalition as the Executive Director of the American Center for Law and Justice. This statement of his appears on the dustcover of the book. "It's high time that all of us who are Christians come together regardless of the difference of our confessions and our traditions and make it our common cause to bring Christian values to bear in our society."

A few excerpts from Fournier's book will point out his particularly Catholic views on ecumenism. "All families, regardless of their apparent or real health, are dysfunctional. Granted, the type, number and degree of the dysfunctions vary from family to family, but they are always present. . . The family of God, the church, is no different. . . This problem began in the eleventh century when some disputes over political, ecclesiastical, theological, and even liturgical issues finally led to a split between Western and Eastern Christians. Known as the Great Schism of 1054, it created the first break in the unity of the church. From that moment, the Roman Catholic Church and the Greek Orthodox Church went different ways. Although much reconciliation and healing still need to take place between Catholics and Orthodox, official steps were begun on December 7, 1965, when Pope Paul VI and Athenagoras revoked the mutual excommunication decrees that had been blocking reunification efforts between the two churches for almost a thousand years.

"The scars left by the Great Schism, however, did not lead to the depth of hurt, anger, and divisiveness that we now see throughout the church. That legacy falls on the shoulders of the Reformation. It began with a call within Catholicism to correct abuses in the church, but it ended with Catholics leaving the church and beginning new movements outside the church's umbrella. The protest leaders and their followers came to be known as Protestants. Once outside the church, however, they had little impetus and no overarching authority to hold them together. They soon splintered into more groups, creating the numerous denominations within Protestantism we see today.

"I have no intention," states Fournier, "to assess blame against

Protestants or Catholics for this terrible split. Enough mistakes were made on both sides. Neither do I ignore the positive impact and necessary correctives the Reformation caused in and outside the Roman Catholic Church (which all leaders, including my own, have acknowledged). But the fact of the matter is that the Reformation movement and the Church's response to it led to a traumatic family split—a radical divorce—and hundreds of years later we are still suffering from its impact. We are children of this great divorce, descendants of a single family tree divided by mistrust, failure, and abuse. We can see its devastation everywhere, even in what is left unsaid or ignored." (Keith A. Fournier, *Evangelical Catholics,* pp. 142, 143)

Many readers will wonder about the role of the Charismatic or Spiritualism in the ecumenical movement. Keith Fournier writes, "Since 1973 I have been involved in what is often called the Catholic Charismatic Renewal or the Catholic Pentecostal Movement. (I guess that makes me a pentecostal, evangelical, Catholic Christian!)." (*Ibid.,* p. 146) A unique combination indeed! It rather reminds one of the three unclean spirits of Revelation, generally interpreted by Adventists to be Spiritism, Catholicism, and apostate Protestantism.

As the wounds of the great divorce fester, Fournier makes an appeal for cooperation in evangelizing the world. "As we stand at the end of one century and the threshold of another, I propose that the opportunity for such a healing has perhaps never been greater. The whole Christian church—Protestant, Catholic, and Orthodox—is in need of reevangelization, renewal, and reformation. The world literally awaits the gospel message. Can we rise to the challenge? Can we cooperate with one another, standing together as a unified beacon of light penetrating the dark with the good news about Christ, our common Savior and Lord? Can we begin to reexamine our long-held prejudices and rediscover our common family heritage? Can we break the insidious cycle of move, countermove, pain, and mistrust? A dying world is waiting for our answer. What will we tell it?" (*Ibid.,* p. 147)

An active and growing group of Protestant leaders in America today is seeking the support of Catholics in full cooperation toward a common goal. Most of the meetings of this group are conducted without press coverage and without the knowledge of the public at large. Fournier described his attendance at such a meeting. "I recently attended a meeting of the American Congress of Christian Citizens, an ecumenical group that Pat Robertson founded to oppose the rising tide of anti-Christian bigotry in the media. In our meeting room were major evangelical leaders I've admired for years—Dr. Charles Stanley, Dr. Jerry Falwell, Dr. D. James Kennedy, Pat Robertson, and many others. I found not only a tremendous openness to my presence, but also a growing respect for my church and a thawing in what had been hard ice in the past. Perhaps the comments by Dr. Falwell were most illustrative. With a sincerity born of battle fatigue, he told the whole group not even to consider trying to affect public policy with only a narrow evangelical Protestant church coalition. He said that from its inception any such effort must include Catholics and consultation with great churchmen such as Cardinal Law and Cardinal O'Connor. Clearly not backing off one bit from his self-described 'narrowness of doctrine,' Dr. Falwell showed a refreshing openness." (*Ibid.*, p. 172)

Regarding his attendance at evangelical Protestant strategy meetings Fournier says, "I am free to move in all these circles because of the increasing realization that we are being led by the same Holy Spirit, we serve the same Savior, and ultimately we will occupy the same Kingdom together. This is no dreamy, wild-eyed ecumenism. I know full well that our bedrock differences in doctrine and practice are serious and must be discussed and worked through. <u>That process is under way</u>. But the missionary challenge of the twenty-first century compels us to come to the foot of the cross together. . . But we can't bring others to the Lord when we can't even live in the Lord together, when we slander each other from our pulpits, when we fail to work together, when we indulge in subtle undertones of bigotry and prejudice. If we are to be true Christians and faithful to our mission, we need to come together. . . <u>Accepting one another is only a necessary first step to positive ecumenism and to our *ultimate* goal—complete unity</u>. We need to pray with each other for the coming about of the full communion in faith and charity of all Christians." (*Ibid.*, pp. 190-192, 197)

As you can see from the remarks and report above the ecumenical movement is alive and well and now finally includes Catholics working with Protestant leaders and groups. Perhaps the most significant factor in the ecumenical movement is that the road is leading "back home" to an unchanged Roman Catholic Church. "Pope John Paul II urged 'all Christians' to mobilize for evangelism and to prepare for what he believes will be 'the dawning of a new missionary age.' . . .The pope stated at one point in his message that the mission of world evangelism must be conducted with the conviction that <u>the Catholic Church 'alone possesses the fullness of the means of salvation.</u>' " (*National & International Religion Report,* Feb. 11, 1991)

Of course, total unity is not necessary for total cooperation. The present level of cooperation is sufficient, and it is still moving ahead rapidly to bring about the fulfillment of Revelation 13. Events are happening so fast it is hard to keep up with them. On March 30, 1994, leading newspapers across the United States posted headlines "Catholics, Evangelicals Huddle—Statement Calls for Acceptance." (*USA Today*) "Christians Herald New Era—U.S. Evangelicals, Conservative Catholics End Discord, Urge Shared Vision." (Denver's *Rocky Mountain News*) In what was called a "historic declaration" signed by thirty-nine leading evangelical Protestants and Roman Catholics the twenty-five-page document urges the nation's 52 million Catholics and 13 million evangelicals to no longer hold each other at theological arm's length and stop aggressive proselytization of each other's flocks—in short, to turn their theological swords into a recognition of a common faith. The signers stated two major goals of the accord—world evangelism and common concerns for society. Those who drafted and signed the declaration are the most visible and influential in their respective organizations today. Men such as Charles Colson, Pat Robertson, John Cardinal O'Conner, Richard John Neuhaus, and the director of the Southern Baptist's Home Mission Board. This is now making public and official what the Christian Coalition has been doing behind the scenes for several years. It is high time that we realize what is happening and equip ourselves by the study of God's Word for what is just ahead of us.

It has long been recognized by many that the Charismatic movement may well be the glue that brings about the unity of "Christians" of all faiths. It seems common to us now but who would ever have thought that the Catholic Church could have been so embracing of this movement. "It was billed as a 'Return to the Upper Room.' About 17,000 priests, nuns, monks, and parish lay leaders convened in Pittsburgh's Civic Arena June 5-7 (1992) to celebrate the Day of Pentecost and the 25th anniversary of the Catholic charismatic renewal movement. The movement began in 1967 when a group of Duquesne University students and professors were 'baptized in the Holy Spirit' during a weekend retreat. An estimated 50 million Catholics worldwide have identified with the movement, including 10 million in the United States." (*National & International Religion Report,* June 15, 1992)

Earlier I discussed the growing awareness that for years Catholic clergy and teachers have been involved in sexual immorality and child abuse. However, in the context of this chapter it should be pointed out that we are not talking about the occasional indiscretion as happens in the Protestant world. The picture that is emerging now is one of pervasive immorality from local parish priest to the archbishops. I mention this now and will share some details at this point for two reasons: first, to underscore that false doctrines bring bad actions, and second, that in spite of a pleasant front, behind that face is a background of very offensive activity.

The reports that we are most familiar with are primarily from the U.S. and Canada. Who knows what the picture is on a worldwide scale? The greatest problem to me is that if the public wasn't crying out right now and even suing the perpetrators and the church, nothing would be done about it. (See Chapter 6, Appendix, for more from the public record on this situation.)

I am not the only one who has noticed the high level of sexual abuse in the Roman Catholic clergy. *Christianity Today*'s January 10, 1994, issue gave a report of the Top Religion Stories of 1993. In a survey of religion writers and editors, three of the five—Peter Steinfels, New York *Times,* Jim Franklin, Boston *Globe,* and Jim Jones, Fort Worth *Star-Telegram*—listed sexual abuse by Roman Catholic clergy as one of the five top religion stories of 1993.

Many have been shocked by the abuses of the Catholic Church. Their confidence in the Catholic system has been shaken. And with the free distribution of Bibles many have found things in God's Word that are different from church dogma. Thousands, yes, millions, of people are leaving the Roman Catholic Church and joining with Protestants. This is especially true in Latin America. A cover and feature article in *Christianity Today* reports that "Latin America Is Turning Protestant." The article points out that "The Pope is concerned. In the aftermath of his second visit to Brazil, his eleventh to Latin America, it is clear that he doesn't pull people in as he used to. In Brazil—supposedly the most Catholic nation in the world—the usual throngs just did not materialize: for one scheduled event, 500,000 people were expected, but only 100,000 showed up. In contrast, on the morning of the Pope's arrival,

200,000 evangelicals packed a soccer stadium for a rally sponsored by a local church, underscoring the fact that over a half-million Brazilians are leaving the Catholic church for evangelical churches *each year*.

"A tidal wave of change is sweeping Latin America and transforming the face of the entire continent.

"In nearly every nation in the region, the number of Protestants has increased significantly. According to Patrick Johnstone of the Worldwide Evangelization Crusade, the number of evangelicals has tripled regionwide in the past twenty-five years and in some countries even sextupled. David Stoll extrapolates from these numbers: 'If it triples again over the next twenty-five years, by 2010 evangelicals will be a third of the population. At that point even slowed growth would soon make Protestants a majority in Latin America.' According to Brazilian Catholic Bishop Boaventura Kloppenburg, 'Latin America is becoming Protestant more rapidly than central Europe did in the sixteenth century.'"

"For centuries, to be Latino was to be Catholic. You were born and baptized, you lived and died with everyone making the sign of the cross. Now young people toting Bibles can be seen in the crammed public buses (Latin Catholics tend to keep their Bibles at home); whole families go to former movie theaters and storefront churches peppering the cityscape, not for mass, but for worship.

"The Catholic church counterattacks evangelical criticisms with paid ads, street marches, and sermons denouncing *los evangelicos.*" (*Christianity Today*, April 6, 1992)

Christianity Today first started printing reports of persecution by Catholics in March of 1990. The Catholic Church has become so upset over its members leaving the church that with its knowledge and, in some cases, encouragement, Catholics are terrorizing and killing Protestants.

"Hostilities between Mexico's Catholics and Protestants reached a new high last month when an interdenominational prayer meeting attended by some 160 evangelicals in the Mexico City area was violently broken up by a mob of several thousand Catholics armed with stones, machetes, and sticks. Virtually all those attending the meeting were injured. 'It was a miracle no one was killed,' said Roxanne Menezes, a young Christian worker who described the scene as 'nightmarish.'

"Witnesses said that an all-night prayer meeting being held on the slopes of the Ajusco volcano in the southeast section of Mexico City had been in progress for several hours when crowds yelling, 'Kill them!' and 'This is a Catholic town!' converged on the group. Townspeople were reportedly told the group consisted of squatters who had come to steal their land. But even after the real identity was explained, the majority of the crowd persisted in its attack.

"Catholic officials in the neighboring suburbs of Xicalco and Magdalena, where most of the mob originated, have made it clear that evangelicals are not welcome. They refused to comment on the Ajusco incident, but a local priest referred reporters to a local government official Guillermo Gutierrez. A report in the influential daily newspaper *Uno mas Uno* quoted Gutierrez as affirming the expulsion: 'We are all Catholic. . . In case someone who lives (in this community) might decide to change religion, the person could be expelled and would have to sell his possessions.'

"In 1989 alone, attacks against evangelicals took the lives of at least five believers, injured dozens more, caused hundreds to flee homelands, and destroyed or closed countless churches." (*Christianity Today,* March 19, 1990)

Two months later it was reported that "The 30 Roman Catholic bishops of northwestern Mexico and California have issued a pastoral letter warning against the proselytizing efforts of groups that 'reject or directly oppose the historical churches.' The letter makes specific reference to the Church of Jesus Christ of Latter-day Saints, Jehovah's Witnesses, Seventh-day Adventists, and Pentecostal groups, according to Religious News Service. Its release comes in the wake of recent attacks on evangelicals that were reportedly instigated by Catholics.

"The letter called clergy and lay leaders to increase activities to counter the missionary work directed at Hispanic Catholics." (*Ibid.,* April 9, 1990)

In a recent visit to Latin America Pope John Paul II mentioned the Protestant defections. "He deplored 'the painful fact' that some Mexicans 'have broken this link of saving unity, joining the sects,' the term the Mexican Catholics hierarchy generally uses for all non-Catholic groups—Jehovah's Witnesses, Mormons, and evangelicals alike.

"Genaro Alamilla, Mexican Catholic church spokesman during the Pope's visit, told the Associated Press that sects 'take advantage of the poverty and ignorance of so many of our brothers.'" (*Ibid.,* June 18, 1990) My question to the Catholic spokesman is Who has kept the people in poverty and ignorance for the last 500 years?

Over the years the Catholic Church has tried to use miracles as a sign of the true church. This phenomenon is often used to bolster confidence where Biblical support is lacking. *U.S. News & World Report* (March 29, 1993) recently devoted its cover and an eight-page article to the present "miracles" happening in Catholic churches across the country. The miracles are varied but the most common ones are "weeping madonnas" (statues of the Virgin Mary), sightings of Mary on hillsides or at shrines, and priests with wrists that bleed like Christ's. I will recount just one such story. "The Rev. Daniel Hamilton was a self-described skeptic, but the Madonna at his church wept so much that staffers had to mop up the water with turkish towels. 'All of us have faith,' he now says, 'but sometimes it's nice to have that faith bolstered by events in the real world.'"

That the Catholic Church would resort to "miracles" to generate support for their claims of being the true church was predicted by Ellen White years ago. (See *The Great Controversy,* p. 588, for example: "Papists . . . boast of miracles as a certain sign of the true church.") She cautions God's faithful, "A prayerful study of the Bible would show Protestants the real character of the papacy and would cause them to abhor and to shun it; but many are so wise in their own conceit that they feel no need of humbly seeking God that they may be led into truth. Although priding themselves on their enlightenment, they are ignorant both of the Scriptures and of the power of God. They must have some means of quieting their consciences, and they seek that which is least spiritual and humiliating. What they desire is a method of forgetting God which shall pass as a method of remembering Him. The papacy is well adapted to meet the wants of all these. It is prepared for two classes of mankind, embracing nearly the whole world—those who would be saved by their merits, and those who would be saved in their sins. Here is the secret of its power." (*The Great Controversy,* p. 572)

We cannot afford to let our people be lured into cooperation with the papacy. In fact we are counseled, "The attention of our churches must be aroused. We are standing upon the borders of the greatest event in the world's history, and Satan must not have power over the people of God, causing them to sleep on. The Papacy will appear in its power. All must now arouse and search the Scriptures, for God will make known to His faithful ones what shall be in the last time. The word of the Lord is to come to His people in power." (*Manuscript Releases,* vol. 2, p. 20)

Obviously, there are many sincere, dedicated, and wonderful people in the Roman Catholic Church. It is the system, not the members, that is corrupted both theologically and organizationally. It is this system with the pope at its head that "all the world wonders after." We should pray earnestly for the individuals involved in this organization that they will hear the call of God saying, "Come out of her my people."

CHAPTER 7

Economic Armageddon

World economic conditions point to catastrophic financial problems in the very near future. When the leaders of the world's major industrialized nations, commonly known as the G-7, met together in Tokyo in July of 1993 their major activity was commiserating on the dreadful economic conditions that each faced. The main topic of discussion quickly became "How can we create more jobs for our people?" In fact, one of the most unusual features of the occasion was the fact that Boris Yeltsin was there from Russia with his hand out pleading for assistance to keep the former "superpower" afloat.

Here in the United States business and personal bankruptcies continue to escalate year after year. In 1992, for example, there were over 20,000 personal bankruptcies filed—*every week!* This growing list of personal bankruptcies has a rippling effect on the entire economy. With real estate mortgage defaults by the thousands, banks are failing at record rates. Businesses must consolidate or die, and even major corporations are experiencing setbacks, plant closures, unheard of losses, and thousands being laid off.

Perhaps the magnitude of our financial problems today can be underscored by the announcement made just prior to the 1992 elections by New Hampshire Republican, Senator Warren Rudman, that he would not seek a third term. Easily re-electible, Rudman, along with colleague Phil Gramm, tried to seek fiscal responsibility with the Gramm-Rudman initiative to balance the federal budget. Rudman stated as his reason for leaving the U.S. Senate: "The problem is the various special-interest groups. . . It's hard to get anything done here. . . We are literally ignoring our single most pressing problem—the deficit—which is going to destroy the country and cause the financial markets at some point to collapse, the currency to be devalued; all that people have saved will be worthless unless we do something about it. We are reaching the thin edge, and every economist knows it. You're talking a national debt that will equal the annual GNP by 1999." (*U.S. News and World Report,* April 6, 1992, p. 19)

The state of the economy played a major role in the 1992 presidential election. No president in recent history had a higher approval rating (90%+) than George Bush just one year before the election. However, when the dust settled and the election results were in President Bush was defeated. Why? Exit polls revealed that in spite of all the rhetoric about abortion and family values during the campaign, only 12% of voters had these factors in mind when casting their votes, but an amazing 68% voted with the economy and its problems as the number one factor.

In spite of the pre-election rhetoric, president-elect Bill Clinton, even before his inauguration, stated that things were worse than he had believed and that we should not expect any miracles. His plan was to assemble a large group of financial experts to study the situation and make recommendations. The bottom line became: "We really don't know exactly what to do. We are going to try one thing first, and if that doesn't work, then we will try something else."

Many Biblical descriptions of our day, the last days, indicate that people will be what we call materialistic. "But know this, that in the last days perilous times will come: For men will be lovers of themselves (selfish), lovers of money (materialistic), boasters, proud. . . lovers of pleasure rather than lovers of God." (II Timothy 3:1, 2, 4)

In this materialistic, money-oriented, society men place a high priority on possessions, earning power, and lifestyle. Those who cannot afford to live as they would like to will borrow, or go into debt to secure those things which they feel they must have. Even many apparently wealthy people have debt loads that threaten to swamp them. Donald Trump with his investments in real estate in Atlantic City is leveraged in debt up to the very limits of his ability to pay.

People or families that are living in debt, on borrowed money, are really living today on money they expect to earn in the future. If one or a number of factors change in their life, then serious financial embarrassment can result. Many feel that bankruptcy is their only option at that point.

Late in her life, Ellen White, in writing about "The Last Crisis," pointed out that money problems would be very evident. "There are not many, even among educators and statesmen, who comprehend the causes that underlie the present state of society. Those who hold the reins of government are not able to solve the problem of moral corruption, poverty, pauperism, and increasing crime. They are struggling in vain to place business operations on a more secure basis. If men would give more heed to the teaching of God's word, they would find a solution to the problems that perplex them.

"The Scriptures describe the condition of the world just before Christ's second coming. Of the men who by robbery and extortion are amassing great riches, it is written: 'Ye have heaped treasure together for the last days. Behold, the hire of the laborers who have reaped down your fields, which is of you kept back by fraud, crieth: and the cries of them which have reaped are entered into the ears of the Lord of Sabaoth. Ye have lived in pleasure on the earth, and been wanton; ye have nourished your hearts, as in a day of slaughter. Ye have condemned and killed the just; and he doth not resist you.' (James 5:3-6)

"But who reads the warnings given by the fast-fulfilling signs of the times? What impression is made upon worldlings? What change is seen in their attitude? No more than was seen in the attitude of the inhabitants of the Noachian world. Absorbed in worldly business and pleasure, the antediluvians 'knew not until the Flood came, and took them all away.' (Matthew 24:39) They had heaven-sent warnings, but they refused to listen. And today the world, utterly regardless of the warning voice of God, is hurrying on to eternal ruin." (*Testimonies for the Church,* vol. 9, pp. 13, 14)

Christian financial counselor, Larry Burkett, describes the precarious state of the American economy this way: "So how do we break out of this debt spiral? We don't. Unfortunately we have no choice but to continue with more of the same. It's as one of my economics professors liked to say: 'He who rides on the back of a tiger cannot dismount.' . . . It's a little like a cowboy in the old west riding his horse to death trying to avoid the Indians chasing him. He knows if he keeps on riding, his horse will eventually collapse. But he also knows that if he stops, he will die. So he rides on, hoping for a miracle." (Larry Burkett, *The Coming Economic Earthquake,* pp. 90, 91)

So what is the prognosis for our debt-ridden society? Burkett sums it up this way: "Eventually the majority of households will reach the stage where they cannot repay what they owe, nor will they be able to borrow more. At that point, the economy must stop while the debt is either repudiated (by a depression), devalued (by hyperinflation), or repaid (unthinkable)." *(Ibid., p. 106)*

The present crisis puts a compounding effect upon the government. Many counselors are beginning to warn, "Don't rely on the government for your financial security." They base this counsel on the following reasons:

The Tremendous Debt Load—When George Bush first took office he stated that during his first term he would balance the federal budget. However, his first budget was $65 billion dollars in the red, and it has gone from bad to worse since. Of course, he didn't count on the collapse of the savings and loan industry, which added another $500 billion plus to the problem. In addition, there has been the expense of the Middle East War, Hurricane Andrew, lower revenues from taxes because of the high unemployment brought on by the recession, etc. With over four trillion dollars in debt the government is actually bankrupt, but it can't just declare bankruptcy, pass "go," and collect two hundred dollars, because most of the debt is now owed to foreign countries like Japan.

No money has been paid on the principle to reduce the debt since 1974. And so, today many economists are predicting that because we are now borrowing to pay the interest on the national debt that the compounding effect of the debt will, in less than seven years, require all of the revenues generated by the tax system just to pay the interest on the national debt. You can only imagine the effect this will have on society when the welfare, social security, and the entitlement programs go unfunded.

The Welfare Burden—When the welfare system was established in 1935, there were 143 people working for each person drawing welfare benefits. Now the ratio is one to one! There is one person drawing some form of welfare or entitlement money for each person working.

The Social Security System Is Insecure—"If you were born after 1936, don't count on Social Security to make your retirement years comfortable. The Social Security system will be in serious trouble within ten years, and the crunch will be devastating when the baby boomers start arriving at retirement age around 2010.

"Social Security has expanded coverage and benefits so much that this year it will pay out $302 billion! That is $830 million dollars a day to retired workers and their spouses, widows and dependent children, and the disabled.

"As matters now stand, there simply will not be enough money to pay promised benefits." (*Bottom Line Personal,* vol. 13, No. 19, Oct. 15, 1992)

You have heard some folks say that there is enough money in the Social Security system to last for twenty more years, and others say the system is broke. What is the truth? The truth is they are both right. On paper the system has a good surplus. However, by law, the extra funds must be invested in Special Issue Government Bonds. These bonds have been sold to pay interest on the national debt. The money is all gone! We only have IOU's from the government. Those presently working are paying in to assist those who are drawing benefits.

The Graying of America—In just a few years when the baby boomers begin to retire, there will be twice as many people retired as there are today, and only half as many people working as there are today. This will have a devastating effect on the economy.

Education Crisis—In May of 1988 the Commission on Minority Participation in Education and American Life rendered its report to the president of the United States in a book entitled *One-Third of a Nation.* The bottom line is that unless something very drastic is done to the American Educational system, by the year 2000 one-third of the workforce will be minorities—Blacks, Hispanics, Asians, and American Indians, who for whatever reason have not been able to avail themselves of the educational system and will be working at minimum wage. Imagine, one-third of our work force working at subsistence income or below.

I have helped many families work out a budget and turn things around financially. But, unless a family is completely debt free, including no home mortgage, it is nearly impossible to develop a family budget on minimum wage. Minimum wage is primarily for entry level jobs for young people and older folks who need to supplement their income.

I realize that this is a very depressing view of the future. However, I believe it is an accurate one. The primary question then is what can one do to prepare for the future time? The obvious inclination would be to hoard money. There are a number of reasons why that would be the worse thing to do!

The Bible encourages us to save. "The wise man saves for the future, but the foolish man spends whatever he gets." (Proverbs 21:20, *The Living Bible*) Savings is the opposite of debt. Saving is making provision for the future, while debt presumes upon the future.

Hoarding, on the other hand, defined as saving for security, could cause serious problems in the future. There are at least four major problems with hoarding money—saving beyond our personal, basic needs:

First, one could lose all he has saved (hoarded) in a failed economy. By now you are surely aware that our U.S. economy is in a very precarious position. It would be very unfortunate indeed to lose our entrusted capital. In the event that each person wanted to actually hold all the money that he "owned," there is not enough money printed to accommodate such a situation. Eighty percent or 4/5 of our "money" is really only paper on computer records in the banks. We all know now that it is possible to lose "paper" investments overnight in the event of a collapse of the stock market.

Note Ellen White's counsel in this regard. "The very means that is now so sparingly invested in the cause of God, and that is selfishly retained, will in a little while be cast with all idols to the moles and the bats. Money will soon depreciate in value very suddenly when the reality of eternal scenes opens to the senses of man. God will have men who will venture anything and everything to save souls." (*Evangelism*, p. 63) "It is a snare of the last days, to involve God's people in loss of their Lord's entrusted capital, that should be used wisely in the work of winning souls." (*Counsels on Stewardship*, p. 243) "Those who hold fast their property till the last moment, surrender it to death rather than to the cause. Losses are occurring continually. Banks fail, and property is consumed in very many ways. . . . Satan works to prevent the means from coming into the treasury at all." (*Testimonies for the Church*, vol. 5, p. 154)

The second problem with hoarding is that some will hold on to their money so long that it cannot be used to benefit the cause of God. Ellen White was given a vision of the Rich Young Man who came to Jesus. The vision, given to young Sabbath keepers, is recorded in *Testimonies for the Church*. I will share here only a portion that is pertinent to the topic at hand. "Here is the reward for those who sacrifice for God. They receive a hundred fold in this life, and shall inherit everlasting life. . . . Those who still cling to their earthly treasure, and will not make a right disposition of that which is lent them of God, will lose their treasure in heaven, lose everlasting life. . . The work is closing; and soon the means of those who have kept their riches, their large farms, their cattle, etc., will not be wanted. I saw the Lord turn to such in anger, in wrath, and repeat these words: 'Go to now, ye rich men.' (James 5:1) He has called but you would not hear. Love of this world has drowned His voice. Now He has no use for you, and lets you go, bidding you: 'Go to now, ye rich men.'

"Oh, I saw that it was an awful thing to be thus forsaken by the Lord—a fearful thing to hold onto a perishable substance here, when He has said that if we will sell and give alms, we can lay up treasure in heaven. I was shown that as the work is closing up and the truth is going forth in mighty power, these rich men will bring their means and lay it at the feet of the servants of God, begging them to accept it. The answer from the servants of God will be: 'Go to now, ye rich men. Your means is not needed. Ye withheld it when ye could do good with it in advancing the cause of God. The needy have suffered; they have not been blessed by your means. God will not accept your riches now. Go to now, ye rich men.'" (*Testimonies for the Church,* vol. 1, pp. 173-175)

This statement is awesome in its power, boldness, and implications.

The third problem with hoarding money is the Revelation 13:17 scenario. Let's say that the economic problems with our country that I have described in this chapter no longer exist. You have $300,000 invested in mutual funds and can live comfortably on the interest. Then as "an overwhelming surprise" end-time events begin to unfold, and it is declared that no one can buy or sell unless he receives the mark of the beast. In other words, your money that you have worked so hard to save up and are depending upon to take care of you is worthless unless you compromise your standards and receive the Mark of the Beast. What are you going to do? Are you going to turn your back on your $300,000 and walk away. Remember, that amount represents thirty years' worth of house payments! This is why Jesus said, "Remember Lot's wife." (Luke 17:32)

It boils down to the question "Do I want to be able to spend my hard earned money, or give it up and depend 100% on the providence of God, and maybe even lose my life as a result?" The sad part is that many Christians with money hoarded will go for the money and turn their backs on God and eternal life. And then to add insult to injury they will lose it all in a few months or weeks anyway. "For what will it profit a man if he gains the whole world, and loses his own soul? Or what will a man give in exchange for his soul." (Mark 8:36, 37)

The fourth problem with hoarding is that our savings will be evidence of our selfishness and will be a witness against us in the judgment. Note the comments from Scripture in this regard. "Come now, you rich, weep and howl for your miseries that are coming upon you! Your riches are corrupted, and your garments are moth-eaten. Your gold and silver are corroded, and their corrosion <u>will be a witness against you</u> and will eat your flesh like fire. You have heaped up treasure in the last days." (James 5:1-3)

None of us would ever deposit money in a bank without first opening an account and securing a receipt for each deposit that is made. Our passbook or statement then is the official evidence of our funds in the account. I get the impression from the following statement that this evidence of our account of funds, if they have been hoarded for our personal use, will document our selfishness.

"Hoarded wealth is not merely useless, it is a curse. In this life it is a snare to the soul, drawing the affections away from the heavenly treasure. In the great day of God its witness to unused talents and neglected opportunities will condemn its possessor." (*Christ's Object Lessons*, p. 352)

So, if we don't store up money to assure our own security how should we prepare for the times ahead?

Honor your covenant relation with God. When Jesus returns in the near future He will call out from the heavens to His angels, "Gather My saints together to Me, those who have made a covenant with Me by sacrifice." (Psalm 50:5) In the Bible there were certain offerings including the tithe that were "vowed offerings." In other words, they really weren't offerings at all. They were part of the covenant relation with God. So what does this have to do with the topic at hand? A great deal. In the same chapter God says, "Offer to God thanksgiving, (not worry), and pay your vows (tithe) to the Most High. (Then you can) Call upon Me in the day of trouble; I will deliver you, and you shall glorify Me." (Psalm 50:14, 15)

What I am saying here in very plain language is—make sure you are square with God in your financial dealings. If you have withheld or diverted tithe or felt that you couldn't afford to tithe because of your personal financial situation, I urge you to do an accounting and make things right with God. God doesn't need the money (see Ps. 50:12) nearly as much as we need the blessing and security that faithfulness brings.

Get out of debt. "Why don't we all borrow up to our credit limits and use the money to finish the work," some have asked me, "and then we can thumb our noses at the devil on the way to heaven." What is wrong with that reasoning? There is the Biblical counsel to avoid debt— Proverbs 22:7, "The borrower is the slave of the lender," and Romans 13:8, "Owe no man anything except the continuing debt to love one another." And we know that just before Jesus comes there will be a time of trouble such as never was since there was a nation. (See Dan. 12:1) I believe that those who are out of debt will be much better off during this time than those in debt. Someday, just before Jesus comes, His faithful people will not be able to buy or sell. Why not beat the devil to the punch and get rid of our "stuff" while it can still do some good? "The work of God is to become more extensive, and if His people follow His counsel, there will not be much means in their possession to be consumed in the final conflagration. All will have laid up their treasure where moth and rust cannot corrupt; and the heart will not have a cord to bind it to earth." (*Testimonies,* vol. 1, p. 197)

It is a rather sobering thought that we, like faithful Noah, will be asked to spend all we have to prepare the world for the Second Coming. Responding to indications that the return of Jesus was near at hand Ellen White made the following statement: "The Lord is soon to come, and before His advent the message of warning is to be proclaimed to all nations, tongues, and peoples. While God's cause is calling for laborers and means to carry the gospel to lands lying in darkness, what are those doing who are living under the full light of gospel truth? There are some who feel no burden for souls. They profess to believe that the end of all things is at hand, but covetousness has blinded their eyes to the needs of the cause of God. The means that He has placed in their hands to be used to His glory, they are tying up in houses and lands (Context indicates real estate beyond our primary home), while the proclamation of the truth that God has entrusted to them to be given to the world, is delayed by a lack of means. Every believer is to do his utmost to advance the cause, and is then in faith to ask God to do what man can not do."

(*Review and Herald*, April 14, 1910)

We all must recognize that the opening providences of God are presently way ahead of our willingness to respond. These opportunities call for our wholehearted support.

"We are not to spend means unnecessarily, but <u>we must do an extensive work to gather in souls, for time is short. The Lord is coming.</u> He that is to come will come and will not tarry. We are not told the appointed time, but we know that the coming is very near. We have been so backward in giving the real message! Unless we arouse, we can not be saved ourselves, for we have not gained the experience of being workers together with God. We are to be His instrumentalities, His agents. With all the strength of our influence, we are to try to bring souls to a knowledge of the truth." (*Manuscript Releases*, vol. 3, p. 290)

The financial picture and somewhat careless routine that we are all accustomed to will soon take a serious turn for the worse. Those who have maintained their covenant relation with God, are out of debt, and have utilized their assets for the furtherance of the work of God will be in a position to trust Him to provide for their needs when they can't buy or sell. It is not difficult to see that this method of forcing compliance is already being used by the United Nations and the United States with embargo policies toward "rebellious" nations or governments like Haiti and Iraq. And now both Protestant and Catholic interests are entering the political arena to "legislate" their agenda and "straighten out" the problems in this country and "bring our nation back to God." When the faithful cannot buy or sell, they must trust God fully for their support. Why not begin trusting Him now?

CHAPTER 8

The Appointed Time

Some have advanced the idea that because God is eternal He is not bound by time. They apparently believe that things happen in a rather random manner whenever God gets the whim. However, when we observe God's dealings with mankind and the history of the earth, it is certainly evident that He is very timely and precise when dealing with us. In fact, God has a way of doing things that is very predictable. God has a "modus operandi" by which you can set your watch.

Man did not invent the mathematical precision of the natural world; he merely discovered what God had already put in motion. For example, man does not keep track of accurate time. Rather, we set our timepieces by the stars. I recall visiting the United States Naval Observatory in Washington, D.C., and seeing the great timepieces there. One telescope there is focused on a very small and precise spot in the heavens, and when a certain star passes over that spot, a beam of light is transmitted through the telescope to a cross hair "bull's eye" on a chart. At that precise second (or millisecond) real earth time is set.

If God's timing with respect to the movement of the heavenly bodies was off in the slightest degree, then we would not have been able to put a man on the moon as we have. Are you aware that we are able to predict the sunrise and sunset and the high tide and low tide of a coastal city with precise accuracy years in advance? This is no particular credit to man. It is simply that we have discovered God's precise timeliness.

God tries to tell us about Himself in Scripture. With regard to His sense of mission and timing He says,

"I am God, and there is no one like Me;
I reveal the end from the beginning,

from ancient times I reveal what is to be;
I say, 'My purpose shall take effect,
I will accomplish all that I please.'
I summon a bird of prey from the east,
one from a distant land to fulfill my purpose.
Mark this; I have spoken, and I will bring it about,
I have a plan to carry out, and carry it out I will."
(Isaiah 46:9-11, NEB)

The same view of God is given repeatedly by Ellen White. "In the past the Lord God of ages revealed His secrets to His prophets. The Omniscient looked down the centuries, and predicted through His prophets the rise and fall of kingdoms, hundreds of years before the events foretold took place. The present and the future are equally clear to God, and He shows His servants what shall be. His voice echoes down the ages, telling man what is to take place. Kings and princes take their position at the appointed time. They think they are carrying out their own purposes, but in reality they are fulfilling the word God has given through His prophets. They act their part in carrying out God's great plan. Events fall into line, fulfilling the word the Almighty has spoken." (*Review and Herald*, Feb. 6, 1900)

Interestingly, the Bible also states that, though God is eternal, He deals with men within the parameters of time. "But You, O Lord, shall endure forever, and the remembrance of Your name to all generations. You will arise and have mercy on Zion; Yes, the set time has come." (Psalm 102:12, 13)

Evidently, from earliest memory God had devised a plan with very accurate precision as to timing to put down the rebellion and atone for the sins of mankind. There was:
a time for the flood;
a time for the exodus;
a time for Christ to come to the earth;
a time for Him to be baptized;
a time for the crucifixion;
a time for the resurrection;
a time for the ascension;
a time for the Holy Spirit to come;
a time for the "time of the end" to begin;
a time for the judgment to begin; and

a time for the Second Coming—though only God knows the exact day and hour.

As William Miller concluded his prophetic studies that led to the proclamation of the first angel's message he stated, "Another kind of evidence that vitally affected my mind was the chronology of the Scriptures. . . I found that predicted events, which had been fulfilled in the past, often occurred within a given time. The one hundred and twenty years to the flood (Genesis 6:3); the seven days that were to precede it, with forty days of predicted rain (Genesis 7:4); the four hundred years of the sojourn of Abraham's seed (Genesis 15:13); the three days of the butler's and baker's dreams (Genesis 40:12-20); the seven years of Pharaoh's (Genesis 41:28-54); the forty years in the wilderness (Numbers 14:34); the three and a half years of famine (I Kings 17:1); [See also Luke 4:25]. . . the seventy years' captivity (Jeremiah 25:11); Nebuchadnezzar's seven times (Daniel 4:13-16); and the seven weeks, threescore and two weeks, and the one week, making seventy weeks, determined upon the Jews (Daniel 9:24-27),— the events limited by these times were all once only a matter of prophecy, and were fulfilled in accordance with the predictions." (*The Great Controversy*, p. 323)

The Bible tells us plainly in Habakkuk 2:3 that, though God's time table may appear to us to be long, in fact, it really is not delayed because at the appointed time God's plans will take place. "For the vision is yet for an appointed time; but at the end it will speak, and it will not lie. Though it tarries, wait for it; because it will surely come, it will not tarry."

Adventists have identified the beginning and ending dates for the two longest time prophecies—the "1260 days" and the "2300 days." We feel quite comfortable with these dates and they occur consistently in our communications. We believe that the 1260 day/year prophecy began in 538 A.D. with the Papacy's official rise to power and ended in 1798 when the Papacy received the deadly wound—yet still lived. Accordingly, we believe that "the time of the end" began in 1798. How long will "the time of the end" last? Could it go on for hundreds of years, or will it really be only a relatively short period of time at the end of a relatively long period of time? By its very description the "time of the end" sounds like a climax or conclusion of time. The *Daniel and Revelation Committee Series* agree with this basic understanding.

"The main lines of prophecy in Daniel outline the rise and fall of the major powers that were to rule first the Near Eastern and then the Mediterranean world from the prophet's day to the end of time. . . In his opening statement of explanation in Dan. 8, Gabriel told the prophet that the vision given to him was for the 'time of the end' (Hebrew: *et-qes*, vs. 17). His explanation then began with the first element, the Persian Ram (vs. 20), and continued on down to its last element—the time factor of 'evening-mornings' (vs. 26). The obvious inference of Gabriel's explanation is that the time element presented with this vision leads the interpreter along to that 'time of the end' in human history.

"The same point is brought out in the explanation of this vision given in Dan. 11, 12. The final activities of the king of the north are described as occurring in the 'time of the end' (11:40). At that time Michael stands up and delivers His living saints and resurrects His dead saints (12:1-2). The reference here is to the establishment of the final kingdom of God, and this occurs at the **end** of 'the time of the end.' Within that same 'time of the end' the prophecies of Daniel were to be unsealed, studied, and understood (12:4, 9).

"These references in Dan. 11:40 and 12:4, 9 indicate that the 'time of the end' was to be **a period of time,** and that the prophetic time periods referred to in Dan. 8:14, 26 and 12:7, 11 lead up to that final period.

"Since the prophecies in Dan. 7-8, and 10-12 all lead up to the 'time of the end' which is to be followed by the setting up of God's final kingdom, the time periods mentioned in these prophecies should naturally be seen as extending through history to that 'time of the end.'" (William H. Shea, "Selected Studies on Prophetic Interpretation," *Daniel and Revelation Committee Series,* vol. 1, pp. 59, 60)

Later in his study Shea indicates again that the 'time of the end' has limitations. He states, "Furthermore, the emphasis on 'the time of the end' in some of the prophecies of Daniel implies that their time periods extend down to that 'time of the end' and delimit it." (*Ibid.,* p. 86) *Delimit* is defined by Webster as "to fix or define the limits of." "The time of the end" is a fixed period of time that precedes the second coming of Christ.

In the same manner, we believe that the beginning of the 2300 day/year and the 70 week prophecies began in 457 B.C. The 2300 day prophecy continued down to the fall of 1844. As I mentioned earlier, the 1844 date stands without impeachment. The unfolding of the great 2300 day prophecy is described as follows:

"The 2300 days had been found to begin when the commandment of Artaxerxes for the restoration and building of Jerusalem, went into effect, in the autumn of B.C. 457. Taking this as the starting point, there was perfect harmony in the application of all the events foretold in the explanation of that period in Daniel 9:25-27. Sixty-nine weeks, the first 483 of the 2300 years, were to reach to the Messiah, the Anointed One; and Christ's baptism and anointing by the Holy Spirit, A.D. 27, exactly fulfilled the specification. In the midst of the seventieth week, Messiah was to be cut off. Three and a half years after His baptism, Christ was crucified, in the spring of A.D. 31. The seventy weeks, or 490 years, were to pertain especially to the Jews. At the expiration of this period, the nation sealed its rejection of Christ by the persecution of His disciples, and the apostles turned to the Gentiles, A.D. 34. The first 490 years of the 2300 having then ended, 1810 years would remain. From A.D. 34, 1810 years extend to 1844. 'Then,' said the angel, 'shall the sanctuary be cleansed.' <u>All the preceding specifications of the prophecy had been unquestionably fulfilled at the time appointed</u>. With this reckoning, all was clear and harmonious, except that it was not seen that any event answering to the cleansing of the sanctuary had taken place in 1844. To deny that the days ended at that time was to involve the whole question in confusion, and to renounce positions which had been established by unmistakable fulfillments of prophecy." (*The Great Controversy*, p. 410)

Now, of course, as a matter of historical record we know, as they learned later, that their dates were correct and only the event to culminate the prophecy was misunderstood. We now know that 1844 marked the beginning of the investigative portion of the judgment.

"At the time appointed for the judgment—the close of the 2300 days, in 1844—began the work of investigation and blotting out of sins. All who have ever taken upon themselves the name of Christ must pass its searching scrutiny. Both the living and the dead are to be judged 'out of those things which were written in the books, according to their works.' Revelation 20:12." (*Maranatha*, p. 250; see also Acts 17:31)

The purpose of this chapter is to document from Scripture and the Spirit of Prophecy that God's method of operation is to set up a time table and to do everything right on time.

"Christ, as Commander of heaven, was appointed to put down the rebellion. Satan and all his sympathizers were cast out of heaven. Then was begun the work which, before the foundations of the world were laid, Christ had engaged to do. At the appointed time He came to our world in human flesh, that He might become man's substitute and surety." (*Review and Herald,* May 30, 1899)

As the one in charge of the timetable from the foundation of the world, it was Christ's responsibility to oversee every detail of the history of the great controversy. Accordingly, at the end of the forty years of wandering in the wilderness, "the Lord announced to Moses that the appointed time to deliver Israel was at hand, and as the aged prophet stood upon the heights overlooking the river Jordan and the promised land, he gazed with deep interest upon the inheritance of his people. That vast, garden-like plain, with its deep verdure and feathery palm trees, spread out invitingly before him, and he felt an intense longing to share with Israel in the possession of that land which had been the object of their efforts, the goal of their hopes, for so many years." (*Signs of the Times,* Jan. 13, 1881)

I believe that once again God's people are on the very borders of the promised land which has been the object of our efforts and the goal of our hopes for so many years.

While doing the research for this book I was amazed at the intricate detail and timeliness of God's plan for this earth. "God had ruled the events clustering around the birth of Christ. There was an appointed time for Him to appear in the form of humanity. A long line of inspired prophecy pointed to the coming of Christ to our world, and minutely described the manner of His reception. Had the Saviour appeared at an earlier period in the world's history, the advantages gained to Christians would not have been so great, as their faith would not have been developed and strengthened by dwelling upon the prophecies which stretched into the far future, and recounted the events which were to transpire." (*The Spirit of Prophecy,* vol. 3, p. 180)

Evidently, time is a factor in the decisions of heaven, because we are told that God does not become impatient, neither does He delay to act once the time comes. "Like the stars in the vast circuit of their appointed path, God's purposes know no haste and no delay. Through the symbols of the great darkness and the smoking furnace, God had revealed to Abraham the bondage of Israel in Egypt, and had declared that the time of their sojourning should be four hundred years. 'Afterward,' He said, 'shall they come out with great substance.' Gen. 15:14. Against that word, all the power of Pharaoh's proud empire battled in vain. On 'the self-same day' appointed in the divine promise, 'it came to pass, that all the hosts of the Lord went out from the land of Egypt.' Ex. 12:41. <u>So in heaven's council the hour for the coming of Christ had been determined.</u> **<u>When the great clock of time pointed to that hour, Jesus was born in Bethlehem.</u>**" (*The Desire of Ages*, p. 32) "When the fullness of time had come, God sent forth His Son, born of a woman, born under the law." (Galations 4:4).

Not only was Christ's birth timely, but all heaven was involved in its announcement. Angels announced His birth to the shepherds, then the heavenly choir sang songs of praise. (See Luke 2:8-14.)

It is interesting to note that Jesus was taught the prophecies by His mother while He was growing up, and that, at least by the age of twelve, He knew that He was the Messiah (Luke 2:49), but He patiently waited until He was about thirty years of age (Luke 3:23) to begin His ministry. "He who had been the Commander of Heaven was on earth a loving and obedient son. The great things brought to His mind by the service of the temple were hidden in His heart. He waited until God's time to begin His appointed work."(*The Story of Jesus*, p. 34)

"Jesus did not ignore His relation to His earthly parents. From Jerusalem He returned home with them, and aided them in their life of toil. <u>He hid in His own heart the mystery of His mission, waiting submissively for the appointed time for Him to enter upon His work.</u> For eighteen years after He had recognized that He was the Son of God, He acknowledged the tie that bound Him to the home at Nazareth, and performed the duties of a son, a brother, a friend, and a citizen." (*The Desire of Ages,* p. 82)

On numerous occasions during the ministry of Jesus, particularly following one of His miracles, the disciples and others urged Jesus forward to "take up His kingdom." Yet until His very last trip to Jerusalem, He would always tell them, "Mine hour is not yet come." Why did He say that? Was He on some great time schedule? Indeed He was! "The words 'Mine hour is not yet come,' point to the **fact** that every act of Christ's life on earth, was in fulfillment to the plan that had existed from the days of eternity. Before He came to earth, the plan lay out before Him, perfect in all its details. But as He walked among men, He was guided, step by step, by the Father's will. He did not hesitate to act at the appointed time. With the same submission He waited until the time had come." (*The Desire of Ages,* p. 147)

Both the resurrection and the ascension of Christ were again attended, right on time, by the heavenly angels. I found an absolutely awesome statement from the pen of Ellen White, recorded in *The Youth's Instructor*, that gives a most vivid description of the timely resurrection of Christ. "Christ had declared that He would be raised from the dead on the third day; **and at the appointed time a mighty angel descended from heaven,** parting the darkness from his track, and resting before the Saviour's tomb. 'His countenance was like lightening, and his raiment white as snow; and for fear of him the keepers did shake, and became as dead men.' Brave soldiers, who had never been afraid of human power, were now as captives taken without sword or spear. The face they looked upon was not the face of a mortal warrior; it was the face of a heavenly messenger, sent to relieve the Son of God from the debt for which He had become responsible, and for which He had now made a full atonement. The heavenly visitant was the angel that on the plains of Bethlehem had proclaimed Christ's birth. The earth trembled at his approach, and as he rolled away the stone from Christ's grave, heaven seemed to come down to earth. The soldiers saw him removing the stone as he would a pebble, and heard him call, 'Son of God, thy Father saith, Come forth.' They saw Jesus come from the grave as a mighty conqueror, and heard Him proclaim, 'I am the resurrection, and the life.' The angel guards bowed low in adoration before the Redeemer as He came forth in majesty and glory, and welcomed Him with songs of praise." (*The Youth's Instructor*, May 2, 1901)

Following the resurrection Jesus spent time with the disciples encouraging and reaffirming them. Then He let it be known that it was time for Him to return to heaven. Before His death Jesus had designated a time and place where He would meet with the believers one last time before His ascension. Then apparently only the eleven remaining disciples were with Him at the ascension. (See Acts 1:9-14.) Again, the angels were there at the ascension to sing and talk with the disciples. But this special appointment of Jesus with a larger group of believers was quite unique. "At the time appointed, about five hundred were collected in little knots on the mountain-side, eager to learn all that could be learned from those who had seen Christ since His resurrection. From group to group the disciples passed, telling all that they had seen and heard of Jesus, and reasoning from the Scriptures as He had done with them. Thomas recounted the story of his unbelief, and told how his doubts had been swept away. <u>Suddenly Jesus stood among them</u>. No one could tell whence or how He came. Many who were present had never before seen Him; but in His hands and feet they beheld the marks of the crucifixion; His countenance was as the face of God, and when they saw Him, they worshipped Him." (*The Desire of Ages*, pp. 818, 819)

Two statements of Jesus were repeated over and over in the minds of the disciples after Jesus' ascension. They were, "Lo, I am with you always," and "I will come again to receive you unto Myself." And just as the characters of the Old Testament longingly looked for the first advent of Christ, each generation of Christians has longingly looked for the second advent. But there would be a long delay—nearly 2000 years. The apostle Paul warned the folks in his day that Christ would not return until after the great apostasy and the man of sin was revealed. Luther stated that he felt it was at least 300 years away from his day. And as we noted earlier, Ellen White said that the nearness of the advent could not even be preached until after 1798. Then we are told that in the last days—following 1798—there would be those who, because of the long delay, in their minds at least, would scoff at the very notion of an imminent second coming. But in reality, as we have seen, God is still on schedule!

It may be hard for us to realize that this old world is quickly running out of time. The devil knows it all too well. "Therefore rejoice, ye heavens, and ye that dwell in them. Woe to the inhabiters of the earth and of the sea! for the devil is come down unto you, having great wrath, <u>because he knoweth that he hath but a short time.</u>" (Revelation 12:12) What is there to rejoice about? Rejoice because time is short!

"The crisis is stealing gradually upon us. The sun shines in the heavens, passing over its usual round, and the heavens still declare the glory of God. Men are still eating and drinking, planting and building, marrying and giving in marriage. Merchants are still buying and selling. Men are jostling against one another, contending for the highest place. Pleasure lovers are still crowding to theaters, horse races, gambling-hells. <u>The highest excitement prevails, yet probation's hour is fast closing, and every case is about to be eternally decided.</u> **Satan sees that his time is short.** <u>He has set all his agents to work, that men may be deceived, deluded, occupied, and entranced, until the day of probation shall be ended, and the door of mercy be forever shut.</u> The time is right upon us when there will be sorrow that no human balm can heal. Sentinel angels are now restraining the four winds, that they shall not blow till the servants of God are sealed in their foreheads; but when God shall bid His angels loose the winds, there will be a scene of strife such as no pen can picture." (*Review and Herald*, March 14, 1912)

What a statement! Satan sees that time is short, and he has all his agents at work that men may be deceived, deluded, occupied, and entranced until probation closes. That's what this book is all about. To believe that we have lots of time left is a delusion. To be too busy to study is to be occupied. To believe that things are going to get better is to be deceived. And to stand by and do nothing is to be entranced.

Another interesting note from this statement is that Satan realizes that he doesn't have to work clear to the Second Coming. He only has to work until the close of probation! After that, it will be eternally too late to get ready, because the door of mercy will be eternally shut! It is my personal belief that no one will be surprised by the second coming of Christ but rather by the close of probation. Let's face it. After the seven last plagues have come with the water turned to blood, the sores, the great heat, the hailstones, and the great earthquake that causes islands to disappear and mountains to be moved out of their places, even the most ignorant and unbelieving will realize that the end of the world has come. What will overtake people is the close of probation—some time before the Second Coming. When the plagues start to fall, the door of mercy has forever closed.

"Many who profess to believe the Word of God do not seem to understand the deceptive working of the enemy. They do not realize that the end of time is near, but Satan knows it, and while men sleep he works. Satan is at work even among the people of God, to cause disunion. Selfishness, corruption, and evil of every kind are taking a firm hold upon hearts. With many the precious Word of God is neglected. A novel or a storybook engages the attention. . . That which excites the imagination is eagerly devoured, while the Word of God is set aside." (*In Heavenly Places*, p. 309)

Satan realizes not only that time is short but also that there is an appointed time for him to do his terrible work. It is very unfortunate that he has been so successful in attracting the attention of men and women from the prize of the high calling in Christ. "Today, Satan has great power in the world. He has been permitted to have proprietorship of this earth **for an appointed time**. During this period, when iniquity prevails, men and women are given a chance to take sides. In every possible way, Satan tries to make the broad road attractive and the narrow road grievous, humiliating, and objectionable. He lays ingenious plans to allure men and women to indulge appetite. Cheap, unsatisfying pleasures are made all and in all in this degenerate age. Satan throws his glamour about these amusements, which eclipse eternal things. Many will sell their birthright, as did Esau, for trifling consideration by the indulgence of appetite. Worldly pleasure will appear more desirable to them than the heavenly birthright." (*The Upward Look*, p. 39)

Why is it that we are just now beginning to realize how near we are to the literal second coming of Christ? One answer is that God allows each generation to have just the knowledge they need for their time. "In the vision the plan of redemption was presented to Jacob, not fully, but in such parts as were essential to him at that time." (*Patriarchs and Prophets,* p. 184)

Perhaps because of the apparently long delay, God's people, those who are to give the last warning message to the world, have become tired, lethargic, apathetic. With the signs of the end fast fulfilled around us, other Christians are heralding their ideas of the advent more than we are. Why is this the case, and what should we do about it? There is an answer. "God's people have lost their first love. They must now repent and make steady advancement in the path of holiness. God's purposes reach to every phase of life. They are immutable, eternal; and at the time appointed they will be executed. For a time it may seem that Satan has all the power in his hands; but our trust is in God. When we draw near to Him, He will draw near to us, and will work with mighty power to accomplish His gracious purposes." (*Review and Herald,* Feb. 25, 1902)

After being given the vision of the 2300 days in Daniel 8:14, Daniel desperately wanted to understand its meaning. "Now it happened, when I, Daniel, had seen the vision and was seeking the meaning, that suddenly there stood before me one having the appearance of a man. And I heard a man's voice between the banks of the Ulai, who called and said, 'Gabriel, make this man understand the vision.' So he came near where I stood and when he came I was afraid and fell on my face; but he said to me, 'Understand, son of man, that the vision refers to the time of the end.' Now, as he was speaking with me, I was in a deep sleep with my face to the ground; but he touched me and stood me upright. And he said, 'Look, I am making known to you what shall happen in the latter time of the indignation; for at the appointed time the end shall be.'" (Daniel 8:15-19)

Ellen White makes a significant comment about this great prophecy and the "appointed time" of the end. "It cannot now be said by the Lord's servants, as it was by the prophet Daniel: 'The time appointed was long.' Daniel 10:1. **It is now but a short time till the witnesses for God will have done their work in preparing the way of the Lord.**" (*Testimonies for the Church,* vol. 6, p. 406)

This next statement puts this entire chapter into perspective. "But there is a day that God hath appointed for the close of this world's history: 'This gospel of the kingdom shall be preached in all the world for a witness unto all nations; and then shall the end come.' Prophecy is fast fulfilling. More, much more, should be said about these tremendously important subjects. **The day is at hand when the destiny of every soul will be fixed forever.** This day of the Lord hastens on apace. The false watchmen are raising the cry, 'All is well;' but the day of God is rapidly approaching. Its footsteps are so muffled that it does not arouse the world from the death-like slumber into which it has fallen. While the watchmen cry, 'Peace and safety,' 'sudden destruction' cometh upon them, and they shall not escape; 'for as a snare shall it come on all them that dwell on the face of the whole earth.' It overtakes the pleasure lover and the sinful man as a thief in the night. When all is apparently secure, and men retire to contented rest, then the prowling, stealthy, midnight thief steals upon his prey. When it is too late to prevent the evil, it is discovered that some door or window was not secured. 'Be ye also ready: for in such an hour as ye think not the Son of Man cometh.' People are now settling to rest, imagining themselves secure under the popular churches; but let all beware, lest there is a place left open for the enemy to gain an entrance. Great pains should be taken to keep this subject before the people. The solemn fact is to be kept not only before the people of the world, but before our own churches also, that the day of the Lord will come suddenly, unexpectedly. The fearful warning of the prophecy is addressed to every soul. Let no one feel that he is secure from the danger of being surprised. Let no one's interpretation of prophecy rob you of the conviction of the knowledge of events which show that this great event is near at hand." (*Special Testimonies on Education,* p. 107)

I believe that very soon Jesus will stand up and say that His work of mediation is finished and "he who is unjust, let him be unjust still; he who is filthy, let him be filthy still; he who is righteous, let him be righteous still; he who is holy, let him be holy still. And behold, I am coming quickly, and My reward is with Me, to give every one according to his work." (Revelation 22:11, 12) The close of probation is the event that will catch the world off guard. When the plagues begin to fall, it seems to me, people will begin to realize that it is all over. And soon Jesus will come for His faithful people.

The prophet Daniel puts it this way: "And at that time Michael shall stand up, The great prince who stands watch over the sons of your people; And there shall be a time of trouble such as never was since there was a nation, Even to that time. And at that time your people shall be delivered, Everyone who is found written in the book." (Daniel 12:1, 2) When Michael stands up it's all over but the plagues. The angels loose the winds of strife, and the great time of trouble begins. Then, in a short time Jesus comes to rescue those whose names are written in the book. What a day that will be!

Right up to the end of her life Ellen White urged preparation for the imminent return of Jesus Christ. She wrote this in a *Review* article printed in the year of her death. "We must cherish and cultivate the faith of which prophets and apostles have testified,—the faith that lays hold on the promises of God, and waits for deliverance in His appointed time and way. The sure word of prophecy will meet its final fulfillment in the glorious advent of our Lord and Saviour Jesus Christ, as King of kings and Lord of lords. The time of waiting may seem long; the soul may be oppressed by discouraging circumstances; many in whom confidence has been placed may fall by the way: but with the prophet who endeavored to encourage Judah in a time of unparalleled apostasy, let us confidently declare, 'The Lord is in His holy temple: let all the earth keep silence before Him.' Hab. 2:20. Let us ever hold in rememberence the cheering message, 'The vision is yet for an appointed time, but at the end it shall speak, and not lie: though it tarry, wait for it: because it will surely come, it will not tarry. . . The just shall live by his faith.' Hab. 2:3, 4." (*Review and Herald,* July 15, 1915)

EATD-4

CHAPTER 9

A Real Time-Lord

W hen we read the Bible devotionally we are inspired by the acts of God in human history. We are encouraged by the stories of how God protected Daniel in the den of lions, how He saved the three Hebrew young men from the fiery furnace, and how Jesus found Zacchaeus in the sycamore tree. But the Bible is more than just a record of God's dealings with people one to one. God also has a way of dealing with temporal rulers and nations. God has these superlative qualities that go way beyond what we expect from our fellow human beings. One of these qualities is that God never changes. "Jesus Christ is the same yesterday, today, and forever." (Hebrews 13:8) With God "there is no variableness or shadow of turning." (James 1:17) And the God who never changes says, "Surely the Lord God does nothing, unless He reveals His secret to His servants the prophets." (Amos 3:7)

The unchanging God has a methodology, a way of doing things, a modus operandi, if you please. And one of His methods is that if He is going to do something, He will give a preview of it through a prophet.* The Lord planned to destroy the world by a flood. To which prophet did He reveal this fact? Most of us would quite naturally think of Noah. But actually he made a prior prediction present truth. Nearly a thousand years before the destruction of the unrepentant world by the deluge, God sent mankind a warning of their impending doom. Jude reminds us that the prophet Enoch, who lived only seven generations following Adam (Jude 14; *Patriarchs and Prophets,* p. 85) "was the first prophet." (*SDA Bible Commentary,* vol. 1, p. 1088) "Enoch learned from the lips of Adam the painful story of the fall, and the precious story of God's condescending grace in the gift of His Son as the world's Redeemer. He believed and relied upon the promise given. . . He waited before God, and prayed to know His will more perfectly, that he might perform it. God communed with Enoch through His angels, and gave him divine instruction. He made known to him that He would not always bear with man in his rebellion—that it was His purpose to destroy the sinful race by bringing a flood of waters upon the earth." (*Signs of the Times,* Feb. 20, 1879)

In addition to the destruction of the world by water, Enoch was also shown the second coming of Christ and the second destruction by fire. "The Lord opened more fully to Enoch the plan of salvation, and by the spirit of prophecy carried him down through the generations which should live after the flood, and showed him the great events connected with the second coming of Christ and the end of the world." *(Ibid.)*

So the first prophet, the seventh from Adam, was shown all these things. Now how does God reveal His secrets to His people? At different times and in many ways. Bible students understand that inspired writers have used personal names to convey messages. For example, when God told Isaiah that the Assyrians were coming and that they were going to destroy Damascus, how did He do it? By instructing Isaiah to name his son the longest name in the Bible—Maher-shalal-hash-baz. (Isa. 8:1-4) It meant "the enemy is coming from the north and is going to cause you great trouble; the riches of Damascus and Samaria will be taken away by the king of Assyria." The story was told by the name of Isaiah's son.

Other prophets were asked to name their children for a specific reason to convey a particular message. He told Hosea, "You shall call your daughter 'Lo-ammi' and your third son 'Lo-ruhamah.'" He told Zachariah, "His name shall be called John." And he told Joseph and Mary, "His name shall be called Jesus." Every time they called out, "Jesus Emmanuel," they were preaching a sermon.

In the days before the flood the world attained a level of wickedness comparable to the last days. As Jesus said, "As it was. . .   so shall it be." (Matthew 24) The Lord told Enoch to call his son Methu-selah. *Methuselah* comes from two words *salah*—"to send" and *methu*—"his death" or "at his death." The name literally means, "When he dies, it will be sent." (See *Cruden's Complete Concordance of the Old and New Testaments,* pp. 709-718; Alfred Jones, *The Proper Names of the Old Testament,* (1865), p. 249)

Evidently, Enoch named his son Methuselah as a vehicle to predict the flood. We can test this meaning within the facts of the flood narrative as presented by inspiration. (See Gen. 5:25-29; 7:11.) Methuselah was 187 at the birth of his son, Lamech, who, in turn, was 182 when his son, Noah, was born. Adding these figures together, we find that Methuselah was 369 at the birth of his grandson, Noah. When Noah reached age 600, the flood commenced, at which time Methuselah would be 969, the year of his death.

Did anyone know when he would die? No, of that day and hour knew no man. But the year he died—it was sent.

A hundred and twenty years before the end of Methuselah's life, God raised up another prophet. His name was Noah. He preached and built for 120 years. His present truth message was, "yet 120 years and the flood will come," and "at his death it will come." Noah took prophetic truth and made it present truth. He made it relevant for his day. That is what present truth is. Relevantly applied prophetic truth is present truth. And when Methuselah died, the flood came—with absolute mathematical precision!

When we analyze this story a picture of God's methodology appears. The Lord first predicted the coming event through a prophet, Enoch, and set a time span for its fulfillment. Although unknown to man, its duration was buried in the lifespan of Methuselah whose cryptic name was a warning filled with solemn and mysterious significance. Near the end of the prophecy the prophetic truth was proclaimed as present truth by a second prophet, Noah. Conceptually the model looks like this:

The Flood Prediction

Methuselah
(The year he dies, it will be sent)

Enoch	Noah
Prediction	Application

There are a number of other prophetic epochs that follow the same method of revealing God's secrets. The plan usually involves a group of faithful believers who believed the present truth and met the crisis as the believing remnant. We can apply this principle to any age that God has predicted.

The next great epoch was the Exodus. Abraham was told of the Exodus. He predicted 400 years of affliction and 430 years of sojourning. Abraham was recognized as a prophet. God told Abimalek, "He is a prophet and he will pray for you." (Gen. 20:7) Moses made Abraham's prediction present truth. He declared in Exodus 12:40, 41 that the Israelites left Egypt on the selfsame day that was predicted. This epoch appears as follows:

The Exodus Prediction
430 years of pilgrimage
400 years of affliction

Abram	Moses
Prediction	Application
Gen. 15:13	Ex. 12:41

Imagine you are one of the Israelites leaving Egypt. You have just witnessed the water turning to blood, jillions of frogs, jillions of lice, great darkness along with the other plagues, and now it is just past midnight, and the Egyptians are wailing and crying with the death of their firstborn. Finally Pharaoh gives the approval to leave, and the great procession begins to move with its goods and animals. Somehow you manage to get close to "General" Moses. Then to your great astonishment you hear him say, "This is awesome, absolutely awesome! This is the exact date God predicted through Abraham 400 years ago! Praise God!"

That is the kind of God we serve. He does everything precisely on time. Satan, Pharaoh, and his counselors did their utmost to prevent the Exodus, but it came to pass on the exact day God had predicted the hosts of God went out.

Another of the significant epochs in the history of God's dealings with man is the Babylonian exile. As you would expect, knowing now how God operates, this is what the epoch looks like:

The Babylonian Exile Prediction
70 years captivity

Jeremiah	Daniel, Haggai, Zechariah
Prediction	Application

As you recall, Jeremiah made the prediction, and then at the end of the 70 years, God sent several prophets to make the present truth application.

The 70 week or 490 year prophecy is one of the central prophecies of Scripture because it predicts the coming of "Messiah the Prince."

The Messiah Prediction
70 weeks/490 years

Daniel	John the Baptist, Christ
Prediction	Application

John was named by God before he was born. Raised following special instructions to his parents, he devoted his entire ministry to the present truth that the Messiah was coming. Jesus called him the greatest prophet. (See Matthew 11:11.)

The next great epoch has great significance to us today, because it reaches all the way from the time of Daniel to end-times—the time of the antitypical day of atonement. We know that we are given the great 2300 day/year prophecy through Daniel, but who is the prophet that makes the present truth application?

The Judgment Hour Prediction
2300 years (2300 Yom Kippurs)

Daniel	William Miller
Prediction	Application

When I first began looking at these great epochs of time, I felt that Ellen White must be the present truth prophet for the 2300 days. However, God did not use Ellen (Harmon) White as a prophet until after the great disappointment. She was actually a convert to "Adventism" through the work of another—William Miller. In fact, Ellen White herself says that Miller was the one who brought the present truth application of the 2300 days.

"The experience of the disciples who preached the 'gospel of the kingdom' at the first advent of Christ, has its counterpart in the experience of those who proclaimed the message of His second advent. As the disciples went out preaching 'The time is fulfilled, the kingdom of God is at hand,' so Miller and his associates proclaimed that the longest and last prophetic period brought to view in the Bible was about to expire, that the judgment was at hand, and the everlasting kingdom was to be ushered in. The preaching of the disciples in regard to time was based on the seventy weeks of Daniel 9. The message given by Miller and his associates announced the termination of the 2,300 days of Dan. 8:14, of which the seventy weeks form a part. The preaching of each was based upon the fulfillment of a different portion of the same great prophetic period." (*The Great Controversy*, p. 351)

In another reference Ellen White likens the reception of Miller's warning to that of Noah's, "As God sent His servant to warn the world of the coming flood, so He sent chosen messengers to make known the nearness of the day of final judgment. But as Noah's contemporaries laughed to scorn the predictions of the solitary preacher of righteousness, so did many in Miller's day treat his words of warning." (*The Spirit of Prophecy*, vol. 4, p. 210)

But now arises the logical question Where does Ellen White fit into all of this? I believe the answer is simple. We call her "the Messenger to the Remnant." She is the Second Coming prophet. But what prophetic prediction does she apply as present truth? We are told, "Enoch was an Adventist. He directed the minds of men forward to the great day of God, when Christ will come the second time, to judge every man's work. Jude tells us, 'And Enoch also, the seventh from Adam, prophesied of these saying, Behold, the Lord cometh with ten thousands of His saints. . ." (*Signs of the Times*, Oct. 12, 1904) The schematic would look something like this:

The Second Coming Prediction
6,000 years

Enoch Prediction	Ellen White Application

Only eight people survived the flood. Only two of those who left Egypt crossed the river Jordan and entered the promised land.

When the seventy year Babylonian captivity was over, unfortunately the majority of Israel decided to stay in Babylon. "This is home for us," they responded to the call to return and rebuild Jerusalem. "We are comfortable here now."

But what about the central prophecy regarding the Messiah? How many welcomed the baby Jesus? Again, only a few. Some shepherds, the wise men, Simeon, and Anna. Even following His ministry, in spite of the work of John the Baptist, there was only a small core group of believers.

And so it was with the judgment hour message. In fact it took nearly twenty years for a remnant of the great disappointment to get together to form the nucleus of the "Remnant" Church. And so, here we are today. Again we have been sent a messenger of warning. She spent her entire adult life speaking and writing about the nearness of Christ's coming. But how many are reading the books she wrote or following the counsel that she gave? I personally believe that to ignore her counsel will be just as costly for those alive today as it was for those who ignored the words of Noah so many centuries ago.

If Ellen White is indeed the Messenger to the Remnant—the one to make the Second Coming prophecies present truth—it occurs to me that her views on the history and scope of the plan of salvation would be extremely valuable to know. This will be discussed in a later chapter. And by the way, since you now understand God's methodology in prophecy and fulfillment, if you question the integrity of Ellen White's gift of prophecy, you had better start looking for another prophet, because there will be one!

I personally have examined her life and writings and have concluded she passes all the tests. Accordingly, I have referred to her works quite extensively in this book. The Scriptures declare: "Believe in the Lord your God, and you shall be established; believe His prophets, and you shall prosper." (II Chronicles 20:20) We are at the end of the last great epic of time, and if we are wise we will heed the counsel of "the Second Coming Prophet."

---

*I am indebted to Dr. Leslie Hardinge for the concepts presented in the basic outline of this chapter.

CHAPTER 10

The Great Week of Time

S ome years ago I attended a ministers' Bible conference sponsored by the General Conference Ministerial Department and held on the campus of Southern College. Contained in the notebook of materials was a section prepared by the White Estate on the 2,000-, 4,000-, and 6,000-year statements made by Ellen White. Eagerly I looked up each one of the quotations in their context and recognized that Ellen White assumed the validity of the 7,000-year time line. Of course, since that time her writings have been made available on the CD-ROM, and now any casual researcher can access her more than seventy-five statements on the topic.

I've heard Evangelist Kenneth Cox, Dr. Jack Blanco, Religion Department Chairman at Southern College, and others give public presentations that also assumed the validity of the approximate 7,000-year time line. Challenging that, others have stated in essence that the fact that the world might last only about 6,000 years in its present state is purely coincidental. I decided to study personally more deeply into prophecy and eschatology. The more I studied the subject of the 6,000 years, the more convinced I became of its general validity. The reason I use the term *general validity* is that I concur with others who have studied this topic in depth, that the 7,000-year time should not and cannot be used to set the exact time for the Second Coming and the end of this world in its present condition.

Some students of this principle have used Genesis as their primary source, others the book of Leviticus, others II Peter, and others the book of Revelation. By putting it all together, a clear picture emerges. In a nutshell, from Genesis, Chapters 1 and 2, one gets the weekly cycle—six days of work and one for rest. From Leviticus, Chapter 25, one gets the sabbatical year—six years to work the land and one to let it rest. From II Peter, Chapter 3, we observe that with the Lord a day is as a thousand years. And from Revelation, Chapter 20, we observe that the "day of the Lord" is one thousand years long. These basic points do leave some missing pieces. In this chapter and others, we'll flesh this principle out more clearly.

"Some portions of Scripture are, indeed, too plain to be misunderstood; but there are others whose meaning does not lie on the surface, to be seen at a glance," Ellen White wrote. "Scripture must be compared with Scripture. There must be careful research and patient reflection. And such study will be richly repaid. As the miner discovers veins of precious metal concealed beneath the surface of the earth, so will he who perseveringly searches the Word of God as for hid treasure, find truths of great value, which are concealed from the view of the careless seeker." (*Review and Herald*, Oct. 9, 1883) She made this statement just a month and a half after the *Review* printed the series of six articles by J. N. Andrews on "The Great Week of Time."

The Great Controversy devotes several chapters to the person and work of William Miller. When commenting on Miller's study methods, Ellen White states, "Endeavoring to lay aside all preconceived opinions, and dispensing with commentaries, he compared scripture with scripture by the aid of the marginal references and the concordance. He pursued his study in a regular and methodical manner; beginning with Genesis, and reading verse by verse, he proceeded no faster than the meaning of the several passages so unfolded as to leave him free from all embarrassment. When he found anything obscure, it was his custom to compare it with every other text which seemed to have any reference to the matter under consideration. Every word was permitted to have its proper bearing upon the subject of the text, and if his view of it harmonized with every collateral passage, it ceased to be a difficulty. . . Link after link of the chain of truth rewarded his efforts, as step by step he traced down the great lines of prophecy," she wrote. "Angels of heaven were guiding his mind and opening the Scriptures to his understanding." (*The Great Controversy*, pp. 320, 321)

William Miller came to the conclusion that the "day of the Lord" was the millennium. Many other Bible scholars, including Ellen White, have come to the same conclusion. They understood that this "day" was a thousand years long. Kai Arasola, in his book, *The End of Historicism.*

Millerite Hermeneutic of Time Prophecies in the Old Testament, says, "The key to Miller's thinking lies in his Old Testament concept of the Day of the Lord. He found two types of Old Testament texts on the subject. One category is on the destruction of the wicked 'Behold the day of the Lord cometh, cruel both with wrath and fierce anger; and he shall destroy the sinners thereof out of it.' (Isa. 13:9) and the other is on the glory of the saints, 'For behold, the day cometh—(when) unto you that fear my name shall the Sun of righteousness arise.' (Mal. 4:1) These two varieties of texts are then interpreted in the light of Revelation 20 which separates the first and the second resurrection by a millennium. (Rev. 20:4, 5) This, Miller asserted, means that the Day of the Lord cannot be an ordinary day. The appearing of the Sun of righteousness 'is a plain figure of the coming of Christ,' but even if the sinners are destroyed at the parousia their ultimate destruction cannot be but a thousand years later (Rev. 20:7-15). <u>The day of the Lord is the Millennium.</u>" (pp. 70, 71)

Significantly, the fourth of Miller's fifteen proof points that the second coming of Christ was near was his understanding of the 7,000-year time line. "Like many before him he believed that 'the sabbath' or rather the weekly cycle is a miniature model and a prophecy of the world's history. 'Christ will also labor six days [1000 years each] in creating the new heavens and earth and rest on the seventh.' . . . At the end of the 6,000 years 'the anti-typical Sabbath of a 1,000 years will commence, the time of peace and rest for the whole universe.'" (Arasola, p. 108)

Of course, William Miller was mistaken in his view of what happened in 1844. He tried to "arrange" Biblical chronology in such a way as to make the 6,000 years end in 1844. This, of course, does not detract from the general validity of the 6,000-year time line from the Creation to the Second Coming.

But Miller was hardly advocating a radical new understanding. In addition to Miller's own research, "The Millerites appealed to the authority of the church Fathers, Irenaeus, Barnabus, Cyprian, Lactantius as well as well known scholars like Mede, Clark, or Gibbon or even Bunyan to exhibit the validity of the 6,000 year theory." (Arasola, pp. 111, 112)

John Nevins Andrews, after whom Andrews University is named, was more than the first Seventh-day Adventist missionary. He was a

Bible student and theologian. Ellen White said of him when writing to the brethren in Switzerland, "Elder Andrews is a conscientious servant of Jesus Christ. . . We sent you the ablest man in all our ranks. . . We needed Elder Andrews here. But we thought his great caution, his experience, his God-fearing dignity in the desk, would be just what you needed. We hoped you would accept his counsel, and aid him in every way possible while he was a stranger in a strange country." (*Manuscript Releases,* vol. 5, p. 436)

Arthur White wrote that "Andrews was mild, submissive, and fearful of making mistakes, but zealous and hard working. He had great intellectual strength and was an indefatigable student and researcher. He could see and understand the deep and wide meaning of truth and searched diligently to find it." (*Ellen G. White in Europe 1885-1887,* p. 19)

The Seventh-day Adventist Encyclopedia gives several interesting details regarding J. N. Andrews. "He enjoyed 'severe study' much more than physical activity; in later years he could read the Bible in seven languages and claimed the ability to reproduce the New Testament from memory. . . In 1867 he became the third president of the General Conference, a position he held for two years. [The term of office was only one year in those days. He was also editor of the *Review and Herald* for ten months while Uriah Smith took a leave of absence for health reasons.]

"As a theologian Andrews made significant contributions to the development of various doctrines of the SDA denomination. For example, for some time after Sabbatarian Adventists had begun to observe the Biblical Sabbath, the seventh day, there was difference of opinion among them as to when they should begin the Sabbath. Joseph Bates in 1851 held that the Sabbath should begin at six o'clock Friday evening. Others held that the Sabbath should be observed from sunset to sunset, as was the custom of the Seventh Day Baptists. In 1855 James White requested Andrews to give the subject a thorough investigation. Andrews published his findings in an article in which he showed on Biblical evidence that the Sabbath begins at sunset Friday evening. His conclusions [using nine texts from the Old Testament and two from the New] became the accepted position of SDA's. [His interpretation was then confirmed by Ellen White.]

"Andrew's extensive writings on the subject of the seventh-day

Sabbath in history were published in October, 1861, in a book of 340 pages entitled, *History of the Sabbath and the First Day of the Week. . .* Andrews was the first among the SDA leaders to publish an article that applied the two-horned beast of Revelation 13 to the United States of America. He also led in a study of what the Scriptures taught concerning the support of the ministry, as a result of which the plan of systematic benevolence was adopted. In 1878 Andrews served on a committee that recommended the tithing system." (p. 35)

J. N. Andrews was not on the fringes of Adventism or on some frolic and banter of his own. So I should not have been surprised to discover his research on the 7,000-year time line and his support of it as a Scriptural teaching. The results of his study were printed in a series of six consecutive articles in the *Review and Herald* starting with the July 17, 1883, issue and concluding August 21, 1883. It was in many ways the crowning work of his life of study and Biblical research. About three months after his articles were printed, he died of tuberculosis on his missionary tour in Switzerland. He was only fifty-four years of age. By the way, at the time of the printing of his articles on this topic, his name appears on the masthead of the *Review* as a corresponding editor. Since this material is not readily available to the student of Adventist history, I have included the complete text of the first and the sixth articles in the Chapter 10 Appendix.

The series of six *Review and Herald* articles authored by Andrews carried the title **"THE GREAT WEEK OF TIME or THE PERIOD OF SEVEN THOUSAND YEARS DEVOTED TO THE PROBATION AND THE JUDGMENT OF MANKIND."** We are not talking here about a casual mention in passing while addressing another subject. Andrews' study consisted of six full articles directly on this topic. I will give just the most significant thoughts from the first and sixth articles.

"When God created our earth, He indicated the period of time which must elapse before the day of Judgment. He employed six days in the work of creation; on the seventh day He rested from all His work. He sanctified the seventh day to be an everlasting memorial of the work of creation. But it appears that God designed by the first seven days of time to indicate the period assigned to the probation and judgment of mankind.

"St. Peter says that one day is with the Lord as a thousand years, and a thousand years as one day. II Pet. 3:8. By this we think he meant, not simply that the day of Judgment will occupy the period of 1,000 years, though this fact seems to be revealed in Rev. 20, in what is said of the two resurrections, but we think St. Peter also signified by it that the period devoted to the history of man before the day of Judgment, was also indicated by the days that God employed in the work of creation. We think, therefore, that at the end of 6,000 years from creation, the day of Judgment will commence, and that that day will last for the period of 1,000 years.

"Thus we have for the probation and judgment of mankind a great week of time,—the period of 7,000 years. This period commenced at creation, when God spake the word which called the elements into existence, and it will end with the destruction of the wicked in the lake of fire. Then God will create new heavens and new earth, which will remain through endless ages the eternal abode of those who have passed the period of their probation, and have been approved in the day of Judgment. Before the commencement of this great week of time, infinite ages had elapsed during all of which God had existed. And after the expiration of this great week, the righteous will enter with Christ upon a kingdom that cannot be moved and that shall never end. Thus the period of 7,000 years is cut off from the eternity of the past and from the eternity of the future, and assigned to the probation and the judgment of mankind.

"It has been the faith of the most eminent servants of God, not only during the entire gospel dispensation but also during some hundred years previous to Christ's first advent, that the period of 6,000 years from the creation would extend to the day of Judgment. And we think that the most careful study of the chronology of the Bible and of the prophetic periods will strongly confirm this view." (J. N. Andrews, *Review and Herald,* July 17, 1883)

Articles two-five in the Andrews' series simply trace the events down through time during each of the successive 1,000-year periods. Those articles make for interesting reading, but the last article, number six, gives the most convincing evidence of the validity of this prophetic interpretation. Therefore, I have quoted the most significant statements from the sixth and final article below.

"We think that God chose the period of six days such as are known to man for the work of creation in order to represent to man that in six days of 1,000 years each, days such as are known to God, He would accomplish the period assigned to man before the Judgment. II Pet. 3:7,

8. That the great week of 7,000 years was indicated by the first week of time has been the judgment of many of the wisest and best of men for the period of more than two thousand years.

"The law of Moses was designed to represent the good things to come through Christ in the same manner that a shadow represents the tree by which it is cast. Heb. 10:1. This was true in a special sense of the three festivals, the passover, the pentecost, and the feast of tabernacles, and of the seven annual sabbaths connected with these feasts, and of the twelve or thirteen new moons of each year, and of the sabbath of the seventh year. These are enumerated in Col. 2:14-17, where the Greek word for sabbath is plural, and all the things mentioned are said to be the shadow of things to come. They are ordained in Lev. 23:4-8, 15-21, 24, 27-43; 25:1-5; Num. 10:10. They are distinguished from the Sabbath of the Lord in Lev. 23:38; for the Sabbath of the Lord only belongs to the moral law (Ex. 20:8-11), and it points backward to the creation and not forward to the renewing of the earth, and it will be an eternal memorial of the Creator in the new earth. Isa. 66:22, 23.

"The week of years in which, after the land had been cultivated six years, it was to remain without cultivation the seventh (Lev. 25:1-7), is certainly a type of the great week of 7,000 years, in which after the earth has been cultivated by its inhabitants during 6,000 years, it will remain uncultivated and desolate during the seventh period of 1,000 years while the Judgment takes place. . . . "The seventh period of 1,000 years commences with the resurrection of the martyrs, and of all those who have not worshiped the beast nor his image. Rev. 20:4. This period terminates at the resurrection of the unjust. Rev. 20:5." (J. N. Andrews, *Review and Herald*, Aug. 21, 1883)

True to his normal mode of writing and scholarship Andrews uses only Scripture with its types and prophecies for the basis of his understanding of the 7,000-year principle. He uses no other authors—though he alludes to the fact that this concept has been the faith of the most eminent servants of God since before the first advent of Christ. In addition, though Ellen White, his close friend and counselor, concurred with his view, he does not quote her.

Here then is a summary of Andrews' reasoning for the teaching of the 7,000 years in history.

The judgment will end the time allotted for the probation of men and angels. The "day of the Lord" was set or reserved before the fall of angels and men. (Jude 6; II Peter 2:4) "He hath appointed a day in the which He will judge the world." (Acts 17:31)

The day of judgment or day of the Lord is a period of time—not just a literal twenty-four-hour day. According to Miller and Andrews, it has a general application to the 1,000 years—the time between the first and second resurrections. (II Peter 3:8; Revelation 20:1-5) This was not a new concept. Ellen White associates the day of the Lord and the 1,000 years. Adventist theologian, Dr. William Shea, states in the *Daniel and Revelation Committee Series,* vol. 1, p. 69, "The poetic statement of Isa. 61:2 presents an uncommon example of the reverse order of the "day" and "year" time elements. The "year of the Lord's favor" is followed by "the day of vengeance of our God." The specific concept from which this use of the word "day" derives is the "day of the Lord," an expression used throughout the prophets to depict a final **time** of judgment for Israel or Judah, or for nations round about God's people, or for kingdoms and peoples seen in prophecy arising in the future."

Andrews concludes that God used the weekly cycle of seven days—six for man and one for God—as a model to indicate the period assigned to the probation and judgment of mankind. Therefore, if God's day is 1,000 years then men's "days" would be 6,000 years, equaling together the great week of time.

Andrews also points out that the weekly seventh-day Sabbath is and has been only and always a memorial of Creation. It is the weekly cycle not the seventh-day Sabbath that is the model for the 7,000-year period.

Additional support for this concept comes from the special holy days or "sabbaths" (small *s*) of the Law of Moses. These typological days are said to be "shadows of things to come." (Col. 2:14-17) They are distinguished from the weekly Sabbath of the Lord but have sabbath-like qualities.

The best explanation of this concept that I am aware of is found again in the studies done by William Shea when he deals with the year/day principle found in Scripture in his comments on Leviticus 25:1-5. Dr. Shea's material is quite technical, but when considered in connection with the Andrews' articles, a solid Biblical basis is established. "This is the earliest biblical text in which the year-day principle is reflected. In this piece of Levitical legislation an institution which has come to be designated as the sabbatical year was established for the Israelite agricultural economy. For six years the Israelite farmer was instructed to sow his fields, prune his vineyards, and gather the harvest into his barns and storehouses. But in the seventh year he was instructed to leave the land to lie fallow and the vineyards and orchards unpruned. What grew of itself could be eaten as food by anyone—the alien, the poor, the slave, as well as the owner; but it was not to be harvested and stored.

"The sabbatical year was marked off as the last or seventh year in a period of seven years. The legislation was introduced with these words: 'When you come into the land which I will give you, the land shall keep a sabbath to the Lord' (v. 2). The 'sabbath' referred to in this instance, however, was not the weekly seventh-day Sabbath but the 'sabbath' of every seventh year. A literal translation of the phrase would read, 'the land shall sabbatize a sabbath to Yahweh.'

"When the command is repeated again in v. 4, it is stated in a slightly different manner: the seventh year was to be 'a sabbath. . . for the land, a sabbath to the Lord.' The comment was also added that it was to be a 'sabbath of solemn rest (*sabbat sabbaton*).' When this latter phrase is repeated in v. 5, the word for 'year' occurs in the same position as the word for 'sabbath.' Thus the two statements read, The seventh year:

'shall be a sabbath of solemn rest for the land' (v. 4).

'shall be a year of solemn rest for the land' (v. 5).

"The grammatical parallelism emphasizes again the identification of that year as a sabbath for the land to Yahweh.

"*Sabbaton* (solemn rest), the second Hebrew word which occurs in these phrases, obviously derives from the root word for sabbath (*sabbot*). It is commonly translated 'solemn rest' or a similar expression. Andreasen has found this word 'to describe that which really characterize(s) the Sabbath, or any other day which has Sabbath qualities. In that sense it has been termed a *verbal-abstractum,* meaning, 'Sabbath keeping.' We conclude, therefore, that *sabbaton* describes the content of the Sabbath, i.e., it is an abstraction of 'keeping Sabbath. . .'

"The word *sabbaton* occurs only in Exodus and Leviticus, and in those books it occurs in ten passages. It is applied to the weekly Sabbath (Ex. 16:23; 31:15; 35:2; Lev. 23:3), the Day of Atonement (Lev. 16:31; 23:32), the Feast of Trumpets (Lev. 23:24), and to the first and last days of the Feast of Booths (Lev. 23:39), in addition to its two instances in connection with the sabbatical year considered above (Lev. 25:4, 5).

"Since the festival days (Feast of Trumpets, Day of Atonement, first and last days of the Feast of Booths) could fall on days other than the seventh day of the week, it is evident that the word *sabbaton* could also be used for days other than the weekly Sabbath. However, <u>it is evident that the weekly Sabbath has been the **pattern** and that its special significance has been extended to those festival days. It is their Sabbath-day quality that makes them sabbaths of solemn rest.</u>

"More important for the present discussion is the evidence that *sabbaton* (outside our passage in Lev. 25:1-7) is never applied to more than one day at a time. The day of the Feast of Trumpets and the Day of Atonement were individual days which fell on the first and tenth days of the seventh month. It was not the whole Feast of Booths that was a *sabbot sabbaton,* but only the first and eighth days of that festival that qualified for that particular designation. Thus the other usages of this word refer to single or individual days. <u>In like manner, in Lev. 25:4, 5 the word has been taken over and applied to single or individual **years.** In this manner a word with more specific connections to individual days has been applied by analogy in Lev. 25 to individual years.</u>

"<u>It is clearly implied in Lev. 25:1-7 that the sabbatical year is modeled from the sabbatical day, that is, from the weekly Sabbath.</u> Six days of labor were followed by the seventh day of Sabbath rest; six years of farming were to be followed by a seventh year of sabbath rest for the land. The seventh-day Sabbath <u>was to be a Sabbath of 'solemn rest' (Lev. 23:3); and the seventh year, the sabbatical year, was likewise to be a sabbath of 'solemn rest' for the land. (Lev. 25:4, 5).</u>

"Thus there is a <u>direct relationship</u> between the 'day' and the 'year' since the same terminology was applied to both, and the latter sabbatical year was patterned after the former sabbatical day. This relationship becomes clearer quantatively when the next piece of legislation in Lev. 25 pertaining to the jubilee period is considered." (William H. Shea, "Selected Studies on Prophetic Interpretation," *Daniel and Revelation Committee Series,* vol. 1, pp. 69-71)

According to Shea, the seventh year sabbaths of Leviticus 25:4, 5 have the same sabbath-like qualities and in fact are described using the same word (*sabbaton*) as the weekly sabbath and the special feast-day sabbaths. J. N. Andrews stated in his articles that the sabbaths (plural with small *s*) were shadows of things to come. He concluded that since the feast-day sabbaths prefigured the work of Christ in His antitypical ministry, so also must the seventh year sabbaths (also *sabbatons*) prefigure the work of Christ in the overall 7,000-year prophecy.

Dr. Ron du Preez of the Southern College Religion Department has researched Colossians 2:14-17. His conclusion is that the most logical linguistic, grammatical, and contextual interpretation of the Greek *sabbaton* translated "sabbaths" or "sabbath days" in Colossians 2:16 is most likely really a simple transliteration of the Hebrew *sabbaton* from the ceremonial law or "Law of Moses." His research gives added support to the traditional Adventist interpretation of the "sabbaths" of the ceremonial law being types of things to come.

Digging deep into Scripture certainly has its rewards. This is exciting, isn't it! Now let's get back to Andrews' conclusion. Briefly stated: The condition of the earth during the "day of the Lord"—the 1,000 years—the millennium is exactly the same as the condition of the land during the 70-year Babylonian captivity. (See Lev. 26:34, 35; II Chron. 36:20, 21; Jer. 4:23-27.) It is very reasonable to conclude that since the antitypical *sabbaton* is 1,000 years, then the balance of the time in the overall cycle is 6,000 years. And according to Andrews this has been the judgment of many of the wisest and best men for the period of two thousand years.

When the doctrines of the Seventh-day Adventist Church were "studied and prayed out," they were often then endorsed through the modern-day manifestation of the gift of prophecy. This the Adventist pioneers recognized as being manifest in the ministry of Ellen G. White. Many then questioned, in effect, "Why do we have to struggle with all this Bible study and prayer when God could just tell us the true interpretations of Scripture through Sister White?" But God doesn't work that way. This is how Ellen White explained it.

"Many of our people do not realize how firmly the foundation of our faith has been laid. My husband, Elder Joseph Bates, Father Pierce, Elder Edson, and others who were keen, noble, and true, were among those who, after the passing of the time in 1844, searched for the truth as for hidden treasure. I met with them, and we studied and prayed earnestly. Often we remained together until late at night, and sometimes through the entire night, praying for light and studying the Word. Again and again these brethren came together to study the Bible, in order that they might know its meaning, and be prepared to teach it with power. When they came to the point in their study where they said. 'We can do nothing more,' the Spirit of the Lord would come upon me, I would be taken off in vision, and a clear explanation of the passages we had been studying would be given me, with instruction as to how we were to labor and teach effectively. Thus light was given that helped us to understand the scriptures in regard to Christ, His mission, and His priesthood. A line of truth extending from that time to the time when we shall enter the city of God, was made plain to me, and I gave to others the instruction that the Lord had given me." (*Selected Messages*, vol. 1, p. 206)

James White later wrote, "It does not appear to be the desire of the Lord to teach His people by the gifts of the Spirit on Bible questions until His servants have diligently searched the Word." (*Review and Herald*, Feb. 25, 1868)

Since we have already discussed the Biblical basis for the 7,000 years based on the weekly cycle and the seventh-year or sabbatical year as a type or model of the overall time frame for the working out of the probation and judgment of mankind, perhaps it would be good to give an overview of Ellen White's understanding of "types as prophetic guides" In the chapter "Prophecies Fulfilled" in *The Great Controversy* she states, "<u>Arguments from the Old Testament types also pointed to the autumn as the time when the event represented by the 'cleansing of the sanctuary' must take place.</u> This was made very clear as attention was given to the manner in which the types relating to the first advent of Christ had been fulfilled.

"The slaying of the Passover lamb was a <u>shadow</u> of the death of Christ. Says Paul: 'Christ our Passover is sacrificed for us.' I Corinthians 5:7. The sheaf of first fruits, which at the time of the Passover was waved before the Lord, was <u>typical</u> of the resurrection of Christ. Paul says, in speaking of the resurrection of the Lord and of all His people: 'Christ the first fruits; afterward they that are Christ's at His coming.' I Corinthians 15:23. Like the wave sheaf, which was the first ripe grain gathered before the harvest, Christ is the first fruits of that immortal harvest of redeemed ones that at the future resurrection shall be gathered into the garner of God.

"<u>These types were fulfilled, not only as to the event, but as to the time.</u> On the fourteenth day of the first Jewish month, the very day and month on which for fifteen long centuries the Passover lamb had been slain, Christ, having eaten the Passover with His disciples, instituted that feast which was to commemorate His own death as 'the Lamb of God, which taketh away the sin of the world.' That same night He was taken by wicked hands to be crucified and slain. And as the antitype of the wave sheaf our Lord was raised from the dead on the third day, 'the first fruits of them that slept,' a sample of all the resurrected just, whose 'vile body' shall be changed, and 'fashioned like unto His glorious body.' Verse 20; Philippians 3:21.

"In like manner the types which relate to the second advent must be fulfilled at the time pointed out in the symbolic service." (*The Great Controversy*, p. 399)

I understand this to mean that as other *sabbatons* illustrated future antitypical events, which were fulfilled not only as to event but also as to time, so also would the *sabbaton* of Lev. 25:4, 5 that indicated the period of time when the land should rest, and therefore the time for the land to be worked would also be fulfilled at the time pointed out.

We have looked at an overview of the eschatological significance of the *sabbatons* of Leviticus. Next I'll discuss the significance of the jubilee, the Leviticus connection to the interpretation of the time prophecies of the book of Daniel, and also take a close look at the meaning of II Peter 3:8.

CHAPTER 11

A Day As a Thousand Years

Many today see significance in the jubilee cycle as an indication of when Jesus might return to this earth. The 7,000-year prophecy may clarify this concept somewhat. If the sabbatical cycle is typological, as I believe it is, then the Second Coming will introduce the antitypical seventh-year sabbath—not the jubilee. In addition, the jubilee year was not a *sabbaton* as the seventh year sabbaticals were, and may not therefore have been typical as to time but almost surely pointed forward to the meek inheriting the earth. In his sixth article J. N. Andrews stated the same concept.

"After seven of these weeks of years came the year of jubilee. Lev. 25:8-10. In this year liberty was proclaimed throughout all the land to all its inhabitants, and every man returned to his own inheritance. This signifies that after the great Sabbath, during which the earth will remain uncultivated for 1,000 years, the great week of 7,000 years being finished, the curse will cease, after having consumed the earth with all who are wicked. Then the earth will be created anew by the power of God, and all the just will return to their inheritance in the new earth, and never know sin nor sorrow any more." (J. N. Andrews, "The Great Week of Time," *Review and Herald,* Aug. 21, 1883)

The provisions of the jubilee thus reach their logical fulfillment at the creation of the new earth when the meek are granted their inheritance along with Abraham, Isaac, and Jacob. (See Hebrews 11:8-16.)

The second point of discussion in this chapter is how the weekly (seven) cycle and the sabbatical year help us understand the prophecies of Daniel. When we see this connection it is then very clear that the weekly and yearly cycles of seven do indeed have prophetic or predictive elements. William Shea has done a thorough study of this topic. He states, when commenting on Leviticus 25:8, "A literal translation of the opening clause of Lev. 25:8 reads: 'You shall count seven sabbaths of years, seven years seven times, and to you the days of the seven sabbaths of years shall be forty-nine years.'

"The explanation of the first numerical expression, as given in the second phrase of the same clause, indicates that a 'sabbath of years' is to be understood as a *period* of seven years. The Sabbath was the seventh day of the week. In this passage the *seventh day* has been taken to stand for a *seventh year*. As the seventh and concluding day of the week, the Sabbath has been taken over here to stand for the seventh *year* of a period of seven years. Thus *each day* of the 'weeks' which end with these 'sabbaths' in the jubilee cycle stand for *one year*.

". . .Thus the Sabbath day and the six days that preceded it came to be used as the model by which the occurrence of the jubilee year was calculated according to divine directions. Each of these year-days was to extend into the future from the beginning of those cycles to measure off the coming of the jubilee year.

"In prophecy this use of the year-day principle is paralleled most directly by Dan. 9:24-27. A different word (*sabua*) is used in that prophecy, but it means the same thing that the 'sabbaths' mean in Lev. 25:8, that is, 'weeks.' The applicability of the year-day principle to the time periods of Dan. 9:24-27 is especially evident, therefore, from the parallel construction of the Levitical instruction on the jubilee year. One could almost say that the time period involved in Dan. 9:24-27 was modeled after the jubilee legislation.

"Since it is legitimate to apply the year-day principle to the days of the weeks of Lev. 25 to reckon time into the future to the next Jubilee, it is also legitimate to apply that same year-day principle to the days of the weeks in Dan. 9 to reckon time into the future from the beginning of their cycle. By extension, this same principle can be reasonably applied also to the 'days' of the other time prophecies in Daniel." (William H. Shea, "Selected Studies on Prophetic Interpretation," *Daniel and Revelation Committee Series,* vol. 1, pp. 71, 72)

Shea states that the cycle of seven as found in Leviticus 25 is a model to help to properly interpret the book of Daniel. Andrews follows the same reasoning to interpret II Peter 3:7, 8 and to establish an overall prophecy of the history of the great controversy.

"The week of years in which, after the land had been cultivated six years, it was to remain without cultivation the seventh (Lev. 25:1-7) is certainly a type of the great week of 7,000 years, in which, after the earth has been cultivated by its inhabitants during 6,000 years, it will remain uncultivated and desolate during the seventh period of 1,000 years while the Judgment takes place. . .

"The seventh period of 1,000 years commences with the resurrection of the martyrs, and of all those who have not worshiped the beast nor his image. Rev. 20:4. This period terminates at the resurrection of the unjust. Rev. 20:5. As the dead in Christ are raised at the second coming of Christ (II Cor. 15:23, 51, 52; I Thess. 4:16, 17), we know that this period of 1,000 years will commence at the sound of the last trumpet. Peter seems to assign the period of 1,000 years to the day of Judgment (II Pet. 3:7, 8), and John expressly assigns this period to that grand event. Rev. 20:4." (J. N. Andrews, "The Great Week of Time," *Review and Herald*, Aug. 21, 1883)

One key point remains to be made. It appears upon deeper study that the sabbatical and jubilee models were the basis of the prophecy that predicted Christ's first coming, and by extension, why not the second? Let's take a look at the first advent prophecies. Again a good, concise study has been done by the Daniel and Revelation study committee.

"Daniel's prayer in ch 9 begins with an appeal to God for the return of His people to their land on the basis of the 70 years Jeremiah prophesied they would be exiled in Babylon (v. 2; cf Jer. 25:12; 29:10). In answer to his prayer, Gabriel assured Daniel they would return and rebuild the temple and capital city. In doing so, Gabriel also delimited another period of prophetic time: 70 weeks. During that period other events, beyond the previously mentioned ones, would take place (Dan. 9:24-27).

"Since these events could not have been accomplished in 70 literal weeks, it is evident that this later time period was intended to be understood symbolically. The seven-day week provided the model upon which the symbolic units of that time period were based. Thus we find two prophetic time periods in this narrative of Dan. 9—the 70 years at its beginning and the 70 weeks at its end; the one literal, the other symbolic. What is the relationship between these two time periods?

"A relationship between them can be seen from the fact that both are prophetic in nature, and the latter is given in answer to the prayer about the former.

"A relationship between them can also be suggested on the basis of their location in similar positions in the literary structure of the narrative . . .

"Another way these two time periods are linked is through their common use of the number 70. <u>This is no random selection of numbers. The later has been directly modeled after the former</u>. . .

"These two time prophecies are also related by the fact that both are multiples of seven. When the 70 weeks are multiplied by their individual units, they are found to contain seven times more symbolic units than the literal units of the 70 years (70 years: 490 day-years).

"Furthermore, when the symbolic units of the 70 weeks are interpreted according to the literal units of the 70 years, a relationship is produced which parallels the relationship between the jubilee period and sabbatical-year period (Lev. 25:1-19). It may be recalled that the years of the jubilee were also measured off in terms of 'weeks' in the legislation given about them in Lev. 25:8. . .

"Sabbatical year terminology was applied to Jeremiah's 70-year prediction of Babylonian captivity by the chronicler: 'to fulfil the word of the Lord by the mouth of Jeremiah, *until the land had enjoyed its sabbaths.* All the days that it lay desolate *it kept sabbath,* to fulfil seventy years' (II Chron. 36:21, italics Shea). Since the land rested every seventh year, it is evident that the inspired writer viewed the 70 years of captivity as the sum of ten sabbatical-year periods

"Inasmuch as the 70-year period (referred to by Daniel in v 2 just prior to his prayer) was understood to relate to the sabbatical-year legislation (Lev. 25:1-7), it may be expected that the 70-week period (at the close of his prayer) would be related to the jubilee period. This is the sequence in Lev. 25:1-17 (sabbatical year—jubilee). <u>Thus the 70 weeks, or 490 years (on the year-day principle), may be seen as ten jubilee periods even as the 70 years were seen as ten sabbatical-year periods.</u>

"Supplementary support for these sabbatical year-jubilee relationships to Daniel's 70 weeks can be found in the fact that they were fulfilled historically through events that occurred in post-exilic sabbatical years. The years 457 B.C. and A.D. 27 and 34 were sabbatical years." (William H. Shea, "Selected Studies on Prophetic Interpretation," *Daniel and Revelation Committee Series,* vol. 1, pp. 77-79)

This study underlines that there is genuine Biblical support for the predictive use of Leviticus 25:1-17. The *Adventist Review* released a special undated issue in the fall of 1993 titled "LAST-DAY EVENTS

SPECIAL. LOOK UP! JESUS IS COMING." On page 7 Beatrice Neall, Professor of Religion at Union College, in an article titled "Jesus at the Center—How to Interpret Prophecy," states, "Keep in mind that Daniel and Revelation draw upon the typology of the Old Testament—Creation, the Exodus, the sanctuary. This means that type and antitype must be studied carefully."

Every Bible scholar and researcher that I have found who has addressed the 7,000-year time line has considered II Peter 3:8 in the process. Some have advanced the idea that II Peter 3:8, "But, beloved, do not forget this one thing, that with the Lord one day is as a thousand years, and a thousand years as one day," gives support to the 6,000-year theory. Others have said, "No, that's not what it says at all. This text just means that God is eternal and does not think in terms of time as man does." Which view is right? Are either of them? From my perspective having just finished the research for this book, I surely do not believe in the second view. It is obvious that God is operating on a very exact time schedule. His modus operandi is to set a schedule and then follow it very precisely. Though eternal, He always deals with man within the parameters of time and always tells us through the prophets what He is about to do or will do in the future.

In seeking to understand a passage, scholars look at both the internal evidence contained within the text itself and external evidence from outside pertinent sources. Let's follow this method in trying to see what Peter is trying to tell us not to be ignorant of or not to forget.

Peter's second epistle divides itself easily into three sections:

Chapter 1 - Growth in Christ and the cultivation of Christian character

Chapter 2 - The danger of false teachers

Chapter 3 - Confidence in Christ's return.

Peter was not writing to people disappointed after having waited long centuries for Christ's return. His readers needed no reassurance about time being viewed differently by God, or any other explanations for a very long delay, since no long delay had in fact occurred. He was writing to Christians whose hopes had been raised by false teachers to expect Christ's imminent return, and who needed to be guarded against possible disappointment when told that Christ's second coming was in the distant future. In addition, he wanted to turn the believers' heavenly expectations into positive present action.

With this brief historical background clearly in mind let's now turn to consider specific passages in II Peter 3:3-14, where the subject of the second advent is treated most fully.*

Peter pictured a long delay in Christ's coming (II Peter 3:3, 4); he illustrated the delay by the long period from Creation to the Flood (3:5-7); he gave the approximate limits of probationary time by comparing the days of the week with 1,000-year periods (3:8); he gave God's longsuffering as the reason for the delay (3:9). Forestalling the idea of an interminable delay, he declared emphatically that "the day of the Lord will come." He described it as a universal cataclysmic event, not to be confused with the destruction of Jerusalem (3:10). And finally, he used the judgments associated with Christ's coming as the basis for an appeal for holy living (3:11). He tells those "looking for" Christ's imminent return that it was in their power to "hasten the coming of the day of God" by godly lives (3:12-14). We also understand that Peter's statement holding out the possibility for believers in the last days to hasten the coming of Christ disqualifies the use of II Peter 3:8 as a yardstick for fixing the exact time of Christ's return.

In II Peter 3:8 the apostle cannot be referring to the shortness of time with God, for he says, "one day is with the Lord as a thousand years." Seeing that he then repeats the statement in reverse, which would exactly reverse the meaning, we are left with two alternative interpretations. Either Peter is comparing the days of the week with successive 1,000-year periods in human history (possibly based on his knowledge of the day/year and week/sabbatical relationships in Leviticus), or he is saying that time is of no consequence to the Eternal God even when dealing with man and the great controversy on earth.

Let me deal with the second alternative first. It is clear that though God is eternal, He deals with man within the parameters of time. While God is not dependant on the universe He has created, He nevertheless lives within and not apart from His universal creation.

And so the view that "we cannot confine God or His ideas to our scale of days and years" is a confusing half-truth, which does not resolve the problem. We must not forget that the whole Bible witnesses to the fact that in redemption God has chosen to act within the dimensions in which He placed man at Creation; not above and apart from these dimensions, and the Second Advent is as much a part of God's plan of redemption as the incarnation.

The "unlearned" fisherman, Peter, no doubt followed the typical mystical bent of the Hebrew-biblical culture, in which symbols, figures, types, and analogies were reverently used to veil the presentation of sacred truth, rather than the analytical, over-mastering methods of the Greco-European mind, which attempted to penetrate truth, control it, and nakedly expose it for all to see and use—or abuse. In view of this, it is simply out of character for Peter's statement in II Peter 3:8 to be a penetrating philosophical observation on the sacred intimacies of Divine time consciousness. Such concepts were developed only in later years as philosophers tried to interpret Christianity in terms of Greek philosophy. R. H. Strachan concurs, saying, "It can scarcely be said that the writer of II Peter had attained to the conception that the category of time does not exist for the Divine mind." (R. H. Strachan, *The Expositor's Greek Testament*, (1910), p. 144)

Finally, the popular spiritual interpretation of II Peter 3:8 and its supporting arguments, do not fit the historical context. Peter is not addressing "scoffers." (They were to come in the last days according to v. 3.), but believers in Christ's coming, whom he calls "beloved" (3:1, 8). The purpose of his statement is not to rebuke them, but to instruct them to "be not ignorant of this one thing" (3:8). His pointed statement is aimed at removing ignorance about one important aspect concerning Christ's coming.

The believers with misconceptions about Christ's immediate return had experienced no long delay in their expectations, and so, the idea that God is above time would be totally irrelevant to them. The application of Peter's words by many modern commentators gives this scripture relevance for believers today simply because we (unlike Peter's original readers) have experienced a long delay in Christ's return. That delay in the mind of scoffers could be the nearly 2,000 years since the Lord's promise to "come again," or to the nearly 200 years that have elapsed since the "time of the end" Adventists have proclaimed began in 1798.

The other alternative I have stated, namely, that Peter probably was using Hebrew typology to explain the parameters of salvation history, can be defended on five grounds: (1) it fits the immediate context; (2) it fits the historical situation; (3) it is corroborated by the understanding of Christian scholars quite near in time to the historical situation of Peter's second epistle; (4) other statements in the epistle lend support to Peter's time equation; and (5) insights from the Spirit of Prophecy. Let's consider these points individually.

(1) The immediate context requires that we should understand the two uses of "day" in II Peter 3:8 in the light of a further three uses of "day" in II Peter 3:7, 10, 12, or vice versa. Not that they should all have the same meaning, but rather that their use in such close association suggests a deliberately meaningful relationship.

The three terms "the day of judgment" (3:7), "the day of the Lord" (3:10), and "the day of God" (3:12) all refer to Christ's second advent and associated events. The use of "day" here is, of course, figurative and does not refer to a twenty-four-hour period. As we addressed in Chapter 10, the term "day of the Lord" has its origin in the Old Testament and—like most figurative terms which are derived from literal usage—can be traced back to the seventh-day Sabbath of Creation week. "The day of the Lord" in the history of the Jews was primarily the whole period of Babylonian captivity. This 70-year period when "the land enjoyed her sabbaths" (II Chron. 36:21), was the seventh part of a previous six-times-seventy-year period of apostasy and rebellion, during which the Jews refused to "be reformed" to fulfill their calling as God's people (Lev. 25:1-32-35, 43). The local "day of the Lord," was a type of "the great and terrible day of the Lord" ushered in by Christ's return in glory and lasting for 1,000 years.

Finally, the pointedness with which Peter introduces his analogy between a day and a thousand years in the context of his threefold mention of "the day of judgment," "the day of the Lord," and "the day of God," suggests very strongly that "the day of the Lord" IS the "day" that will last for "a thousand years." Since "the day of the Lord," derives its meaning from the seventh-day Sabbath of Creation week, we should also understand him to imply that it will be the seventh part of a previous six-times-1,000-year period.

(2) As we noted earlier, since Peter's readers had been misled into expecting Christ's immediate return, they needed to be taught that a long period lay ahead before Christ would return. By equating the days of the week with 1,000-year periods, Peter satisfies this need in the historical situation. In effect he put "the day of the Lord" about 6,000 years after Creation and about 2,000 years after his own time, thus dispelling the idea of Christ's imminent return. The immediately preceding five verses are all concerned with putting Christ's return in the then distant future.

(3) The fact that there is general support for the 7,000-year time line

in II Peter 3:8 is corroborated by the "early church fathers" or the ante-Nicene fathers. The use these scholars made of II Peter 3:8 is significant since they lived close in time to the historical situation of Peter's second epistle. The following comments are representative:

Justin Martyr (c. 100-c. 165) writes when discussing the millennium in his *Dialogue With Trypho,* "We have perceived, moreover, that the expression, 'The day of the Lord is as a thousand years,' is connected with this subject." (i.e., the 1,000 years.) (Justin Martyr, *Dialogue With Trypho,* Chapter LXXXI. Footnotes cite Ps. 90:4 and II Peter 3:8.)

Irenaeus (c. 130-c. 202) writes, "For the day of the Lord is as a thousand years; and in six days created things were completed; it is evident therefore, that they will come to an end at the six thousandth year." (Irenaeus, *Against Heresies,* Book V, xxviii, 3. Footnote cites II Peter 3:8.)

Hippolytus (died c. 236) writes, "For the Sabbath is the type and emblem of the future kingdom of the saints, when they shall reign with Christ, when He comes from heaven, as John says in his Apocalypse. For a day with the Lord is as a thousand years. Since, then, in six days God made all things, it follows that 6000 years must be fulfilled." (Hippolytus, *Fragments From Commentaries,* Sections on Daniel 2, chapter 4)

No wonder J. N. Andrews could write, "It has been the faith of the most eminent servants of God, not only during the entire gospel dispensation, but also during some hundred years previous to Christ's first advent, that the period of 6,000 years from the creation would extend to the day of Judgment. And we think that the most careful study of the chronology of the Bible and of the prophetic periods will strongly confirm this view." And again he stated, "That the great week of 7000 years was indicated by the first week of time has been the judgment of many of the wisest and best of men for the period of more than two thousand years." By the way, both of these statements are made following comments on II Peter 3:8!

Some critics of the 7,000-year time line have suggested that the early church fathers got their ideas in this regard from ancient Persian traditions or from Jewish literature such as the Slavonic book of II Enoch. However, when you read the ante-Nicene fathers, their only appeal is to Scripture! And if both Jewish and non-Christian traditions mention the 7,000 years, that surely does no more harm to Biblical integrity than mythological flood stories such as the Gilgamish epic or the Enuma Elish do to the credibility of the Biblical account of the flood. Neither is any harm done to the Biblical laws by the Hammurabi Law code, though it precedes the written laws of God and Moses.

Moreover, Barnabus, Justin Martyr, Irenaeus, Hippolytus and Augustine clearly use the phrasing of II Peter 3:8, 10, and not that of II Enoch, as the basis for their teaching that one day is equal to a thousand years, and that "the day of the Lord" represents the Sabbatical Millennium. It is inescapable to conclude that II Peter 3:8 was the source of their idea.

The case of Justin Martyr is particularly significant. His *Dialogue With Trypho* (c. 148) is his effort to convert one of the most learned Jews of his time. With such a delicate task in hand, Justin was particularly careful in his use of sources, preferring whenever possible to quote a Jewish authority to prove a point. Moreover, in discussing the Millennium, Justin assured Trypho, "I choose to follow not men or men's doctrines, but God and the doctrines (delivered) by Him." (Justin Martyr, *Dialogue With Trypho,* Chapter LXXX) Then, without any reference to Jewish canonical or non-canonical sources, Justin added, "We have perceived, moreover, that the expression, 'The day of the Lord is as a thousand years,' is connected with the subject. And furthermore there was a certain man with us, whose name was John, one of the apostles of Christ, who prophesied by a revelation made to him. . ." *(Ibid.,* Chapter LXXXI) It is evident that by "we" and "us" Justin means Christians. By referring to "the expression" without a Jewish source, he must be quoting a widely known Christian saying, as the "furthermore" could also be taken to imply, when he next refers to the Revelation of John. Since he claims to follow only God-inspired doctrines, and since "the expression" he quotes corresponds exactly with a combination of two key phrases from II Peter 3:10 and 8, we are forced to conclude that Peter's second epistle was the source of his idea.

Further evidence that Jewish non-canonical sources were not the origin of the 6,000-year theory among the Church Fathers may be seen in the fact that while they generally held to a temporal millennium, when the world would flourish like Eden, the early Jewish idea was that "the world would last six thousand years and be in chaos during the seventh thousand years." (L. E. Froom, *The Prophetic Faith of Our Fathers,* vol. 2, p. 191)

During and following reformation times Bible scholars continued to hold and teach the general validity of the 6,000-year time line. Latimer (1485-1555) preached the scriptural basis for this idea, saying, "The world was ordained to endure, as all learned men affirm and prove it with Scripture, six thousand years." (H. Latimer, "Third Sermon on the Lord's Prayer," 1552, appearing in *The Works of Hugh Latimer,* vol. 1, p. 356) Thomas Burnet (1635-1715) also cited Scripture as the basis for nearly twenty of the Church Fathers subscribing to the 6,000-year history of the world. He says it was "not so much for the bare authority of the tradition, as because they thought it was founded in the history of the six days of creation and the Sabbath succeeding." (Thomas Burnet, *The Theory of the Earth,* vol. 2, pp. 34, 35)

Thus we are not alone in the view that Scripture in general and II Peter 3:8, 10 in particular are the origin of early Christian ideas that the millennium will be the seventh 1,000-year period of human history, corresponding to the seventh day of Creation and the Sabbatical year. Erroneous views regarding the conditions of the earth during the millennium that many of the Church Fathers associated with this understanding did not arise out of II Peter 3:8, and therefore, do not weaken the validity of their interpretation.

(4) Let's consider other statements in Peter's epistle that lend support to his time equation. Peter identifies Christ's transfiguration "in the holy mount" as a type of the "coming of our Lord" in "power" and "glory" (1:16-18). Holy Scripture indicates that Christ arranged for the transfiguration to occur "six days" "after" He gave His cryptic promise (Matt. 16:28; 17:1; Mark 9:1, 2). Therefore Peter's statement equating one day with a thousand years in the mind of "the Lord" and with special reference to the Second Advent, could also mean that the Second Advent would occur after about 6,000 years.

Next, Peter's reference to Noah as "the eighth preacher of righteousness" (cf. II Peter 2:5 and Jude 14) provides the key to a typological understanding of the genealogy in Genesis 5. Significantly, this results in a 6,000-year typological period from Creation to the Flood, which Peter, like his Lord, identified as a type of the Second Advent (cf. II Peter 3:5-7 and Matt. 24:37).

(5) Finally, what insights into the meaning of II Peter 3:8 can we gain

from the Spirit of Prophecy? There are two very pertinent references in Ellen White's writings.

The first I found while studying the life of Lot and his wife in the fourteenth chapter of *Patriarchs and Prophets*. Abraham had been promised the land of Canaan—hence the name "promised land." But all he ended up with was a cemetery plot for his wife and himself. "But the word of God had not failed; neither did it meet its final accomplishment in the occupation of Canaan by the Jewish people. 'To Abraham and his seed were the promises made.' Gal. 3:16. Abraham himself was to share the inheritance. The fulfillment of God's promise may seem to be long delayed—for 'one day is with the Lord as a thousand years, and a thousand years as one day' (II Peter 3:8); it may appear to tarry; but at the appointed time 'it will surely come, it will not tarry.' Habakkuk 2:3. The gift to Abraham and his seed included not merely the land of Canaan, but the whole earth. . . And the Bible plainly teaches that the promises made to Abraham are to be fulfilled through Christ. All that are Christ's are 'Abraham's seed, and heirs according to the promise'—heirs to 'an inheritance incorruptible, and undefiled, and that fadeth not away'—the earth freed from the curse of sin. Galatians 3:29; I Peter 1:4." *(Patriarchs and Prophets, pp. 169, 170)*

So here is Ellen White's first use of II Peter 3:8, associated in the same sentence by way of explanation with Habakkuk 2:3! "It may appear to tarry; but at the appointed time it will surely come, it will not tarry." The coming of Christ may seem long or delayed but God is right on schedule.

The second reference to this text is right in the middle of an article that Ellen White wrote in the *Signs of the Times* entitled "Noah's Time and Ours," on January 3, 1878. The following four paragraphs are very significant:

"In the days of Noah men followed the imagination of their own hearts, and the result was unrestrained crime and wickedness. The same state of things will exist in this age of the world. . . Of that vast population there was only eight persons who believed the message of Noah and obeyed God's word. . . One marked feature of Noah's day was the intense worldliness of the inhabitants. They were eating and drinking, planting and building, marrying and giving in marriage, not that these things were of themselves sins, but they were, although lawful in themselves, carried to a high degree of intemperance. . . The same evils intensified exist in our world today . . . <u>As the time of Christ's second appearing draws near, the Lord sends His servants with a warning message to the world to prepare for that great event</u> . . . But as in the days of Noah, there is with the majority a total disbelief of the testimony God has in mercy sent to warn the world of her coming destruction."

The seventh paragraph of the article contains the references from II Peter 3 so I will quote this paragraph in full. "<u>When Noah proclaimed the solemn message, yet an hundred and twenty years the judgments of God in a flood of water should destroy the world and its inhabitants, men would not receive it, so it is at the present time.</u> Those who warn the transgressors of law to repent and turn to their allegiance for the Lawgiver is coming to punish the disobedient, will plead and entreat and warn the majority in vain. <u>Peter describes the attitude of the world in reference to the last message:</u> 'There shall come in the last days scoffers, walking after their own lusts and saying where is the promise of His coming? for since the fathers fell asleep all things continue as they were from the beginning of the creation. <u>For this they are willingly ignorant of,</u> that by the word of God the heavens were of old, and the earth standing out of the water and in the water; whereby the world that then was, being overflowed with water perished; but the heavens and the earth, which are now, by the same word are kept in store, reserved unto fire against the day of judgment and perdition of ungodly men. <u>But beloved, be not ignorant of this one thing, that one day is with the Lord as a thousand years, and a thousand years as one day.</u> The Lord is not slack concerning His promise, as some men count slackness; but is longsuffering to us-ward, not willing that any should perish, but that all should come to repentance. But the day of the Lord will come as a thief in the night; in the which the heavens shall melt with fervent heat, the earth also and the works that are therein shall be burned up . . .'

"The men of Noah's time, in their philosophy and worldly wisdom, thought that God could not destroy the world with a flood, for the waters of the ocean could not be sufficient for this . . . <u>And when the great men and the wise men had reasoned before the world the impossibility of its destruction by water, and the fears of the people were quieted, and all regarded Noah's prophecy as the veriest delusion, and looked upon Noah as a crazy fanatic,</u> **God's time had come . . . and the rain began to descend** . . . But let us all bear in mind that those who perished in that awful judgment had an offer of escape.

"While Satan is working to quiet the fears and consciences of men, he is making his last master stroke to retain his power over a world which he sees is about to pass from his grasp . . . He has come down in great power working with all deceivableness of unrighteousness in them that perish. His lying wonders will deceive many . . . Those who would be loyal to the God of heaven will not allow that interpretation of prophecy which will do away with the force of the lesson God designed the prophecy should convey. As the contemporaries of Noah laughed to scorn that which they termed fear and superstition in the preacher of righteousness, so will the solemn messages of warning be ridiculed in our day." *(Signs of the Times,* Jan. 3, 1878)

This article certainly supports the idea that the timely message of Noah was based on a timetable that was growing shorter each day that passed. The same is true of our day. Our message is based on the Bible's time prophecies and the remaining time grows shorter with each passing day. Don't accept an interpretation of the prophecies that will do away with the force of the lesson God designed the prophecy to convey. There is indeed a lesson in the prophecy of II Peter 3!

The general validity of the 6,000-year theory does not need II Peter 3:8 for any additional support. However, I believe it does support the idea. It does not support the "God is eternal" idea—that He will come someday, whenever He gets ready.

Some have asked, "Since part of II Peter 3:8 comes from Psalm 90:4, should not Peter's meaning be the same as Moses' meaning?" While Peter's statement is reminiscent of Psalm 90:4, it is certainly not a quotation. In reality New Testament writers, guided by the Holy Spirit, often bring out meanings not evident to the surface reader. There is no doubt that Psalm 90:4 teaches the shortness of time with God, and if Peter intended merely to assure the believers not to worry at the delay in Christ's coming (which, of course, was not his purpose), then he simply needed to quote Moses' words or repeat his thought. But Peter reverses this thought ("one day is with the Lord as a thousand years") which means that he can no longer be making a simple statement about the shortness of time with God.

Others have stated, "Simply because history is going to work out roughly into a 6,000-year period followed by a 1,000-year period is no evidence that the weekly arrangement was designed to be predictive." Remember the studies done by J. N. Andrews and William Shea on the typological significance of the "sabbaths" of Lev. 23-25? True, God could have allotted a 4,000-year or a 10,000-year probationary period for the human race after its fall. He did not have to allow man 6,000 years. It is also true that on the basis of Genesis 1 and 2 alone, we cannot postulate a 6,000-year history for the world. But on the other hand, we must reject the idea implicit in the above objection, that history is working out according to chance or 'happenstance.' The whole Bible witnesses to the fact that God is in control of history and that history is working out according to a recognizable design. Actually, it is in the light of II Peter 3:8 and 10 as seen against the witness of the Old and New Testaments (Lev. 25, 26; II Chron. 36; Jer. 4; Rev. 20, etc.) that we recognize that God has allotted mankind 6,000 years of probationary time, followed by the 1,000-year "day of the Lord," and that God, in His perfect foreknowledge before the creation and fall of man, foreshadowed this history in the six days of Creation followed by His Sabbath rest upon which the sabbatical cycle was modeled.

Some have said, "Ellen White does not urge the brethren to accept the 6,000-year theory as neglected Biblical truth." But it was not neglected truth in her day! J. N. Andrews, S. N. Haskell, W. H. Littlejohn, John Loughborough, and other Adventist contemporaries of hers taught and wrote about this topic in the *Review* and other publications by our presses. And we have shown that Ellen White did not view her role as bringing new light, but rather pointing out error, and confirming truth. And there is no question that she assumed the general validity of the 6,000 years. Further, in all of the hundreds of letters she wrote to her "pioneer" contemporaries, I find no evidence that she ever attempted to "correct" their views in this matter.

There is much to be learned and gained by reviewing the history of the pioneer work of the Seventh-day Adventist Church. There were about a dozen individuals who began with the Advent movement, went through the 1844 experience, and then went on to help found the Seventh-day Adventist Church. Among those pioneers was J. N. Loughborough. He is now known as the historian of our early church. He was the last survivor of those known as the pioneers, having passed to his rest in 1922.

In 1892 Loughborough wrote a history of the church titled *The Rise and Progress of Seventh-day Adventists.* He revised and enlarged the book in 1905 and reprinted in it with a new title, *The Great Second Advent Movement.*

Ellen White had high regard for Loughborough and encouraged the brethren to circulate his book. "The record of the experience through which the people of God passed in the early history of our work must be republished," she wrote. "Many of those who have since come into the truth are ignorant of the way in which the Lord wrought. The experience of William Miller and his associates, of Captain Joseph Bates, and of other pioneers in the Advent message should be kept before our people. Elder Loughborough's book should receive attention. Our leading men should see what can be done for the circulation of this book." (*The Publishing Ministry,* p. 30)

So what did Loughborough understand about the 6,000 years? He stated when answering the question as to when the saints would be taken to heaven and the events that would take place at the beginning of the millennium, "It is generally agreed that this thousand years is the period when Satan is to be bound, at the end of the six thousand years from creation. (This time is now very nearly expired.) There are very few who do not hold to this theory. The great difference of opinion is more in regard to the work of that period." (J. N. Loughborogh, *The Saints Inheritance or The Earth Made New,* p. 58)

The most weighty objection to the 6,000-year principle is, "This interpretation has often been used to set false dates for Christ's coming and could be so used again." Yes, it would certainly be wrong to use II Peter 3:8, 10 for setting an exact date for Christ's return, as some Bible students have done since the days of Hippolytus. However, the deplorable abuse of this Scripture in the past or a misunderstanding of Biblical chronology should not lead us to rob it of its original meaning. It is not necessary for over-conscientious scholars to attempt to render II Peter 3:8 'harmless' by a spiritual interpretation, for Peter himself made it impossible to use his statement equating one day with a thousand years as a yardstick for determining the exact time for Christ's return.

Peter's use of the Greek participle *speudontas* in verse 12, carries the idea of expediting the coming of Christ. Thus he counsels the believers, "Look eagerly for the day of God and work to hasten it on." (NEB) This hastening of Christ's return can be accomplished by godly lives. (Compare II Peter 3:11, 12, 14 and Mark 4:29.) Moreover, since Peter states that one reason for the delayed advent is God's unwillingness "that any should perish" (3:9), it follows that when all have been reached who can be reached with the message of mercy, Christ will come. (Matt.

24:14) In other words, <u>not a fixed time,</u> but a completed task is the final factor in determining exactly when Christ shall come.

This simply means that the 6,000 years resulting from Peter's equation (3:8, 10) can be regarded as no more than a basic interval of probationary time. There is a time limit which <u>may</u> be hastened by man (3:9, 12), and which Paul declares "will" be "cut short" by God (Rom. 9:28). By exactly how much God will cut short human history has not been revealed in Scripture and is expressly declared to be beyond the ken of "man" and "angels." (Mark 13:32)

---

* Glenn Lello, the late South African Adventist scholar, wrote a paper entitled "Jude or 2 Peter? A Question of Priority and More" in the seventies. Some of the explanations following regarding 2 Peter, chapter 3, I have gleaned from his material.

CHAPTER 12

The Millennium

One of the most misunderstood Bible topics is that of the millennium. The popular beliefs concerning events preceding, happening during, and following this time period are frequently based on the opinions of popular writers and/or preachers and have only a slight resemblance to the biblical truth.

As most Christians realize, the term *millennium* itself does not occur in the Bible. As a stand-alone word it denotes merely a certain stretch of time—1,000 years—without any religious qualification. The major end-time Scripture passage dealing with the millennium is Revelation, Chapter 20. Other passages such as Jeremiah, Chapter 4, give additional details.

There are four major philosophies of history concerning the millennium that have developed. They are historic premillennialism, dispensational premillennialism, postmillennialism, and amillennialism.

Amillennialism: This view considers the millennium as a purely symbolic phase signifying the whole period of the Christian church. It allows for no specific 1,000-year reign of Christ on earth.

Postmillennialism: This view holds that Christ's kingdom is a present reality, because He reigns in the hearts of His believers. It expects a conversion of all nations prior to the Second Advent. It looks forward to a long period of earthly peace without friction among nations, races, or social groups. The millennium will end, according to this view, with the apostasy of the antichrist and the personal return of Christ in glory. Some evangelicals espouse a modified version of this view.

Premillennialism: Basically there are two basic types of premillennialists, and they can be identified as **historicists** and **dispensationalists**. Both believe that the millennium is sharply marked off by two literal resurrections from the dead; the resurrection of the righteous at the beginning, and that of the wicked at the end. Both believe that the millennial kingdom will be dramatically inaugurated by Christ's visible return. A short, fierce persecution of true believers, a so-called great tribulation, will immediately precede the millennium. But here the general agreement between the two premillennial groups ends.

Historic premillennialism has consistently held the church to be the true Israel of God and the focus of the events surrounding the millennium. **Dispensationalism,** on the other hand, is based exclusively on the premise of a consistent literalism in all prophetic applications. This requires that all Israel's kingdom prophecies must be realized in a Jewish kingdom in Palestine. Much of evangelical Christianity today accepts this view, though it is not substantiated by Scripture.

Adventists have traditionally interpreted the Scriptures to present a "historic premillennial" view which has incorporated God's activity regarding the saved and the lost. We understand that the millennium is immediately preceded by the second coming of Christ. At His coming the righteous dead are resurrected, the living wicked are destroyed by the brightness of His coming, and all the righteous are taken to heaven. During the millennium the earth is desolate, all the wicked are dead, Satan is bound by circumstances with no one to tempt, and the righteous live in heaven reigning with Christ and assisting in the work of judgment.

The millennium is 1,000 literal years. Then at the end of the millennium Christ and His saints descend from heaven, the wicked dead are raised, the Holy City, New Jerusalem, descends from heaven, Satan and the wicked are destroyed by fire, and God recreates the earth—that is, the new earth.

This last view is biblically based and fits perfectly with God's great plan for the earth as outlined in the whole Bible.

In a special issue of *These Times,* "Final Events on Planet Earth," an overall view of end-time events is given on a chart with paragraph explanations. When discussing the millennium this article says, "The millennium: Contrary to popular opinion, the earth during the period of 1,000 years between the first and second resurrections will remain desolate and unpopulated, inhabited only by Satan and his evil angels. The righteous will spend this time in heaven with their Creator and Saviour." (pp. 10, 11)

In *The Cross and Its Shadow*, pp. 248, 249, S. N. Haskell states precisely what I believe a thorough study of this topic will support. "The keeping of the weekly Sabbath was a token that the people belonged to God; and in allowing their land to rest during the seventh-year sabbath, they acknowledged that not only they themselves but their land, their time, and all they possessed, belonged to God. (Eze. 20:12, 20)

"The Lord took special delight in the seventh-year sabbath, and the disregard of His command to keep it was offensive in His sight. The children of Israel were carried away into Babylonian captivity because they had not allowed 'the land to enjoy her sabbaths.' (II Chron. 36:16-21) In their love of greed and gain, they had worked the land every year, and God took them away, and let the land lie desolate, that it might keep the sabbath during the seventy years.

"If God's command had always been obeyed and the land had had its rest every seventh year, the earth would not have 'waxed old like a garment,' (Isa. 51:6) but would have remained productive.

"God's commands will all be honored, and as the land lay desolate seventy years, keeping the sabbath during the Babylonian captivity, to atone for the disobedience of ancient Israel; so, after the second coming of Christ, the land will lie desolate for one thousand years, keeping sabbath to atone for the many Sabbaths that have been disregarded since that time. (Rev. 20:1-4; Zeph. 1:1-3; Jer. 4:23-27)

"The weekly Sabbath was a stepping-stone leading up to the other sabbatic institutions; and besides being a memorial of creation, it pointed forward to the final rest of the Jubilee."

Note the parallel condition of the land during the times of Israel's captivity and the land during the millennium. From a biblical standpoint Haskell was on solid ground with his conclusions.

During Israel's Captivity: "I will scatter you among the nations and draw out a sword after you; your land shall be desolate and your cities waste. Then the land shall enjoy its sabbaths as long as it lies desolate and you are in your enemies land; then the land shall rest and enjoy its sabbaths. As long as it lies desolate it shall rest—for the time it did not rest on your sabbaths when you dwelt in it." (Leviticus 26:33-35)

This passage in Leviticus was God's promised prediction or consequence of failure to observe the Sabbatical year. Then in II Chronicles 36 we are told that this condition was brought about during the Babylonian captivity, the 70 years, as a result of their disobedience. Speaking of the destruction of Jerusalem and the taking of the captives by Nebuchadnezzar, we are told, "And all the articles from the house of God, great and small, the treasures of the house of the Lord, and the treasures of the king and his leaders, all these he took to Babylon. Then they burned the house of God, broke down the wall of Jerusalem, burned all its palaces with fire, and destroyed all its precious possessions. And those who escaped from the sword he carried away to Babylon, where they became servants to him and his sons until the reign of the kingdom of Persia, to fulfill the word of the Lord by the mouth of Jeremiah, until the land had enjoyed her Sabbaths. As long as she lay desolate she kept Sabbath, to fulfill seventy years." (II Chronicles 36:18-21)

As Haskell shows, the language used in Scripture to describe the land of Israel during the Babylonian captivity is paralleled in describing the condition of the earth during the millennium—the great antitypical Sabbatical year.

The Millennium Parallel: "I beheld the earth, and indeed it was without form, and void; And the heavens, they had no light. I beheld the mountains, and indeed they trembled, and all the hills moved back and forth. I beheld, and indeed there was no man, and all the birds of the heavens had fled. I beheld, and indeed the fruitful land was a wilderness, and all its cities were broken down at the presence of the Lord, by his fierce anger. For thus says the Lord: The whole land shall be desolate; yet I will not make a full end." (Jeremiah 4:23-27)

This is not at the creation but describes the condition that will exist at "the presence of the Lord," at His coming with power and glory. The mountains and hills have trembled and the cities are broken down. Then the land becomes desolate.

Elder W. H. Littlejohn was the president of Battle Creek College from 1883-1885. During this time he authored over 100 consecutive weekly articles in the *Review and Herald*.

About six months after the J. N. Andrews' articles referred to earlier, the *Review and Herald* published a Littlejohn article titled "Heaven: When Are the Saints to Go There?"

"The saints will be in heaven during the thousand years spoken of in Rev. 20:4, 6. There are excellent reasons for believing that this earth is to be left desolate for a period. The 24th chapter of Isaiah presents this subject in a very clear manner as follows: 'Behold, the Lord maketh the earth empty, and maketh it waste, and turneth it upside down, and scattereth abroad the inhabitants thereof. . .'" [He then quotes from Isa. 24, Jer. 25, Isa. 13, and Jer. 4.]

"Additional proof that the earth is to remain for a time in a desolate condition, can be drawn from the types of the Levitical law. It is well known that many of the provisions of the law which relate to the land of Canaan shadowed forth events to transpire in the future history of this world. Among these were the sabbatical years. Ex. 23:10, 11; Lev. 25:2-7. After the Hebrews had entered the promised land, they were allowed to cultivate the soil for six consecutive years, but were commanded to let it lie waste the next, or seventh, year. This regulation was binding during the whole of the Old Dispensation. During the sabbatical year they could neither plow the land, nor sow it; they could gather neither fruit nor grain. During that year they were to live on the produce of the six preceding years, and the land was to enjoy its sabbath, or rest. II Chron. 36:20, 21.

"The circumstance that this regulation relates so largely to the dispensation to be made of the soil on each seventh year intimates very strongly that it was designed to teach symbolically that the earth after having been occupied by men for six thousand years is to have a grand sabbath or rest in which it is to lie desolate. If so, then the doctrine taught by this type would harmonize with the plain declarations of Isaiah 24, and the other scriptures quoted above." (W. H. Littlejohn, *Review and Herald,* March 4, 1884)

Ellen White affirmed this understanding. In Chapter 41 of *The Great Controversy,* entitled the "Desolation of the Earth," Ellen White quotes Jeremiah 4 as an application to the millennium. It is in this chapter that several of her 6,000-year statements occur in the context of earth's time line.

"For six thousand years the great controversy has been in progress; the Son of God and His heavenly messengers have been in conflict with the power of the evil one, to warn, enlighten, and save the children of men. Now all have made their decisions; the wicked have fully united with Satan in his warfare against God. The time has come for God to vindicate the authority of His downtrodden law." (*The Great Controversy,* p. 656)

In this same chapter she connects the 1,000 years and the 6,000 years. Having just quoted Jeremiah 4:23-27 regarding the condition of the earth during the millennium she states: "Here is to be the home of

Satan with his evil angels <u>for a thousand years</u>. Limited to the earth, he will not have access to other worlds to tempt and annoy those who have never fallen. It is in this sense that he is bound: there are none remaining, upon whom he can exercise his power. He is wholly cut off from the work of deception and ruin which for so many centuries has been his sole delight.

". . .<u>For six thousand years, Satan's work of rebellion has 'made the earth to tremble.'</u> He has 'made the world as a wilderness, and destroyed the cities thereof.' And he 'opened not the house of his prisoner.' <u>For six thousand years his prison house has received God's people,</u> and he would have held them captive forever; <u>but Christ has broken his bonds and set the prisoners free.</u>" (*The Great Controversy*, p. 659)

Ellen White describes the condition of the earth after the Second Coming in this way: "The earth looked like a desolate wilderness. Cities and villages, shaken down by the earthquake, lay in heaps. Mountains had been moved out of their places, leaving large caverns. Ragged rocks, thrown out by the sea, or torn out of the earth itself, were scattered all over its surface. Large trees had been uprooted and were strewn over the land. Here is to be the home of Satan with his evil angels for a thousand years. Here he will be confined, to wander up and down over the broken surface of the earth and see the effects of his rebellion against God's law." (*Early Writings*, p. 290)

Today we are very near a completed 6,000 years and the beginning of the seventh 1,000-year period. Figuratively speaking, we are living in the Friday evening of earth's history. It's almost sundown. The wicked world is really living it up as it typically does on Friday evening, but what the wicked don't know or ignore is that it's almost Sabbath.

The principle of seven is not intended to set the day and hour of Christ's coming, but rather to let us know where we are in time—to let us know that we are at the end of time. Actually, when reading Matthew 24:22 and Romans 9:28, we see that God will cut the time short.

A false concept of the significance and importance of the millennium will ensnare many and cause them eventually to be lost. We have a work to do to get the message out to others. We are told, "The line of distinction between professed Christians and the ungodly is now hardly distinguishable. Church members love what the world loves, and are ready to join with them; and Satan determines to unite them in one body, and thus strengthen his cause by sweeping all into the ranks of

Spiritualism. Papists, who boast of miracles as a certain sign of the true church, will be readily deceived by this wonder-working power; and Protestants, having cast away the shield of truth, will also be deluded. Papists, Protestants, and worldlings will alike accept the form of godliness without the power, and they will see in this union a grand movement for the conversion of the world, and the ushering in of the long-expected millennium." (*The Great Controversy*, p. 588)

In addition, "Christ continues, pointing out the condition of the world at His coming: 'As the days of Noah were, so shall also the coming of the Son of Man be. For as in the days that were before the flood they were eating and drinking, marrying, and giving in marriage, until the day that Noah entered into the ark, and knew not until the flood came, and took them all away; so shall also the coming of the Son of Man be.' Christ does not here bring to view a temporal millennium, a thousand years in which all are to prepare for eternity. He tells us that as it was in Noah's day, so will it be when the Son of Man comes again." (*The Desire of Ages,* p. 633) In other words, the judgment and the end of the world occur on the same day. There is no "second chance" taught in Scripture.

The Scriptures declare, "Blessed and holy is he who has part in the first resurrection. Over such the second death has no power, but they shall be priests of God and of Christ, and shall reign with Him a thousand years." (Revelation 20:6)

CHAPTER 13

The Perfect Number

The number seven occurs often in Scripture. Here is a list of some of the better known Bible references to seven:

Seven days of creation;

Seven days before the flood the animals came into the ark;

Seven days Noah and his family stayed in the ark before the rain started;

Seven fat and seven skinny cows, and seven healthy ears of corn and seven withered ears of corn in Pharaoh's dream;

Seven years times two that Jacob worked for Rachel;

Seven times that Elijah prayed on Mt. Carmel before the rain came;

Seven times Naaman dipped in the Jordan river to be healed;

Seven "sabbaths of years" before the great year of release—the jubilee;

Seven days the Israelites marched around Jericho with seven priests with seven trumpets and then seven times on the seventh day;

Seven years Nebuchadnezzar was humiliated before all the world;

Seven times ten weeks set apart for the Jews;

Seven times the priest cast the blood of the sacrifice toward the temple;

Seven eyes of the Lord run to and fro through the whole earth;

Seven times seventy that we are to extend forgiveness;

Seven devils cast out of Mary Magdalene;

Seven deacons chosen to help with the work of the church;

Seven churches representing seven characteristics and time

periods in the history of the Christian church;
Seven golden candlesticks;
Seven stars in God's right hand;
Seven angels;
Seven thunders;
Seven trumpets;
Seven seals;
Seven last plagues;
Seven hills surrounding the New Jerusalem;
Seven pillars supporting the temple; and
Seven crowns of Jesus—crowns within a crown.

Why is the number seven used so often? Is there some mathematical reason? Are multiples of seven in any way significant in nature? We base our time calculations from the movements of the heavenly bodies and the stars. We call the orbit of Earth around the sun over a time period of 365 days a year. A month is measured by the moon's orbit around the earth every 30 days. And a day passes when the earth rotates on its axis every 24 hours.

But what heavenly body determines the weekly cycle? There is none. There is no mathematical formula or principle that establishes a week. It is based solely upon the weekly cycle established by God at Creation and memorialized by Him in the Sabbath celebration. There simply is no other explanation.

If God had asked us how many days there should be in a week we probably would have chosen five or six, because they both divide evenly into a thirty-day month. But God chose seven days for a week, because to Him that number symbolizes completeness. This completeness is demonstrated both in creation and redemption.

The March 20, 1879, issue of the *Signs of the Times*, contained an article by Ellen White entitled "Disguised Infidelity," which dealt with the Creation week and the seven principle.

"The first week, in which God performed the work of creation in six days and rested on the seventh day, was just like every other week. The great God, in His days of creation and day of rest, measured off the first cycle as a sample for successive weeks till the close of time. 'These are the generations of the heavens and of the earth when they were created.' God gives us the result of His work on each of the days of creation. Each day was accounted of Him a generation, because every day He generated, or produced some new portion of His work. On the seventh day of the first week God rested from His labor, and then blessed the day of His rest, and set it apart for the use of man. The weekly cycle of seven literal days, six for labor and the seventh for rest, which has been preserved and brought down through Bible history, originated in the great facts of the first seven days.

"When God spoke His law with an audible voice from Sinai, He introduced the Sabbath by saying, 'Remember the Sabbath day to keep it holy.' He then declares definitely what shall be done on the six days, and what shall not be done on the seventh. He next gives the reason for thus observing the week, by pointing us back to His example on the first seven days of time. 'For in six days the Lord made heaven and earth, the sea and all that in them is, and rested the seventh day, wherefore the Lord blessed the Sabbath day and hallowed it.' This reason appears beautiful and forcible when we understand the record of creation to mean literal days. The first six days of each week are given to man in which to labor, because God employed the same period of the first week in the work of creation. The seventh day God has reserved as a day of rest, in commemoration of His rest during the same period of time after He had performed the work of creation in six days.

"But the infidel supposition, that the events of the first week required seven vast, indefinite periods for their accomplishment, strikes directly at the foundation of the Sabbath of the fourth commandment. It makes indefinite and obscure that which God has made very plain. It is the worst kind of infidelity; for with many who profess to believe in the record of creation, it is infidelity in disguise. It charges God with commanding men to observe the week of seven literal days in commemoration of seven indefinite periods, which is unlike His dealings with mortals, and is an impeachment of His wisdom.

"Infidel geologists claim that the world is very much older than the Bible record makes it. They reject the testimony of God's word because of those things which are to them evidences from the earth itself that it has existed tens of thousands of years. And many who profess to believe the Bible are at a loss to account for wonderful things which are found in the earth, with the view that creation week was only seven literal days, and that the world is now only about six thousand years old. These, to free themselves from difficulties thrown in their way by infidel geologists, adopt the view that the six days of creation were six vast, indefinite periods, and the day of God's rest was another indefinite period; making senseless the fourth commandment of God's holy law. Some eagerly receive this position; for it destroys the force of the fourth commandment, and they feel a freedom from its claims upon them." *(Spiritual Gifts,* vol. 3, p. 91)

Five years later, in a *Signs of the Times* article entitled "The Creation Sabbath," Ellen White makes the following statement: "When God created the earth and placed man upon it, He divided time into seven periods. Six He gave to man for his own use, to employ in secular business; one He reserved for Himself. Having rested on the seventh day, He blessed and sanctified it. Henceforth, the seventh day was to be regarded as the Lord's rest day, and to be sacredly observed as the memorial of His creative work. It was not the first, second, third, fourth, fifth, or sixth day that was sanctified, or set apart to a holy use, neither was it a seventh part of time and no day in particular; but it was the seventh day, the day upon which God had rested. We are every day to think of God and live as in His sight; but when the six days' work is done, we are to 'remember the Sabbath day to keep it holy'—to cease from labor and devote the day exclusively to meditation and worship." *(Signs of the Times,* Feb. 28, 1884)

Once the cycle of seven was established at Creation God used it in other ways in dealing with man. He used it not only every seventh day but also every seventh year. "Six years you shall sow your field, and six years you shall prune your vineyard, and gather its fruit; but in the seventh year there shall be a sabbath of solemn rest for the land, a sabbath to the Lord. You shall neither sow your field nor prune your vineyard. What grows of its own accord of your harvest you shall not reap, nor gather the grapes of your untended vine, for it is a year of rest for the land." (Leviticus 25:3-5)

God even took further steps to emphasize the cycle of seven in the fiftieth year Jubilee which, of course, was preceded by seven times seven years. "And you shall count seven sabbaths of years for yourself, seven times seven years; and the time of the seven sabbaths of years shall be to you forty-nine years. Then you shall cause the trumpet of the Jubilee to sound on the tenth day of the seventh month, on the Day of Atonement you shall make the trumpet to sound throughout all your land. And you shall consecrate the fiftieth year, and proclaim liberty throughout all the land to all its inhabitants. It shall be a Jubilee for you; and each of you

shall return to his possession, and each of you shall return to his family."
(Leviticus 25:8-10)

Do we have any clues as to why God chose seven for His "cycle number"? I believe we do.

"Christ fulfilled still another feature of the type. 'His visage was so marred more than any man, and His form more than the sons of men; so shall He sprinkle many nations.' Isaiah 52:14. In the Temple service, when the animal brought as a sacrifice was slain, the high priest, clothed in white robes, caught in his hand the blood that gushed forth, and cast it in the direction of the tabernacle or Temple. This was done seven times, as an expression of perfection. So Christ, the great antitype, Himself both High Priest and Victim, clothed with His own spotless robes of righteousness, after giving His life for the world, cast the virtue of His offering, a crimson current, in the direction of the holy place, reconciling man to God through the blood of the cross." *(Manuscript Releases,* vol. 12, p. 397)

With regard to the number of times one should forgive another, the significance of the number seven again is pointed out. "Peter had come to Christ with the question, 'How oft shall my brother sin against me, and I forgive him? Till seven times?' The rabbis limited the exercise of forgiveness to three offenses. Peter, carrying out, as he supposed the teaching of Christ, thought to extend it to seven, the number signifying perfection. But Christ taught that we are never to become weary of forgiving. Not 'until seven times seven,' He said, 'but, until seventy times seven." *(Christ's Object Lessons,* p. 243)

We are also told, "The names of the seven churches are symbolic of the church in different periods of the Christian Era. The number seven indicates completeness, and is symbolic of the fact that the messages extend to the end of time, while the symbols used reveal the condition of the church at different periods in the history of the world." *(The Acts of the Apostles,* p. 585) It is very significant in light of this statement that we, by common consensus in our church, recognize that we are living in the time of the Laodicean church—the very last one in the cycle.

By looking at the seven principle we can see that:

God uses the number seven throughout the Bible as a cycle or chronological sequence;

The seven cycle is based on the Creation week model of six days for work and one day for rest;

The seven-day cycle is repeated in a seven-year cycle, six years to work and the seventh year—the "sabbath of years"—as a rest year. Then there is the seven times seven-year cycle culminating in the Jubilee "sabbath year";

As we saw earlier, the description of the land of Israel during the "sabbath of years" parallels the desolate description of the earth during the millennium;

Seven indicates completeness or perfection;

It is the worst kind of infidelity to believe that Creation took place over seven indefinite periods of time;

It is not like God to deal with men in indefinite periods of time;

God divided time into seven periods—six for work and one for rest; and

We are living in the time of the seventh and last church.

The various "seven cycles" listed in this chapter demonstrate that God frequently uses a cycle of seven for a complete picture of a given illustration. The seventh item in each cycle was the final event or era of each sequence. The cycles listed are of various lengths but each is complete in itself.

It follows by logical extension that God will use His cycle of seven, in this case 7,000 years, to complete the cycle of the great controversy—6,000 years for the great controversy struggle with evil followed by the sabbath rest of 1,000 years for the earth.

CHAPTER 14

Biblical Chronology

M any today are eager to set a date for Christ's coming. Many scholars and authors have set dates for the termination of the 6,000 years. It is my personal conviction that if we could know when Christ will return, then He would not have to announce the day and hour of His coming during the time of trouble. (See *Early Writings,* pp. 15, 34, 285; *The Great Controversy,* p. 640.) I also believe that God would not have us know exactly the day and hour of Christ's coming ahead of time.

This chapter, then, will state only in general terms where we are in time from the information provided by the Bible and the Spirit of Prophecy.

J. N. Andrews wrote: "It has been the faith of the most eminent servants of God, not only during the entire gospel dispensation, but also during some hundred years previous to Christ's first advent, that the period of 6,000 years from the creation would extend to the day of Judgment. And we think that the most careful study of the chronology of the Bible and of the prophetic periods will strongly confirm this view." (J. N. Andrews, "The Great Week of Time," *The Review and Herald,* July 17, 1883)

Ellen White believed that the end would come at the conclusion of the 6,000 years; however, she did not, as William Miller and others did, set a year for the termination of this period. She did state, as we have noted previously, that the great controversy had been carried on for "nearly six thousand years" and was "soon to close." This is also the position that I am taking in this book. However, over a hundred years have passed since she wrote those words, so our salvation is much nearer than when we first believed.

One point that is clear from Andrews and Ellen White is that there is a record of chronology in Scripture, and we are on safe ground only when we use this record as the basis for our views of earth's history.

"While chronology is seldom a subject for sermons, and rightly so, it is important to the Christian faith," wrote Glenn Lello in a 1976 study entitled "Some Guidelines Towards a Reliable Sacred Chronology."

"First: it portrays the Bible as a reliable historical record from God, and any weakening of the historicity of the Bible weakens the Christian's faith (Rom. 10:17). The discounting of Genesis as history undermines human personality at its deepest level, which concerns the origin and purpose of life. Moreover, if Genesis is not a reliable record of the origin of man, the fall, and God's plan to save man, then, to be logical, we must reject the New Testament theology of salvation, which is built on the Genesis record—Adam and Eve, the Serpent, the genealogies, the flood, and all (Matt. 19:3-6; 24:37-39; Luke 3:23-38; Rom. 5:14-21; I Cor. 15:21, 45; I Tim. 2:13; II Pet. 3:5, 6; Jude 14, etc.). And, to be consistent, we must reject the Sabbath as well, since it is also rooted in Genesis as history (Gen. 2:1-3; Ex. 20:8-11). An important bulwark against such conclusions is the Genesis Chronology, which brings us step by step from the unverifiable past into the reasonably familiar terrain of ancient history. Those who think they can hold onto the historicity of Genesis, while they regard the genealogies of Genesis 5 and 11 as having some purpose other than the historico-chronological connection of the past to the present, are playing dice with the Devil.

"Second: sacred Chronology is important because it is closely bound up with Bible prophecy, through which God has revealed His purposes in His faithful children throughout the ages. Chronology is particularly important to the Seventh-day Adventist Church because it is a movement that was born as fulfillment of prophecy, much of its message consists of prophecy, and its destiny is bound up with important prophecies concerning the end of the world and the second coming of Christ. In view of the close connection between prophecy and chronology, it is not surprising that Satan has seriously undermined the historicity of the Bible in these last days. Particularly Genesis, the book of beginnings, is being strongly contested as we approach the end of the drama of salvation history. Nor should it surprise us that Satan's attack on Genesis has extended to God's people of prophecy in these last days, coming, characteristically, as a message of light." (Lello, p. 1)

Some students of Biblical chronology are somewhat baffled by the so-called "second Cainan" mentioned in Luke's chronology. Really there is no major problem either with or without the second Cainan. The genealogies of Genesis 5 and 11 are unique—unparalleled throughout the entire Bible. Here alone are we given a list of ages in such a way as to point to an obvious chronological sequence. Their very form requires that we treat these genealogies differently from all others and accept them as a complete historical sequence, <u>unless there is incontrovertible evidence of abridgment.</u> The only possible evidence of abridgment is the Septuagint's "second Cainan." Adventist scholars are in general agreement that the chronological accounts in Genesis 5 and 11 with no gaps and the Masoretic Text calculation of the dates is to be preferred.

The scope of this book does not have room for a lengthy study of this particular issue; however, it appears to me that it would be well for any student of Biblical chronology to understand the purpose of Biblical Chronology and to understand certain principles that make its study more meaningful. Again let me quote from Glenn Lello's paper: "A most remarkable thing about the Bible is that it gives so many <u>specific</u> ages and time periods as round numbers. We read that the Flood came 'in the six hundredth year of Noah's life, in the second month, and the seventeenth day of the month' (Gen. 17:11). Isaac was born when 'Abraham was an hundred years old' (Gen. 21:1-5). Moses fled Egypt at forty (Acts 7:23), led the Exodus at eighty (Acts 7:7), and died at 120, when 'his eye was not dim, nor his natural force abated' (Deut. 34:1-7). The Babylonian captivity lasted 70 years (II Chron. 36:21-23; Jer. 29:10). Moreover, much of Scripture's <u>concealed</u> time data also work out exactly as round numbers. Shem lived 600 years (Gen. 11:11). The confusion of the languages at the tower of Babel occurred 100 years <u>after</u> the Flood (Gen. 10:25; 11:16). God's covenant with Abram and the destruction of Sodom and Gomorrah both occurred 450 years <u>after</u> the Flood (Gen. 17:17).

"The patterns are too numerous and remarkable to explain as mere chance or coincidence. Moreover, 'coincidence' is an irreverent, infidel word, when applied to history (especially sacred history), for it belittles God's power to control human affairs (Gen. 15:13-16; Dan. 4:17, 25, 32, 35; 5:21). Rather we should ask, What is God's purpose in the remarkably precise patterns that characterize much of the Old Testament narrative? What is He teaching us through chronology?

". . . The design associated with so much Old Testament time data should not discredit these data as contrived or inaccurate, but should rather make us examine the <u>meaning</u> of the history being measured. And so, <u>the ultimate purpose of sacred chronology is not merely to measure time, but to reveal the design of God in history, and through this, to identify the message He has for His children.</u>" (Lello, pp. 2, 3)

I realize that we are diving down deep into the Word when we study chronology. However, I believe that it is good for us to see that our beliefs have a solid basis in Scripture. There are amazing discoveries for the student of the Bible. When I realize that the devil will attempt to deceive even the very elect (Matt. 24:24) and that none but those who have their minds fortified with God's Word will stand in the coming crisis *(The Great Controversy,* pp. 593, 594), I am concerned that my own mind be fortified. Then I think of those whose only Bible study is a quick look at the Sabbath School lesson. And what about those who don't even study the prepared lesson? Please consult the Appendix for Chapter 14 to discover seven principles for studying Biblical chronology.

My reason for including a chapter on chronology in this book is not to lay down a definitive chronology, which would probably take the whole book to do, but rather to lay down some guidelines that will let you know how to tell truth from error. These principles have convinced me that the Bible is dependable and is the final authority. And my study of them leads me to conclude that we are definitely within the 6,000-year period, though we are very near the end of it.

There is no question that Ellen White assumed the general validity of the 6,000-year probationary time line. The question for our discussion here, then, is to determine just where on this line we find ourselves today.

Warren H. Johns, the seminary librarian at Andrews University, wrote an article entitled "Ellen G. White and Biblical Chronology," which was printed in *Ministry* magazine in the April 1984 issue. He states in part, "Scholars have offered a greater variety of opinion upon the date for Creation than for any other single event in sacred history. Robert Young in his *Analytical Concordance* (p. 210) lists thirty-seven suggested dates for Creation, but he states that a nineteenth-century work, Hale's *A New Analysis of Chronology and Geography, History and Prophecy,* lists some 120 possible dates and admits that the list might be swelled to three hundred. Of the 120 different chronologies, did Ellen

White choose any particular one? Or did she establish an independent chronology that followed no humanly devised scheme? Are her statements authoritative yet today?

"We are now in a position to provide a definitive answer to such questions. Owing to the recent development and marketing of the laser-disc Ellen G. White concordance. . . we can compile for the first time a complete set of all Ellen G. White statements relative to Biblical chronology. (The laser-disc concordance lists the occurrence of virtually every one of the 35,000 key words used by Ellen White—some 9 million references in all!) It may come as a surprise to some, but Ellen White makes more than 2,500 references to Biblical chronology. . .

"Of particular interest are the Ellen G. White statements that have a bearing on the age of the earth. Thanks to the assistance of the laser-disc concordance, we now have located a total of forty-two 6,000-year statements published by her in primary sources before her death in 1915. Of course, these do not include any compilations or reprints of her works made after 1915. In addition, we have forty-one 4,000-year statements— all of which are pertinent to the question of determining what was Ellen White's view on the age of the earth.

"Having recently completed an examination of all 2,500 references to Biblical chronology made by Ellen White, I can state unequivocally that her chronology matches that of Archbishop Ussher more closely than perhaps any other of the dozens of chronologies in use in the nineteenth century. Ussher's chronology so dominated that era that his dates were printed in the margins of most Bibles. Ellen White must have been aware of at least a few chronologies other than Ussher's. Of the 1,200 books by non-SDA authors in her library as of 1915, several were devoted entirely to chronology, and others contained discussions of chronology. For example, she was familiar with the Scottish preacher John Cumming, whose works she read and borrowed material therefrom on occasion, but she did not adopt his chronology. The 6,000 years for Cumming ended in 1864. She had in her office library R. C. Shimeall's *Age of the World,* but Shimeall in Millerite fashion placed the end of the world at the close of the 6,000 years which he calculated to be the year 1868. Ellen White also seemed to have parted company with William Miller, who placed the end of the 6,000 years in 1843. For her as for Ussher there were exactly 4,000 years between the creation of man and the birth of Christ, thus making the earth 5,900 years old at the close of the nineteenth century. [Johns' third footnote given at this point states, "Ellen White's final position on the age of the earth was that it was 'nearly six thousand years' old as of 1913."] *(Counsels to Parents and Teachers,* p. 467) This comes closer to Ussher's figures than to any other chronology. In nine of her 6,000-year statements she used the qualifier *nearly* and in three she used *about. It is significant,* I believe, that in *none* of the 4,000-year statements did she use the words *nearly* or *about.* Why? Because according to her chronology [and Ussher's] there were exactly four millenniums between Creation and the birth of Christ.") Cumming, Shimeall, and Miller differed with Ussher by more than one hundred years on their dates for creation.

"A careful analysis of all 2,500 chronological references made by Ellen White leads one to conclude that she sided with Ussher not only on the issue of the 6,000 years but also upon the dating of numerous Biblical events. Some Seventh-day Adventists have suggested that Ellen White utilized her chronological expressions very loosely, speaking in generalities rather than specifics. But that is not generally true. Generally she used chronology with exactness and skill. Except for a few rare cases, she would round off larger numbers to the nearest century and smaller figures to the nearest decade. Even in the use of terms like 'nearly a thousand years,' 'more than a thousand years,' 'nearly two thousand years,' 'three thousand years,' or 'more than four thousand years,' her figures are not much more than a hundred years from those in Ussher and quite often less than twenty-five years removed. Her dates for the building of the Temple, the writing of Deuteronomy, the Exodus from Egypt, the time of Jacob, the Abrahamic covenant, and the Noachian flood are all in accord with Ussher's dates. In only 1 to 2 percent of all her chronological statements did she deviate significantly from Ussher's chronology. Ellen White had other options; she did not have to follow Ussher. One authoritative chronological study was William Hale's *A New Analysis of Chronology,* which was in her library. However, she definitely did not follow Hale's schema." *(Ministry,* April 1984, pp. 20, 21)

Warren Johns writes that some have regarded Ellen White's chronological statements with "inspiration/full authority" and others with "inspiration/limited authority." Under the second view one takes into account time and place and then decides for himself which to believe. This may be a proper method when principles are involved such as problems with pride and proper stewardship as demonstrated by the "bicycle craze" commented upon by Ellen White. But chronology is not a matter of principle—it is a matter of fact. If it was ever right, it is still right.

He also discusses the possibility that the 4,000-year statements were a *literary linkage* between the days of Adam and Christ. This position is, of course, contrary to the conclusions of the first part of his study in which, as quoted above, he states that Ellen White believed that there were exactly four millenniums between Adam and Christ. Then he discusses the possibility that the 6,000-year statements amount to *literary emphasis* and are used instead of the words "for thousands of years." This position also is contrary to the conclusions he draws earlier in his study where he states that she maintained the position that the length of earth's present state—that is the time between Creation and the Second Coming—would be 6,000 years and that the earth was 5,900 years old at the end of the nineteenth century.

Johns concludes the article by stating, "Notwithstanding all the criticisms that have been leveled at the work of Archbishop Ussher, his chronology has suffered less from the impact of modern archeological discoveries than most other chronologies in use in the nineteenth century. In other words, Ellen White, I believe, was <u>divinely guided to use the best available to her.</u> Ussher's chronology needed less revision because of his meticulous fidelity to the scriptural data and his refusal to interject conjectures and suppositions. If Ellen White were alive today, she would no doubt advocate that chronology that holds the closest fidelity to the scriptural record." *(Ministry,* April 1984, p. 23)

There are just enough questions regarding an exact chronology that we cannot determine with precision when the 6,000 years will end. However, we surely can understand enough to see that we are not living in the first, second, third, fourth, or fifth millenniums. We are living at the end of the sixth millennium! The time is at hand!

CHAPTER 15

Ellen White's View of
Salvation History

W e have reviewed the research of several Adventist Bible scholars on the 6,000-year time span. We have looked at the great epochs of time in terms of prophetic testimony. Now let's see how the messenger to the remnant viewed the overall history of God's plan for mankind.

Remember the perspective of James and Ellen White we discussed earlier. They felt that the gift of prophecy was given to follow up good biblical research to (1) point out the error of wrong conclusions, (2) give more detail in a particular area of study, or (3) confirm or affirm correct decisions. I believe that she assumed the general validity of J. N. Andrews' research. You can decide for yourself after reading the following statements from her work.

It is only human nature to be so involved in our own day-to-day problems that we see only the present and the recent past. As a result we often become discouraged, disheartened, and depressed in regard to our present condition. By standing back and taking a look at the big picture of history, we gain a perspective that would otherwise escape us. Early in the ministry of Ellen White, God allowed her to have an overview of history to see just where we were in time. Her grandson, Arthur White, was elected in 1937 as a lifetime member of the board of the White Estate and secretary of the estate, a position he held for forty-one years. In his six-volume biography of Ellen White he stated:

"The vision at Lovett's Grove, Ohio, on a Sunday afternoon in mid-March, 1858, was one of great importance. In this the theme of the great controversy between Christ and His angels on the one side and Satan and his angels on the other, <u>was seen as one continuous and closely linked chain of events spanning six thousand years.</u> This vision has put

Seventh-day Adventists into a unique position with clear-cut views on the working of providence in the history of our world—a viewpoint quite different from that held by secular historians, who see events of history as the interplay between the actions of men, often seemingly the result of chance or natural developments. In other words, this vision and others of the great conflict of the ages yield a philosophy of history that answers many questions and in prophetic forecast gives the assurance of final victory of good over evil." (Arthur L. White, *Ellen G. White: The Early Years Volume I—1827-1862,* p. 366)

This idea of a prophetic chain is also mentioned in the book *Education,* where she points out that God's dealing with the great controversy stretches from eternity in the past to eternity in the future. Please note the portion of the statement that I have underlined. "The history which the great I AM has marked out in His word, uniting link after link in the prophetic chain, <u>from eternity in the past to eternity in the future,</u> tells us where we are today in the procession of the ages, and what may be expected in the time to come. All that prophecy has foretold as coming to pass, until the present time, has been traced on the pages of history, and we may be assured that all which is yet to come will be fulfilled in its order." (p. 178)

This passage in *Education* appeared in 1903, twenty years after the Andrews' articles in which he stated, "Before the commencement of this great week of time, infinite ages had elapsed during all of which God had existed. And after the expiration of this great week, the righteous will enter with Christ upon a kingdom that cannot be moved and that shall never end. Thus the period of 7,000 years is cut off <u>from the eternity of the past and from the eternity of the future,</u> and assigned to the probation and judgment of mankind." (J. N. Andrews, *Review and Herald,* July 17, 1883) In other words, Ellen White confirms the fact that though God is eternal, He deals with man within the parameters of time as we have noted in Chapter 8.

It seems clear from the writings of Ellen White that she perceived time—God's dealings with earth and its inhabitants—as being a great time line that stretches for 7,000 years. The first 6,000 years consist of the great controversy on earth and the seventh 1,000-year period—which we usually call the millennium—being the Sabbath of the earth or the "seventh year" when the land will rest while God's people are spending a long sabbath with God in heaven. Sometimes we have a tendency to think that the great events of earth's history "just happen" as some sort of fate. We shall see, however, that Ellen White's view of history was one in which God has laid out a strategy with a very definite timetable in which the events of history were ordained of God. The following are some representative statements in this regard:

"In the past ages the Lord God of heaven revealed His secrets to His prophets, and this He does still. The present and the future are equally clear to Him, and He shows to His servants the future history of what shall be. The Omniscient looked down the ages, and predicted through His prophets the rise and fall of kingdoms, hundreds of years before the events foretold took place. The voice of God echoes down the ages, telling man what is to take place. Kings and princes take their places at their appointed time. They think they are carrying out their own purposes, but in reality they are fulfilling the word God has given through His prophets. They act their part in carrying out God's great purposes. Events fall into line, fulfilling the word God has spoken." *(The Upward Look,* p. 96)

Several times, as in the statement above and the one to follow, she uses the word "line," as in "time line," as if time could be graphed with world events and fulfilled prophecies charted. "The voice of God, heard in past ages, is sounding down along the line, from century to century, through generations that have come upon the stage of action and passed away. Shall God speak, and His voice not be respected? What power mapped out all this history, that nations, one after another, should arise at the predicted time and fill their appointed place, unconsciously witnessing to the truth of that which they themselves knew not the meaning." *(The Youth's Instructor,* Sept. 29, 1903)

God's plan of putting the right people in the right place at the right time is shown in the story of the Egyptian Pharaoh at the time of the Exodus. The plagues of God were falling upon Egypt in order to encourage Pharaoh to let God's people go. In the midst of the plagues we are told, "Still the heart of Pharaoh grew harder. And now the Lord sent a message to him, declaring, 'I will at this time send all My plagues upon thy heart, and upon thy servants, and upon thy people. . . And in very deed for this cause have I raised thee up, for to show in thee My power.' Not that God had given him an existence for this purpose, but His providence had overruled events to place him upon the throne at the very time appointed for Israel's deliverance. Though this haughty tyrant had by his crimes forfeited the mercy of God, yet his life had been preserved that through his stubbornness the Lord might manifest His wonders in the land of Egypt. The disposing of events is of God's providence. He could have placed upon the throne a more merciful king, who would not have dared to withstand the mighty manifestations of divine power. But in that case the Lord's purposes would not have been accomplished." *(Patriarchs and Prophets,* pp. 267, 268)

There are many statements made by Ellen White regarding the time period covered by Bible history. Here is a sample:

"During the first twenty-five hundred years of human history, there was no written revelation. Those who had been taught of God, communicated their knowledge to others, and it was handed down from father to son, through successive generations. The preparation of the written word began in the time of Moses. Inspired revelations were then embodied in an inspired book. This work continued during the long period of sixteen hundred years,—from Moses, the historian of creation and the law, to John, the recorder of the most sublime truths of the gospel." *(The Great Controversy,* p. v)

In a number of places Ellen White places the events surrounding the birth of Christ as being 4,000 years after the time of Adam and Eve. "The Son of God humbled Himself and took man's nature after the race had wandered four thousand years from Eden, and from their original state of purity and uprightness." *(Selected Messages,* book 1, p. 267)

The great matchless love of God is pointed out in this statement from *The Desire of Ages.* "The story of Bethlehem is an exhaustless theme. In it is hidden 'the depth of the riches both of the wisdom and knowledge of God.' Romans 11:33. We marvel at the Saviour's sacrifice in exchanging the throne of heaven for the manger, and the companionship of adoring angels for the beasts of the stall. Human pride and self-sufficiency stand rebuked in His presence. Yet this was but the beginning of His wonderful condescension. It would have been an almost infinite humiliation for the Son of God to take man's nature, even when Adam stood in his innocence in Eden. But Jesus accepted humanity when the race had been weakened by four thousand years of sin. Like every child of Adam He accepted the results of the working of the great law of heredity. What these results were is shown in the history of His earthly ancestors. He came with such a heredity to share our sorrows and temptations, and to give us the example of a sinless life." *(The Desire of*

Ages, pp. 48, 49)

"Christ, in the wilderness of temptation, stood in Adam's place to bear the test he failed to endure. Here Christ overcame in the sinner's behalf, four thousand years after Adam turned his back upon the light of his home." *(Selected Messages,* book 1, p. 267)

With regard to the age of the earth Ellen White states, "Infidel geologists claim that the world is very much older than the Bible record makes it. They reject the Bible record, because of those things which are to them evidences from the earth itself, that the world has existed tens of thousands of years. And many who profess to believe the Bible record are at a loss to account for (the) wonderful things which are found in the earth, with the view that creation week was only seven literal days, and that the world is now only about six thousand years old. These, to free themselves of difficulties thrown in their way by infidel geologists, adopt the view that the six days of creation were six vast, indefinite periods, and the day of God's rest was another indefinite period; making senseless the fourth commandment of God's holy law. Some eagerly receive this position, for it destroys the force of the fourth commandment, and they feel a freedom from its claims upon them. They have limited ideas of the size of men, animals, and trees before the flood, and of the great changes which then took place in the earth." *(Spiritual Gifts,* vol. 3, p. 91)

Satan also understands the time frame of the great controversy and as the sixth millennium draws to a close he realizes that his time is short. Note the increased intensity of the struggle in the great controversy as we near the close of time.

"The great controversy between good and evil will increase in intensity to the very close of time. In all ages the wrath of Satan has been manifested against the church of Christ; and God has bestowed His grace and Spirit upon His people to strengthen them to stand against the power of the evil one. When the apostles of Christ were to bear His gospel to the world and to record it for all future ages, they were especially endowed with the enlightenment of the Spirit. But as the church approaches her final deliverance, Satan is to work with greater power. He comes down 'having great wrath, because he knoweth that he hath but a short time.' Revelation 12:12. He will work 'with all power and signs and lying wonders.' II Thessalonians 2:9. For six thousand years that mastermind that once was highest among the angels of God has been wholly bent to the work of deception and ruin. And all the depths of satanic skill and subtlety acquired, all the cruelty developed, during these struggles of the ages, will be brought to bear against God's people in the final conflict. And in this time of peril the followers of Christ are to bear to the world the warning of the Lord's second advent; and a people are to be prepared to stand before Him at His coming, 'without spot, and blameless.' II Peter 3:14. At this time the special endowment of divine grace and power is not less needful to the church than in apostolic days." *(The Great Controversy,* pp. ix, x)

There are numerous statements regarding man's original physical power and that which he now possesses after six thousand years of sin. "Man came from the hand of his Creator perfect in organization and beautiful in form. The fact that he has for six thousand years withstood the ever-increasing weight of disease and crime is conclusive proof of the power of endurance with which he was first endowed." *(Counsels on Health,* p. 19)

"The controlling power of appetite will prove the ruin of thousands, when, if they had conquered on this point, they would have had moral power to gain the victory over every other temptation of Satan. But those who are slaves to appetite will fail in perfecting Christian character. The continual transgression of man for six thousand years has brought sickness, pain, and death as its fruits. And as we near the close of time, Satan's temptation to indulge appetite will be more powerful and more difficult to overcome." *(Counsels on Diet and Foods,* p. 59)

"Never has the world's need for teaching and healing been greater than it is today. The world is full of those who need to be ministered unto—the weak, the helpless, the ignorant, the degraded. The continual transgression of man for nearly six thousand years has brought sickness, pain, and death as its fruit. Multitudes are perishing for lack of knowledge." *(Counsels to Parents, Teachers, and Students,* p. 467)

We are now ready to consider some statements that point particularly to the close of the sixth millennium as the close of earth's history, the defeat of the devil, and the final deliverance of God's faithful people. Please read the following statements slowly and carefully to get their full impact.

"The great controversy between Christ and Satan, that has been carried forward for <u>nearly six thousand years, is soon to close;</u> and the wicked one redoubles his efforts to defeat the work of Christ on man's behalf, and to fasten souls in his snares. To hold the people in darkness and impenitence till the Saviour's mediation is ended, and there is no longer a sacrifice for sin, is the object which he seeks to accomplish." *(The Great Controversy,* p. 518)

"The great controversy between Christ and Satan, that has been carried on for <u>almost six thousand years, is soon to close.</u> And yet how few have their attention called to this matter, <u>how few realize that we are living amid the closing scenes of earth's history!</u> Satan is working diligently, binding his sheaves preparatory to gathering in his harvest. He is uniting the elements of his kingdom for the <u>final struggle.</u>" *(Signs of the Times,* May 8, 1884)

"<u>For six thousand years the great controversy has been in progress;</u> the Son of God and His heavenly messengers have been in conflict with the power of the evil one, to warn, enlighten, and save the children of men. <u>Now all have made their decision;</u> the wicked have fully united with Satan in his warfare against God. <u>The time has come for God to vindicate the authority of His downtrodden law.</u>" *(The Great Controversy,* p. 656)

The following three statements are given in the context of a finished great controversy and final deliverance of God's people. This is a time of great rejoicing! And we are almost there!

"For six thousand years, Satan's work of rebellion has 'made the earth to tremble.' He has 'made the world as a wilderness, and destroyed the cities thereof.' And he 'opened not the house of his prisoners.' <u>For six thousand years his prison house has received God's people,</u> and he would have held them captive forever; <u>but Christ has broken his bonds and set the prisoners free</u>." *(The Great Controversy,* p. 659)

The statement just quoted above is in Chapter 41 of *The Great Controversy* entitled the "Desolation of the Earth." As we noted in Chapter 11 on this same page (659), having just quoted Jeremiah 4:23-26 regarding the condition of the earth during the millennium she states, "Here is to be <u>the home of Satan</u> with his evil angels <u>for a thousand years.</u> Limited to the earth, he will not have access to other worlds to tempt and annoy those who have never fallen. It is in this sense that he is bound: there are none remaining, upon whom he can exercise his power. He is wholly cut off from the work of deception and ruin which for so many centuries has been his sole delight." So she uses the 6,000 years of the great controversy and the 1,000 years of the millennium together on the same page which together make 7,000 years—the great week of time.

This next statement is the basis of what we all refer to as "the blessed hope." I think it is cause for rejoicing even now. "Satan's work of ruin is forever ended. For six thousand years he has wrought his will, filling the earth with woe, and causing grief throughout the universe. The whole creation has groaned and travailed together in pain. Now God's creatures are forever delivered from his presence and temptations. 'The whole earth is at rest, and is quiet; they (the righteous) break forth into singing.' Isaiah 14:7. And a shout of praise and triumph ascends from the whole loyal universe. 'The voice of a great multitude,' 'as the voice of many waters, and as the voice of mighty thunderings,' is heard saying, 'Alleluia; for the Lord God omnipotent reigneth.'" *(The Great Controversy,* p. 673)

And finally we will note that the purpose of the great plan of redemption—the restoration of man—is accomplished within the 6,000-year time frame. "The great plan of redemption results in fully bringing back the world into God's favor. All that was lost is restored. Not only man but the earth is redeemed, to be the eternal abode of the obedient. For six thousand years Satan has struggled to maintain possession of the earth. Now God's original purpose in its creation is accomplished. 'The saints of the Most High shall take the kingdom, and possess the kingdom forever, even forever and ever.' Daniel 7:18." *(Patriarchs and Prophets,* p. 342)

It is significant that not only does Ellen White utilize some of the wording of the Andrews' articles as I noted earlier in this chapter, but I have just discovered that while she was in Europe she used J. N. Andrews' library to write *The Great Controversy!* Arthur White states, "It was while Ellen White was in Europe and had access to the library left by J. N. Andrews at the denomination's publishing house in Basel, Switzerland, that the manuscript for the 1888 edition [of *The Great Controversy]* was largely prepared." (Arthur L. White, *Ellen G. White: The Later Elmshaven Years Volume 6—1905-1915,* p. 308)

Ellen White had great confidence in the scholarship of J. N. Andrews. In fact God had shown her that he was a chosen servant for work in the last days. She wrote to her husband, James, "From what God has shown me from time to time, Brother [J. N.] Andrews was His chosen servant, to do a work others could not do. I have testimonies where the most distinct reference is made to his precious gift. The experience he has obtained has qualified him for the important work for these last days." *(Manuscript Releases,* vol. 13, p. 32)

Summarizing the views of Ellen White in regard to the age of the earth and the duration of the events of the great controversy we can state that she believed:

- Time is outlined as a closely linked chain of events spanning 6,000 years;
- Jesus could not have come before 1798;
- Jesus acted precisely on time;
- God put people and circumstances into place at the appointed time;
- Jesus lived on earth 4,000 years after Adam;
- The great controversy that has been carried on for almost 6,000 years is soon to close;
- We are living amid the closing scenes of earth's history;
- When 6,000 years are past, all have made their decision, the time has come for God to vindicate the authority of His downtrodden law, Christ has broken Satan's bonds and set the prisoners free, Satan's work of ruin is forever ended, now God's creatures are forever delivered from Satan's presence and temptations, all that was lost is restored, and now God's original purpose in earth's creation is accomplished;
- God's plan for man and earth are following the great clock of time;
- Time has almost run out; and
- The earth will lie desolate during the millennium.

CHAPTER 16

Shadows of Things to Come

After years of wandering in the desert Israel approached the Jordan river, the entrance to the promised land. Moses reminded them again of God's leading and blessing and emphasized the importance of being faithful and obedient to Him. One of the most interesting texts that comes to us from this setting is Deuteronomy 29:29, " The secret things belong to the Lord our God, but those things which are revealed belong to us and to our children forever, that we may do all the words of this law."

This text says two things to me. First, we must recognize that there are some things, at least this side of heaven, that will remain a mystery to us. We will never have all the answers that we seek for some of life's hard questions. And, second, that what God has revealed should be eagerly studied and taken into our understanding. I believe that with proper study there is much that God intends to reveal to us that we have yet to discover.

It goes almost without saying that given the present state of society, the world, and the Christian church in general that it is extremely important for each one of us to study to show ourselves approved unto God. We share a lot with other Christians in our understanding of spiritual things—topics like the fall of Satan and his angels, the creation and fall of man, the flood, the call of Abraham, the Exodus, the giving of the Ten Commandments, conversion, forgiveness, baptism, tithing, and many others. However, Adventists hold unique views on—the Sabbath, the second coming of Christ, the state of the dead, the sanctuary, and the Spirit of Prophecy.

One text, very interestingly, impacts on nearly every one of these unique subjects. The text is Colossians 2:16, 17, "Let no man therefore judge you in meat or in drink or in respect of an holyday or of the new moon or of the sabbath days, which are a shadow of things to come, but the body is of Christ." (KJV)

What do you make of this particular text? Many Sabbath keepers have shared with others the great joy and blessings that they experience on the Sabbath. They have recounted the history of the Sabbath from Creation, to Sinai, through the life of Jesus, and on to the New Earth. A portrayal of the Sabbath's history and significance is generally well received by individuals. It makes sense to them. It sounds great. Some even comment, "Why didn't I ever see this before?" And you think to yourself, "Well, there's going to be another Sabbath keeper." However, the next time you see that person they ask you about Colossians 2:16, 17. "It sounded good," they tell you, "but have you read this text? Evidently, it doesn't make any difference anymore which day you keep."

The best biblical background to understand this text is found in Leviticus 23. In addition to the regular weekly Sabbath of the Lord, Leviticus 23 establishes six ceremonial festivals or sabbaths that were observed on an annual basis by the Israelites. There were six feasts or special events, and within these festivals were seven sabbaths.

In Leviticus 23:37 we read, "These are the feasts of the Lord, which ye shall proclaim to be holy convocations, to offer an offering made by fire unto the Lord, a burnt offering, and a meat offering, a sacrifice, and drink offering, everything upon his day."

These special days were to be celebrated on certain days of the month, like the fourteenth day of the first month, or the tenth day of the seventh month. Everyone knows where they were born and the date of their birthday. But what day of the week is your birthday? It can be any day of the week because it is a date, a day of the month, not a day of the week, and the same was true of these special sabbath days.

Now let's look at the next verse. These "sabbaths" were to be celebrated, "Besides the Sabbaths of the Lord (or in addition to the Sabbaths of the Lord), besides your gifts, besides all your vows, and besides your freewill offerings which you give to the Lord." (Leviticus 23:38) In other words, these ceremonial sabbath days were in addition to the weekly Sabbath.

Turning our attention back to Colossians, we can now see from the perspective of Leviticus, and also from the very context of the chapter in Colossians, that this text is not counseling people to eat anything they want to, or to throw away the weekly seventh-day Sabbath. But if

Colossians 2:16, 17 is not talking about food and "the" Sabbath, what is it talking about? Why did God give His people these special feast days that came on specific days of the month? Were they given these events just to occupy their time during the wilderness wanderings? Remember, they wandered around for forty years and idle minds are the devil's workshop. For some reason God wanted them to have the same round of ceremonies year after year. Evidently, God wanted them to learn an important lesson in these services.

Let's look at Colossians 2:16, 17 again, "Let no man therefore judge you in meat, or in drink, or in respect of an holyday, or of the new moon, or of the sabbath days, which are a shadow of things to come; but the body is of Christ."

The key phrase in the internal interpretation of these verses is in verse 17—"which are a shadow of things to come." All of the items that the apostle has mentioned in the verse above (v. 16) are shadows or types, illustrations, if you please, of things to come in the future, symbolizing the work of Christ in the plan of salvation.

Now a shadow has no substance, but it is cast by something tangible. The Jewish ceremonies were shadows cast by heavenly realities. Christ's life, His ministry, His death, and His kingdom are the realities, and the portrayals of this in the ceremonial law were only shadows.

The typical Jewish year was an outline of the entire plan of salvation. It was the gospel in sand-box illustration. "Christ was the foundation of the Jewish economy. The whole system of types and symbols was a compacted prophecy of the gospel, a presentation in which were bound up the promises of redemption." *(The Acts of the Apostles,* p. 14) Each one of these "shadows" was a prophecy of what Christ would do in the future reality of the gospel. All of the types of the Old Testament would have antitypes in the New Testament. (See Chapter 16, Appendix, for background on this from *Christ's Object Lessons,* p. 34)

Why don't we modern Christians celebrate the Passover and the other ceremonial sabbaths? The answer is very simple. Type has met antitype in the ministry of Christ on our behalf. To remember the Passover in a commemorative way may still be appropriate for some, but to continue to sacrifice the Passover lamb today would in fact deny the death of Christ on our behalf as a matter of completed fact. We now celebrate His death as our passover by the Lord's Supper.

This "compacted prophecy of the gospel" can be illustrated by a simple time-line chart which also puts this prophecy in perspective. The six ceremonial festivals or sabbaths were actually chronological events on a great eschatological calendar as God's plan of salvation was opened up before the world.

The Beginning of the Christian Era	The End of the Christian Era

ANTITYPE

Crucifixion	Great Awakening
Resurrection	Investigative Judgment
Holy Spirit Sent	Marriage Supper—Lamb

Spring Feasts	Fall Feasts

Passover	Feast of Trumpets
Unleavened Bread	Day of Atonement
Pentecost	Feast of Tabernacles

TYPE
(long summer)

The events below the line depict the typical Jewish feast days. In the Spring there were three feast days—Passover, Unleavened Bread, and Pentecost. In the Fall there were also three feasts—Feast of Trumpets, Day of Atonement, and Feast of Tabernacles. These six holydays were celebrated each year by God's people with the regularity that we observe our holidays today. In the early part of the year we have Martin Luther King Day, President's Day, and Memorial Day. In the last part of the year we have Labor Day, Thanksgiving, and Christmas. These typical Jewish year festivals were only shadows or illustrations of heavenly realities that God would do on man's behalf.

As we look at each of these ceremonial feast days we will begin to see the antitypical counterpart in the work of Christ. As you look back at the chart above you can see that above the line I have listed the New

Testament counterpart of the Old Testament feast days/sabbaths. At the beginning of the Christian era we have the Crucifixion, the Resurrection, and Pentecost. Then way down at the end of the Christian era we have the antitype of the Fall feast days—the Great Awakening, the Investigative Judgment, and the Marriage Supper of the Lamb.

Passover

The Passover was the opening feast in the yearly round of these services, and it was celebrated on the fourteenth day of the first month, the month of Abib. Actually, the month of Abib corresponds roughly to our March and April today, because when the Israelites left Egypt, God had told them to commemorate that experience by beginning the new year right then. The Passover was both commemorative and typical. It was commemorative of the deliverance of Israel from Egypt. God had promised, "When I see the blood, I will pass over you." No one was exempt from participating in this particular service, because the destroying angel had passed over every home in Egypt, from the house of the king to the prisoner in the dungeon—every home!

From our point of view, however, the typical significance of the Passover is most interesting. The Bible clearly tells us that Jesus was typified by the sacrificial lamb that was slain.

The key phrases from several different texts point this out. Revelation 13:8, speaking of Christ says, "The lamb slain from the foundation of the world." In the Old Testament the gospel prophet writes, "He is brought as a lamb to the slaughter." (Isaiah 53:7) The most profound introduction of any man that has ever walked the earth was spoken by John the Baptist when he introduced Jesus, "Behold the Lamb of God which taketh away the sin of the world." (John 1:29) And the apostle Paul states in explicit language, "Christ, our Passover, is sacrificed for us." (I Corinthians 5:7)

Christ was crucified on the actual Passover day as our Passover, our substitute, thus initiating the actual redemptive activity on man's behalf and the antitypical fulfillment of the Old Testament types and shadows.

Unleavened Bread

The second feast in the Spring was the Feast of Unleavened Bread. Remember the Passover was the fourteenth day of the first month. The Feast of Unleavened Bread was the next day, the fifteenth, but it was seven days long. The first of those seven days was a ceremonial sabbath.

Now take careful note. Whenever one of these ceremonial sabbath days came along on its particular day of the month, if it was a Tuesday, Wednesday, or Thursday, it didn't matter. It was kept like the Sabbath. They didn't do any work on that day. But what would happen if one of the ceremonial sabbaths happened to land on a weekly Sabbath? What did they call that day? It was a "high day" or "high Sabbath." When studying the life of Christ in the New Testament, one discovers that the Sabbath on the weekend that Jesus was crucified was a high Sabbath. The weekly Sabbath that weekend was the ceremonial sabbath of the first day of the Feast of Unleavened Bread. Jesus rested in the tomb on that day after His work of redemption, just as He rested after the Creation.

The second day of the Feast of Unleavened Bread was called the day of the wave sheaf, or sometimes called the first fruits. It was still about two months until the spring wheat harvest, but some of the barley grain had ripened, and the priest would take a handful of that ripened grain— not just one head, but a handful—and take it into the sanctuary. He paused in front of the golden alter and waved that grain before the Lord. Just as the first handful of grain was a pledge of the coming harvest, so the resurrection of Jesus and others on that day as the wave sheaf or the firstfruits was a pledge of the resurrection of the righteous.

Paul states this concept very plainly in I Corinthians 15:20, "But now is Christ risen from the dead, and become the firstfruits of them that slept." He was the antitypical fulfillment of the Feast of Unleavened Bread. Christ was crucified on Friday, which that year was the Passover. He rested in the grave on the Sabbath, which was the antitypical Feast of Unleavened Bread, and He was raised from the tomb on Sunday as the antitypical wave sheaf!

Pentecost

The third Spring feast was Pentecost. Many Christians mistakenly believe that the Pentecost experience of the New Testament disciples was the first Pentecost ever celebrated. As a matter of fact, the New Testament Pentecost was simply the antitype of the third yearly feast that had been celebrated by Israel for centuries. Pentecost came fifty days after the wave sheaf. In other words, it was a little over a month and a half from the time those first grains ripened until the whole harvest was ready. All men were required to appear in Jerusalem for the celebration of Pentecost.

Pentecost is sometimes called the Feast of Harvest, because it celebrated the Spring harvest. And so, as a result of Jesus' preparatory ministry, the preaching of the disciples on that day resulted in a great harvest of 3,000 souls. This harvest was the antitypical Feast of Harvest, and it also typified the great final harvest at the end of the world.

Before Jesus ascended to heaven He promised His disciples the gift of the Holy Spirit. "But when the Comforter is come, whom I will send unto you from the Father, even the Spirit of Truth, which proceedeth from the Father, He shall testify of me." (John 15:26) And the coming of that Comforter was an indication to the disciples that Christ was with the Father. He was beginning His ministry as our High Priest in heaven.

Looking at the chart you will note that after the long Summer and into the early Fall, the next festival occurs. Just as the Spring feasts initiated the Jewish year, the Fall feasts closed it out. So we can expect that toward the close of time would come the antitypical fulfillment of the Fall festivals.

The Feast of Trumpets

The trumpet was used not only as a musical instrument among the Israelites, but it also played an important role in their religious and civil ceremonies. The blasts of the long herald trumpets was often heard sending messages over the land of Israel.

One specific day each year was set aside for the blowing of the trumpets. It is recorded, in Leviticus 23, and also in Numbers 29:1 which I will quote here. "In the seventh month, on the first day of the month, ye shall have a holy convocation; ye shall do no servile work: it is a day of blowing the trumpets unto you."

It is quite evident that the Feast of Trumpets, like the Passover, was both commemorative and typical. It came ten days before the Day of Atonement, the type of the great investigative judgment which opened in 1844, at the end of the long 2300 day prophecy. (See Daniel, Chapters 7-9)

Now in the type the trumpets were blown throughout all Israel. When the people heard these trumpet sounds throughout the land, they knew that the great, solemn Day of Atonement was coming. In the antitype, then, we should expect a worldwide message to be given in every corner of the earth in trumpet tones, announcing the great antitypical Day of Atonement in heaven.

Beginning with the years 1833 and 1834 and extending down to 1844, just such a message was given to the world. In the ten years preceding 1844 every civilized nation on this earth received the message that "The hour of His judgment is come."

Joseph Wolff was converted to Christianity from Judaism and became an Episcopal missionary to the Middle East. He was often called the "Missionary to the World." He spent hours studying the prophecies of Daniel and Revelation. In those days all of the churches believed that the cleansing of the sanctuary was this earth being cleansed by fire at the end of time when Jesus returns. Wolff went about preaching that Jesus was coming in 1843.

At the very same time, Edward Irving, an Anglican minister in England, was independently studying these same prophecies, and he, too, began to preach that Jesus was coming in 1843. He preached this all over the British Isles with the result that 500 other ministers joined him in preaching this message throughout the British Empire.

At the same time, not connected with Joseph Wolff or Edward Irving in any way, Manuel De Lacunza, a Roman Catholic priest in South America, carefully studied the prophecies of Daniel and Revelation, also coming to the conclusion that the end of the world was near. He published a book under the name of Rabbi Ben Ezra. It went all over South America. Thousands read it and believed that Jesus was coming soon.

At the very same time Baptist minister William Miller was just concluding a seven-year study of the prophecies. He, too, had traced them down and came to the conclusion that Jesus was coming in 1843. Thousands and thousands of people gathered in huge tent presentations all over the United States to hear this message preached. In fact, some of the railroad companies actually built railroad spurs out to these big tents in the country, so that people could get to the meetings. Historians still refer to this experience as "The Great Awakening."

Young Methodist minister S. S. Snow attended one of Miller's meetings and went home to study it out for himself. Using calculations given in the prophecies, he came to the conclusion that Jesus would really come on October 22, 1844.

A Bible conference was called, and Snow presented his findings to others. They agreed that the event at the end of the 2300-day prophecy would be the cleansing of the sanctuary. Thousands believed with all their hearts that Jesus was coming on October 22, 1844.

But Revelation 10:10 accurately predicted the result. That understanding which had been sweet in their mouths became bitter in their bellies. The date was right, but they were mistaken as to the event that would take place. But please note carefully this point. The fact that the men who proclaimed this message misunderstood the full importance and significance of it did not prevent them from fulfilling the antitypical Feast of Trumpets.

This can be illustrated from the prophetic fulfillments surrounding the life of Christ. The followers of Christ cried out, "Blessed be the King that cometh in the name of the Lord," on the occasion of the triumphal entry into Jerusalem. They laid their coats down on the road in front of Him and waved palm branches over His head. They believed that Jesus was entering Jerusalem to be recognized as the king of Israel. They were fulfilling Zechariah 9:9. If they had known that in only a few days Jesus would be hanging on a cross, they would not have been able to fulfill the prophecy of Zechariah 9:9 "rejoicing greatly." That was a high day, with children and adults singing praises. It is interesting to note that in the great antitypical Feast of Trumpets there were child preachers in Sweden and many other places praising God by their testimony of His soon return.

The message due to the world between 1834 and 1844 could never have been given with the power and joyfulness that it demanded to fulfill the antitype of the Feast of Trumpets if those who gave the message had understood that Jesus, instead of coming to this earth, was to enter the most holy place of the heavenly sanctuary to begin His work in the investigative judgment.

Day of Atonement

The Day of Atonement was the fifth of the six feasts. It came in the middle of the Fall feasts. It came on the tenth day of the seventh month. The Day of Atonement is known to us today as Yom Kippur. It was the most important and solemn of all the Jewish festivals. Take note when the next Yom Kippur comes around and see how even modern-day Jews regard it.

The placement of the Day of Atonement near the end of the year is significant. It was a time of investigation, vindication and restoration, followed by the joyous procession into Jerusalem to celebrate the harvest.

On the solemn Day of Atonement the entire congregation—not as families, but as individuals—recognized that their personal fate was in the balance. It was a time of evaluation and separation.

First there was a judgment involving the representatives of the people, symbolized by goats. One was declared worthy to provide payment for the sins of the camp, while the other one was declared responsible for all the wickedness. We should carefully note that the one regarded as responsible for sin did not atone for it. That goat was simply banished into the wilderness. The other goat, as an innocent substitute, paid in blood for the transgression of the people.

The most holy place in the sanctuary typified the throne from which God dispenses judgment. Only on the Day of Atonement was this place of judgment used, and it became the focal point of attention as the blood of reconciliation was presented in the presence of God.

A fascinating parallel exists between the gospel's sparkling truths and the truths that were taught on the Day of Atonement. Blood also provided atonement for the holy place, not because the building itself had sinned, of course, but because it had served as the headquarters and clearing house for the redemptive activity throughout the year. During the Day of Atonement the people participated by setting aside the things of the world and coming together in humility while trusting in the blood of their substitute for a favorable verdict.

It was a time of judgment. "If there is any person who will not humble himself on this day, he shall be cut off from the people." (Leviticus 23:29) Anyone who refused to apply the merits of that sacrifice to his own account was cut off.

Much incense was used on the Day of Atonement, symbolizing the merits of Christ. "For on that day shall the priest make atonement for you, to cleanse you, that you may be clean from all your sins before the Lord." (Leviticus 16:30) The saints were clean because of the blood shed for them, not because of the work of sanctification done in their lives. Because of what God had done for them, they stood perfect.

Sometimes men have imperfect standards, but God's standard is always perfect. Only He can meet it. I remember that when I was a student at Loma Linda some twenty years ago, one of my teachers in the

School of Health was a grain inspector for the federal government during the summer. He worked in the Columbia River basin in the Northwest. Federal standards required that all of the grain shipped overseas had to be 97% pure wheat kernels. That meant that there could be briars, little sticks, and some dirt, but 97% of it had to be wheat. It was my teacher's responsibility to make sure that the standard was upheld.

Great barges would be towed up the Columbia River to loading areas where the wheat was delivered from Idaho, Montana, and Washington. American technology was so sophisticated that they could make the thrashed wheat 100% pure! Accordingly they met the standard by filling the 100-ton barge with 97 tons of wheat kernels. Then they would back up a dump truck to the barge and dump in 3 tons of dirt on top of the wheat. No one could argue, because they were meeting the standard and living up to the contract with the purchasers. They were getting wheat prices for dirt! By the time the barges arrived at their overseas destinations the dirt had sifted down into the wheat, and it just looked like dirty wheat.

But on the Day of Atonement it was not man's standard that was used. Men could not say, "I don't have anything to worry about. I've been a good Israelite all year." No, it was God's standard, and they must look to the blood for atonement. The only thing that counted was the blood. To pass the test of the judgment they were not asked to recite Scripture from memory. They were not investigated to see if they had met their fund-raising quotas. They were not asked to present fruit that they had raised with God's cooperation, nor were they supposed to wave palm branches of personal victory through the Spirit's power in their lives. The only thing that counted was the blood! Judgment was based exclusively on their willingness to lay aside everything else and trust in the atonement for them. Once it was apparent in their behavior that they had, indeed, chosen to participate in salvation, no further investigation was made. "He that believes in Him is not judged; but he who does not believe has been judged already." (John 3:18) They remembered the words "When I see the blood, I will pass over you."

The great antitypical Day of Atonement that began in 1844 was properly preceded by the antitypical Feast of Trumpets and properly followed by the preaching of Revelation 14:6 and 7, that "the hour of His judgment _is_ come."

When Paul spoke before King Agrippa as recorded in the book of

Acts, he spoke of "righteousness and temperance and judgment to come," but now after 1844, there is a worldwide movement to preach the hour of His judgment <u>has</u> come.

The Feast of Tabernacles

Now that we have covered the foregoing explanation in this chapter we are ready for the real purpose for including this material in this book. The antitypical Feast of Tabernacles is the last event in the parallel to the Jewish feast days. It typified the consummation of the entire plan of redemption. But when will it be celebrated in antitype? Has it already happened? Will it be celebrated on this earth? Remember, it was a time of great rejoicing in the type.

"The Feast of Tabernacles was not only commemorative but typical. It not only pointed back to the wilderness sojourn, but, as the feast of harvest, it celebrated the ingathering of the fruits of the earth, and pointed forward to the great day of final ingathering, when the Lord of the harvest shall send forth His reapers to gather the tares together in bundles for the fire, and to gather the wheat into His garner." The author adds, "At that time the wicked will all be destroyed. They will become 'as though they had not been.' Obadiah 16. And every voice in the whole universe will unite in joyful praise to God." *(Patriarchs and Prophets,* p. 541) Apparently this joyful celebration will begin in heaven but continue on into the new earth because here Ellen White refers to the fact that the wicked will be "as though they had not been," which in its complete fulfillment will not take place until the end of the millennium. In addition, Revelation 21 and 22, dealing with the new earth, are saturated with the Feast of Tabernacles imagery.

The Feast of Tabernacles began five days after the Day of Atonement. All the Israelites rejoiced in their acceptance with God and also in the bounties of the Fall harvest.

The antitypical Feast of Tabernacles will not be celebrated on this earth!   As spoken of so many times in the New Testament, it will be fulfilled antitypically in the Marriage Supper of the Lamb that will take place in heaven. And this is only the beginning! Jesus is now calling. "Come," He says, "for all things are now ready." It will be the best He can do, a welcome home for earth's hostages after 6,000 years.

God's loving welcome will be, "Come My people, you have come out of great tribulation, and done My will; suffered for Me; come in to supper, for I will gird Myself, and serve you.

"We shouted, Alleluia! Glory! and entered into the city, and I saw a table of pure silver. It was many miles in length, yet our eyes could extend over it." *(Early Writings,* p. 19)

I have often thought that it is interesting that God chose a woman to have this particular vision. A man might have taken a long look at the silver table and begun to calculate its value based on the sterling market today. But the lady saw what was for supper! It is very fascinating, because the plan of salvation and redemption is not to start all over again with a new plan. It is to restore man back to his original creation, and that includes his original diet. In describing the banquet Ellen White wrote, "I saw the fruit of the tree of life, the manna, the almonds, figs, pomegranates, grapes, and many other kinds of fruit." *(Ibid.)*

I want to be there, don't you? It won't be long now. It's supper time!

It all fits together. When you line up the antitypical feast days in eschatological order they have all been fulfilled except the last one. The very next event is the Marriage Supper of the Lamb. And it will be celebrated in heaven!

Now as you picture Jesus hanging on the cross you can realize that He is the beginning and the end of the antitypical fulfillment of those great Old Testament types and shadows.

His death, His resurrection, His gift of the Comforter, His warning to the world of the end of time, His mediation on our behalf with His own blood as our high priest, and His preparation for the heavenly banquet were all foretold in the ceremonial services.

CHAPTER 17

It All Fits Together

O ne of the most satisfying things about the beliefs of the Seventh-day Adventist Church is the harmony of the doctrinal understanding. Many remark when they join the Adventist Church, "Now it all makes sense; everything fits so well together." For example, the resurrection at the Second Coming is so biblical and practical. Ellen White stated the problem of conflicting doctrines that others face this way. "If the dead are already enjoying the bliss of heaven or writhing in the flames of hell, what need of a future judgment?" *(The Spirit of Prophecy,* vol. 4, p. 368) One can quickly see that our interpretation of Christian Anthropology—man's conditions in birth, life and death—makes sense because it is true to Scripture.

Adventists love Scripture. We enjoy reading it. It is our standard of faith and practice. We accept the counsel of Ellen White as inspired, because it meets the Scriptural tests like Isaiah 8:20—"To the law and to the testimony: if they speak not according to this word, it is because there is no light in them." Accordingly, in my study of end-time events I am very eager to be sure that the material presented in this book is in harmony with the fundamental teachings of Scripture and have the additional affirmation of the Testimony of Jesus which is the Spirit of Prophecy. With this in mind the manuscript was submitted to various readers: laymen, pastors, church leaders, and religion professors. It is my firm conviction that no prophecy is of any private interpretation so that if what I am presenting in this book is true, then others would recognize and support it as well. This has been the case.

This book does not in any way disparage our basic prophetic understandings. No attempts are made in this book to set the day and hour of Christ's coming. No dates are set for anything—the close of probation, the National Sunday Law, etc. The point of this book is very simple. We have not followed cunningly devised fables in our prophetic interpretations. As I mentioned earlier, "1844 stands without impeachment." The point is that because of the "delay" many Adventists have become apathetic and disinterested in the Second Coming. And yet all the while, the devil, knowing that time is short, has marshalled his forces for the final events. The 6,000-year time line lets us know for sure that the events we are now seeing are the "real thing." The end of all things is at hand!

The idea that we are at the end of time is nothing new to Adventist understanding. In 1980 *Review* editor, Kenneth H. Wood, prepared a series of six articles that were published in the *Review* entitled "Church of Destiny" in which he pointed out the uniqueness of the Seventh-day Adventist Church and its role as the end-time "remnant" church. In the final article printed in the August 21, 1980, issue he printed a chart showing that the major prophecies of Daniel, Matthew, and Revelation point to the present period of history as the end-time. The chart's caption reads "This chart helps underscore one point that has been emphasized throughout this series of six articles: All the major time prophecies of the Bible make clear that we are living in the last days; earthly nations have virtually run their course; soon God will set up His everlasting kingdom." (*Adventist Review*, Aug. 21, 1980, p. 9)

In the official program prepared for the 1990 General Conference session in Indianapolis, Indiana, is the following statement on page ten: "The world is rushing to its premillennial climax. There are awesome signs for which we have waited, telling us that the end is nearing."

The material in this book does no harm to our commonly held beliefs. It only allows us to back up and see all the prophecies in perspective. Take a look at the chart on the next page and you will see that every documented historical date or fact that you know can be placed on the time-line of history—all the great time prophecies, all the great epics of time, the rise and fall of nations, and the record of God's dealings with man. The entries I have put on the chart simply show a few commonly accepted events and prophecies and their approximate times. That the time of the end began in 1798 is a well accepted fact in Adventist prophetic interpretation because both Daniel and the Revelation mention this period of time in various passages.

The Great Week of Time
The Antitypical Sabbatical Cycle

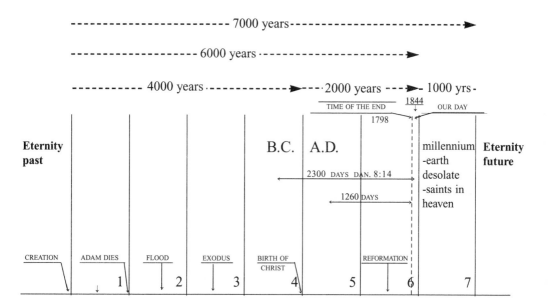

So, by placing the 1798 "time of the end" date on the 7,000-year time line we come up with essentially the same chart as Kenneth Wood prepared for his *Review* articles in 1980. The bottom line is that approximately 20 percent of the sixth millennium is the "time of the end." The significant fact of all this is that we are now over 195 years into "the time of the end." The last great epoch of time is drawing quickly to a close. Surely the appointed time is almost here.

CHAPTER 18

What Is God Waiting For?

If any generation since 1844 could have witnessed the second coming of Jesus, and Jesus really wants to come back, what is He waiting for? Why hasn't the work been finished? Why hasn't Jesus come, and why aren't the saints in the kingdom? Does the wickedness in the world need to increase? Is it a matter of character development? Is it because we have not taken the gospel commission seriously? Is God behind schedule on building the mansions? Why has the time of the end already extended to nearly 200 years? Why are we still here? Let's examine some material that might help answer these questions and give us even greater insight to the fact that the end of all things is at hand.

The biblical illustration most well-known for a delay is the forty-year wilderness wandering of Israel after being right at the borders of the promised land. We have had a very similar situation if the words of Ellen White are to be taken at face value.

"Had Adventists, after the great disappointment in 1844, held fast their faith and followed on unitedly in the opening providence of God, receiving the message of the third angel and in the power of the Holy Spirit proclaiming it to the world, they would have wrought mightily with their efforts, the work would have been completed, and Christ would have come ere this to receive His people to their reward. But in the period of doubt and uncertainty that followed the disappointment, many of the advent believers yielded their faith. . . Thus the work was hindered, and the world was left in darkness. Had the whole Adventist body united upon the commandments of God and the faith of Jesus, how widely different would have been our history!

"It was not the will of God that the coming of Christ should be thus delayed. God did not design that His people, Israel, should wander forty years in the wilderness. He promised to lead them directly to the land of Canaan, and establish them there a holy, healthy, happy people. But those to whom it was first preached, went not in 'because of unbelief.' Their hearts were filled with murmuring, rebellion, and hatred, and He could not fulfill His covenant with them.

"For forty years did unbelief, murmuring, and rebellion shut out ancient Israel from the land of Canaan. The same sins have delayed the entrance of modern Israel into the heavenly Canaan. In neither case were the promises of God at fault. It is the unbelief, the worldliness, unconsecration, and strife among the Lord's professed people that have kept us in this world of sin and sorrow so many years." *(Evangelism,* p. 696)

In commenting on this failure of Israel to enter into the land of Canaan Ellen White later stated, "The lesson of this record is for us. The Lord had prepared the way before His people. They were very near the promised land. A little while and they would have entered Canaan. They themselves delayed the entering. In the first place, it was they who requested that spies should be sent up to search the land." *(The General Conference Bulletin,* March 30, 1903)

Who would deny that as a people we have exhibited unbelief or lack of faith, that we have become worldly and materialistic, that we have exercised only half hearted response to the great commission, and that we have had almost continuous internal strife. Let's pray that we can reverse these four problems.

The Matthew 24:14 Connection

Jesus told His disciples, "And this gospel of the kingdom will be preached in all the world as a witness to all the nations, and then the end will come." This is a promise for the final generation.

"And yet there remains much to be done. In the past we have not been as diligent as we ought to have been in seeking to save the lost. Precious opportunities have been allowed to pass by unimproved. This has delayed the coming of our King. Had the people of God constantly preserved a living connection with Him from the beginning of the great advent movement, had they obeyed His word and advanced in all His opening providences, they would today be in the heavenly Canaan." *(An Appeal to Ministers and Church Officers,* p. 3)

The point is God loves every person on the earth as much as He loves you and me, and He is longsuffering, not willing that any should perish. What a loving God! He wanted to come many years ago, but His mercy to the unready has delayed His return.

Other statements underscore this fact. "Because the people are disobedient, unthankful, unholy, as were ancient Israel, time is prolonged that all may hear the last message of mercy proclaimed with a loud voice. The Lord's work has been hindered, the sealing time delayed. Many have not heard the truth. But the Lord will give them a chance to hear and be converted." *(The Faith I Live By,* p. 288) "Why has the Lord so long delayed His coming? . . . It is because missionaries are few." *(Review and Herald,* March 27, 1894) "It is because the work has not been done for the wicked that time delays." *(Manuscript Releases,* vol. 10, p. 275)

The evil servant and the scoffer blame God for the delay. (See Matt. 24:48; II Pet. 3:3, 4.) This is similar to the accusation Ahab made to Elijah, "Are you the one who troubleth Israel?" It is easy to blame God or someone else, but the fact remains that because His people have not taken seriously the great gospel commission, God in His mercy has delayed His coming.

"God is calling His people at this time to a long-delayed work. Decided efforts are to be made to enlighten those who have never yet been warned. The work in the cities is now to be regarded as of special importance." *(Review and Herald,* April 7, 1910)

We may have a tendency to think that the greatest sins of the day are problems in the large cities of the world. But terrible crime, violence, and immorality are eclipsed by something else. "The warning of Christ sounds down along the lines to our day. He would arouse the people for whom He gave His life, and attract their attention to Himself, the source of all wisdom, righteousness, strength, hope, and peace. He would have His people let their light shine forth to the world in good works. The sins of Sodom are repeated in our day, and the earth is destroyed and corrupted under the inhabitants thereof; but the worst feature of the iniquity of this day is a form of godliness without the power thereof. Those who profess to have great light are found among the careless and indifferent, and the cause of Christ is wounded in the house of its professed friends. Let those who would be saved, arouse from their lethargy, and give the trumpet a certain sound; for the end of all things is at hand." *(Signs of the Times,* Oct. 16, 1893)

One of the biggest problems in the delay scenario is that because of our failure to warn the world, people think that we are not serious and that Christ will never return. "And because, in His mercy, He delays His coming to give the world a larger span for repentance, sinners flatter themselves that He will never come." *(Manuscript Releases,* vol. 10, p. 265)

One of the major points of this book is that the so-called "delay" in the Second Coming only underscores the fact that the end of all things is at hand, first from the perspective that the scoffers are a sign of the last days and also because each day that passes puts us that much nearer to the final day. But we can make a difference!

"God 'hath appointed a day, in the which He will judge the world' (Acts 17:31). Christ tells us when that day shall be ushered in. He does not say that all the world will be converted, but that 'this gospel of the kingdom shall be preached in all the world for a witness unto all nations; and then shall the end come.' By giving the gospel to the world it is in our power to hasten our Lord's return. We are not only to look for but to hasten the coming of the day of God. (II Peter 3:12, margin) Had the church of Christ done her appointed work as the Lord ordained, the whole world would before this have been warned, and the Lord Jesus would have come to our earth in power and great glory." *(The Desire of Ages*, pp. 633, 634)

Immorality Plays a Role

There is another factor to consider in the delay. God's mercy has limits as illustrated in His dealings with the antideluvians and the cities of Sodom and Gomorrah. Man's degradation in sin today is surely at God's boundary line.

A special report in *Reader's Digest* entitled "Asia's Shocking Secret" revealed the depths to which sinful man has fallen. Not only do men repeat the sins of Sodom on a regular basis, but such sins are recorded in movies and videos that are shown to millions. The article stated that depraved men have turned to innocent children. "Throughout southern Asia every year, thousands of children are delivered into sexual slavery. Girls and boys as young as four are bought, sold, and stolen to serve this repellant trade. . . According to the Bangkok-based international organization ECPAT (End Child Prostitution in Asian Tourism), there are about 500,000 prostitutes 16 years old or younger in Thailand, the Philippines, and Sri Lanka. At least 50,000 are under 13.

"Fueling this child-sex industry are tens of thousands of pedophile tourists from the United States, Canada, Britain, Germany, Sweden,

Japan, Australia, and New Zealand. Often assisted by clandestine pedophile networks, they fly to southern Asia for child sex, knowing they face little risk of being caught and small penalty if they are. The lure of tourist dollars leads government and law-enforcement officials in these countries to look the other way." *(Reader's Digest,* October 1993, pp. 69, 70)

I wonder what God thinks of all of this. "The angel that stood by my side then instructed me that but few have any conception of the wickedness existing in our world today, and especially the wickedness in the large cities. He declared that the Lord has appointed a time when He will visit transgressors in wrath for persistent disregard of His law." *(Testimonies for the Church,* vol. 9, p. 93) This wickedness is yet another sign that the coming of Christ will not be delayed much longer.

The point here is not that such wickedness has not existed previously, but now it is becoming more open and bold. For example, just a few years ago homosexuality was hidden in the "closet." Today the homosexual lobby is highly visible and active. Not only did the gay community have a contingent in President Clinton's inaugural parade, but they assembled an estimated 350,000 homosexuals and their supporters for a march on Washington, D.C., on Memorial Day, 1993! And to top this, planners are estimating 1,000,000 in the 1994 "Gay Pride" march in New York City! What an insult to the Creator.

The judgments of God are already at work. In the 1994 Los Angeles earthquake initial coverage of the damage failed to mention that the quake's epicenter was the hub of America's $3,000,000,000 X-rated video industry. According to newspaper reports, "The triangle formed by the San Fernando Valley communities of Chatsworth, Northridge, and Canoga Park—tightly encircling the epicenter of the powerful quake—contains nearly seventy companies that crank out more than 95% of the roughly 1,400 sexually explicit videos made every year in the United States." The paper went on to say, "So far, this coincidence of cataclysm-and-Gomorrah appears to have gone unnoticed by California's feisty religious right, but no one in the industry expects that situation to last.

"'Can you imagine how (the fundamentalists) are going to leap on this when the smoke clears?' says a director who works for several Northridge studios. 'They are going to have a field day of "I told-you-sos" down in Orange County. They'll say it's God's retribution, His personal destruction of America's most wicked city.'

EATD-7

"God's will or not, there is no doubt that the devastation in California's adult-video industry has been close to apocalyptic. A telephone survey of valley-area studios discloses that—with no exceptions—every company has suffered some major damage." (The San Jose *Mercury,* Jan. 25, 1994)

"Everything is preparing for the great day of God. Time will last a little longer until the inhabitants of the earth have filled up the cup of iniquity, and then the wrath of God, which has so long slumbered, will awake, and this land of light will drink the cup of His unmingled wrath. The desolating power of God is upon the earth to rend and destroy. The inhabitants of the earth are appointed to the sword, to famine, and to pestilence." *(Testimonies for the Church,* vol. 1, p. 363)

The End Is Coming!

"We cannot afford to live with no reference to the day of judgment; for though long delayed, it is now near, even at the door, and hasteneth greatly. The trumpet of the Archangel will soon startle the living and wake the dead. At that day the wicked will be separated from the just, as the shepherd divides the goats from the sheep." *(Child Guidance,* p. 560) In addition, we are told, "Every week counts one week less, every day one day nearer to the appointed time of the judgment." *(Maranatha,* p. 55)

There is good news and bad news when the church finally realizes that the close of probation and the Second Coming are right upon us. The bad news is that a significant proportion, half in the parable of the ten virgins, will find themselves with the knowledge of Bible facts but not the indwelling, life-changing power of the Holy Spirit. And their probation will be closed. The good news is that those who have been truly converted and committed and transformed by the power of God and His Spirit will be roused to a glorious finishing of the work.

"All who wait for the heavenly Bridegroom are represented in the parable as slumbering because their Lord delayed His coming; but

the wise roused themselves at the message of His approach,

and responded to the message,

and their spiritual life was replenished.

Their spiritual discernment was not all gone,

and they sprang into line.

As they took hold of the grace of Christ,

their religious experience became vigorous and abundant,

and their affections were set upon things above.
They discerned where was the source of their supply,
   and appreciated the love that God had for them.
They opened their hearts to receive the Holy Spirit,
   by which the love of God was shed abroad in their hearts.
Their lights were trimmed and burning,
   and sent forth steady rays into the moral darkness of the world.
They glorified God,
   because they had the oil of grace in their hearts,
   and did the very work that their Master did before them,
   —went forth to seek and to save those who were lost."
(Signs of the Times, Aug. 13, 1894)

What a statement! What a change when the realization of the nearness of the Bridegroom comes! Are we ready to be awakened? I pray that we are and that we will be among the awakened saints.

I have used a number of statements made by Ellen White. I believe she was sent of God to make the great Second Coming prophecies present truth for our day. Her messages were given to encourage us to swell the message of the third angel into the loud cry that enlightens the whole world. And second, she was among those who truly did experience a long delay. From her early teen years around 1844 until she died in her eighties in 1915, Ellen White believed that the coming was near at hand. She also recognized that our failure to warn the world would lengthen the probationary time for this world. The point here is that though the 6,000 years set an outside time limit for Christ's return, God wants to cut it short. We delay His coming by failing to do our appointed work. His cutting the work short may have less to do with shortening the time than interceding in a special way to bring the proclamation to its conclusion.

How did Ellen White relate to all of this? "The angels of God in their messages to men represent time as very short. Thus it has always been presented to me. It is true that time has continued longer than we expected in the early days of this message. Our Saviour did not appear as soon as we hoped. But has the word of the Lord failed? Never! It should be remembered that the promises and threatenings of God are alike conditional." *(Maranatha,* p. 61)

"We have not cast away our confidence, neither have we a message dependent upon definite time, [This regards those who wanted to set the day and hour of Christ's coming.] but we are waiting and watching unto prayer, looking for and loving the appearing of our Saviour, and doing all in our power for the preparation of our fellow men for that great event. We are not impatient. If the vision tarry, wait for it, for it will surely come; it will not tarry. Although disappointed, our faith has not failed, and we have not drawn back to perdition. The apparent tarrying is not so in reality, for at the appointed time our Lord will come, and we will, if faithful, exclaim, 'Lo, this is our God; we have waited for Him, and He will save us.'" *(Manuscript Releases,* vol. 16, p. 178)

God declared in the days before the flood, "My Spirit shall not strive with man forever." (Gen. 6:3) Then, again, through a psalm of David the Scriptures declare, "He will not always strive with us, Nor will He keep His anger forever." (Psalm 103:9) Then, finally, through an angel to John the Revelator we were told that someday time would literally run out, and God would proclaim,

"He who is unjust, let him be unjust still;

he who is filthy, let him be filthy still;

he who is righteous, let him be righteous still;

he who is holy, let him be holy still.

And behold, I am coming quickly, and My reward is with Me,

to give every one according to his work." (Rev. 22:11, 12)

Some day God will have to finally say, "Ready or not, here I come." Your standing that day will determine eternity for you. The long delay will be over. Probation's door will be forever closed. I believe the evidence indicates that this day is near at hand.

CHAPTER 19

The Greatest Sign

There are many signs of the end given in Scripture—wars, famines, pestilence, immorality, crime, family problems, financial problems, persecution, the rise of the beast power after the deadly wound, and the rise of the beast with lamb-like horns. The list is long and quite specific. These signs have become a sometimes ignored weave in the fabric of our tumultuous century. They should tell us in no uncertain way that time is running out—literally. Soon a Great Event will rip into history even more dramatically than the temple curtain tear at Christ's death.

However, Jesus Himself gave the greatest sign. In Matthew 24:14 He tells us: "This gospel of the kingdom will be preached in all the world as a witness to all the nations, and <u>then</u> the end will come." The gospel of Mark repeats this fact, "The end is not yet. . . [because] the gospel must first be preached to all the nations." (Mark 13:7, 10)

The greatest sign that the coming of Jesus is near is the fact that the gospel is now going to all the world in spite of, and in some cases directly because of, war and social upheaval. Missionary activity by the Christian church in general, and specifically by the Adventist Church, is very thrilling.

More than forty separate groups have a goal of taking the gospel to the entire world by the year 2000. Through the untiring efforts of Wycliffe Bible translators and others, the Bible is now available in every written language on earth! Wycliffe is now focusing on taking the remaining languages that are known only in spoken form and reducing them to writing so that they can print Scripture portions for these people groups. This work also requires literacy training for these people, but how exciting that their first reading is done in the Bible! In addition,

Bibles are being printed and circulated worldwide by the millions!

We all recognize that we could do much better, but look at what is being accomplished by God's grace through His remnant church.

For many years we have had a global mission objective. But only in the past few years have we developed a global strategy and a Global Mission Department at the General Conference. Through the combined efforts of many church and supporting ministry organizations, the unreached world is specifically targeted for evangelism.

Ellen White wrote in 1885, "More than one thousand will soon be converted in one day, most of whom will trace their first convictions to the reading of our publications." *(Evangelism,* p. 693) At the time it seemed an almost impossible prediction, yet in 1993 the Seventh-day Adventist Church added a new believer every fifty seconds—that's 1,728 per day! In South Mexico alone, on average 175 are baptized per day, requiring a new organized church daily!

Growth in Chinese believers has been phenomenal in a country without national church organization. During this year (1993) one congregation, led by two local elders, held the second largest single baptism in Seventh-day Adventist history—4,415 were added to the church family! Without enough church buildings, believers in China meet wherever they can—in house churches, Three-self church buildings, or for multiple services in their own sanctuaries.

Membership in Bulgaria has more than doubled in the last fifteen months. While two years ago there were only 500 members in Moscow, there are now more than 5,000. Kenya felt a second Pentecost with the baptism of 3,435 in one day.

The first accessions ever in the former Outer Mongolia came in October (1993)—when two young women were baptized and a young man joined by profession of faith the Adventist family. This followed two years of tent-making evangelism by Brad and Cathy Jolly under the auspices of Adventist Frontier Missions. And church accessions have resumed in Cambodia for the first time in thirteen years.

Three territorial divisons of the General Conference now exceed 1,000,000 members. Africa-Indian Ocean just surpassed that mark, and the Far East will soon reach that figure—thanks in large part to growth in the Philippines. Adventist Church adherents there now equal more than 600,000—making an impact on world church family figures. Today one in twelve Seventh-day Adventists worldwide is a Filipino.

In war-torn Sarajevo and other Bosnian cities Adventist churches are filled to overflowing every Sabbath.

And Native American congregations are growing at the rate of about 10%—especially in the northwestern United States and Canada.

In El Salvador, a country about 45 miles wide and 100 miles long, there are now 400 congregations—too many to manage from one office, so they are preparing to divide into two conferences.

People hungry for the gospel flock to stadiums—more than 30,000 in a single location in Brazil to hear Alejandro Bullon—the largest crusade attendance anywhere in the world. In many countries without church buildings, home churches are thriving, while hundreds of others meet in rented halls.

It is now estimated by Don Noble of Maranatha Volunteers International and Mike Ryan of the Global Mission office that there is a need of over 10,000 new church buildings worldwide—and the need keeps growing daily!

Many Adventists are getting personally involved in short-term mission projects. During 1993 Maranatha Volunteers pursued thirty-four different projects, working on eighty-two buildings. The more than 1,700 volunteers donated nearly 99,000 hours, in addition to paying their own travel expenses, and completed just under 240,000 square feet of buildings valued at nearly US$3.4 million. Most recent of their projects are fifty new church sanctuaries and three new 400-student school buildings in Guatemala. They also completed seventy-five churches which had been started by nationals. In addition, Maranathans built an agriculture facility and eleven staff homes for the orphanage operated by International Children's Care.

In 1993 the *Voice of Prophecy* in Brazil celebrated its fiftieth anniversary with a national campaign to increase church membership. Church members enrolled 1,000,000 persons in Bible courses, and by the end of October, 500,000 had been graduated. More than 750,000 people attended summer evangelistic efforts where more than 25,000 were baptized.

And the newly baptized are becoming involved in media ministries. Julia Utkina, who joined the Adventist family in Nizhne Novgorod, Russia, began a television ministry in her area—sponsored by viewers of 3ABN. Andrei Nikitin did the same in the Ryazan Region—supported by *Faith for Today* viewers.

New Seventh-day Adventist radio stations have begun operating in

Chile, Argentina, Brazil, and Puerto Rico where Adventist believers have also joined the growing family of 3ABN downlinkers with a televison studio at the union office.

The Ukrainian version of the *Voice of Prophecy,* called the *Voice of Hope,* was placed on national Ukraine radio; Middle East College Radio was dedicated in October (1993); and Adventist World Radio more than doubled its broadcasts from four to ten sites.

The humanitarian service by the Adventist Development and Relief Agency has been recognized around the world. Working in more than 100 countries, ADRA provides some kind of assistance to an average of 10,000 people per day.

For example, more than 20,000 Somalis have received care from an ADRA health service, while in Nicaragua more than 900 parents have been trained to teach other parents about nutrition, sanitation, immunization, and birth spacing. Somalia also has eighteen new wells, thanks to ADRA, and there are now 186 ADRA wells in Sudan.

ADRA is the second largest food distributor for USAID in Bolivia, benefitting more than 130,000 people every month. That means that one in three people receives aid from ADRA. The same percentage applies in Ghana, which received more than 51 tons of food.

But perhaps the most impressive success story continues to be in Sarajevo where in addition to humanitarian efforts, ADRA is providing the only mail service the country has; and the international community continues to entrust ADRA with their distribution.

According to an independent polling company, ADRA received at year's end (1993) the highest overall rating and appreciation from among all humanitarian groups.

This report could go on to report dozens of additional exciting developments in the work of the Adventist Church. These examples are simply representative. But I must share one more with you. To me the most exciting development is what is happening in my own home division of North America. In the past materialism and preoccupation have inhibited our public evangelism in this division. But today with one natural disaster after another, financial worries, and crime that by anyone's standard is out of control, folks are beginning to realize that it is time to re-evaluate their spiritual lives in a search for hope and meaning in life.

Public evangelistic meetings are reporting high attendence. For example, in the Spring of 1994, evangelist Mark Finley of *It Is Written* conducted a meeting in Honolulu in which over 150 individuals were baptized.

In the Fall of 1993 church leaders and laymen from across North America met together for three days prior to the regular year-end business session for prayer, praise, worship, and evangelistic planning. Alfred McClure, NAD president, challenged the group to become pro-active in evangelism. Plans were then finalized for "Net '95," the most ambitious evangelistic venture ever undertaken in North America. The Spring of 1995 will find Mark Finley conducting a full evangelistic meeting in Chattanooga, Tennessee. It will be uplinked live via satellite and downlinked simultaneously to hundreds of churches across North America. This project has the potential of being the largest and most successful evangelistic outreach ever in this division. Thousands of volunteers will be needed to help in the implementation of this program.

The General Conference Trust Services department reports that a growing number of members are remembering the work of God in their estate planning. Many are arranging their affairs so that they see the results of their gifts during their lifetime.

The church is waking up! Great things are happening worldwide. Presently with so many doors opening our opportunities are ahead of our efforts. One of the most thrilling promises of the Bible is found in Romans 9:28, "For He will finish the work and cut it short in righteousness, because the Lord will make a short work upon the earth." Apparently as God sees our zeal and the fact that time is running out, He comes in and finishes the work Himself!

"The time will soon come when the Lord will take matters into His own hand; for He has appointed a day in which He will judge the world in righteousness by that man which He has ordained, and it will be demonstrated who is able to govern the heavens and the earth." *(Review and Herald,* Feb. 20, 1894)

"Let me tell you that the Lord will work in this last work in a manner very much out of the common order of things, and in a way that will be contrary to any human planning. . . God will use ways and means by which it will be seen that He is taking the reins in His own hands. The workers will be surprised by the simple means that He will use to bring about and perfect His work of righteousness." *(Evangelism,* p. 118)

Apparently, the outpouring of the Holy Spirit in "latter rain" proportions has the dual purpose of perfecting the characters of the saints and providing the power to "finish the work." Then the most exciting factor comes into play. Evidently, when God sees that time is running out and there is yet work to be done, He employs angels to do the work men should have done. "When divine power is combined with human effort, the work will spread like fire in the stubble. God will employ agencies whose origin man will be unable to discern; angels will do a work which men might have had the blessing of accomplishing, had they not neglected to answer the claims of God." *(Selected Messages,* vol. 1, p. 118)

We have actually been given a pen picture of the end-time work. Read it as a statement of intent by an enabling God. "As the gospel is proclaimed in its purity, men will be called from the plow and from the common commercial business vocations that largely occupy the mind and will be educated in connection with men of experience. As they learn to labor effectively, they will proclaim the truth with power. Through most wonderful workings of divine providence, mountains of difficulty will be removed and cast into the sea. The message that means so much to the dwellers upon the earth will be heard and understood. Men will know what is truth. Onward and still onward the work will advance until the whole earth shall have been warned, and then shall the end come." *(Prophets and Kings,* pp. 223, 224)

Realists look at the staggering number of people unwarned around the world and wonder how the work will ever be finished. Optimists say that God would not give us a task that is impossible to accomplish, and when we all work together in the power of God, that task will be completed. God says He wants us to be involved for our own good but that finally He will take the work into His own hands. He will use simple means to do the job; He will use the angels, and wonderful workings of divine providence will be used. The work will get done and right on time!

CHAPTER 20

Seconds to Midnight

T his book cannot tell you the exact day and hour of Christ's return. Only God knows that. But looking closely at what has been revealed certainly does point out just where we are in time.

The use of the number 2000 in this chapter and the book is only an approximate date, and from my study is a general termination point of the sixth millennium. Certainly Jesus could well come before the year 2000. Even if we could establish that year as the end of the sixth millennium, we are told in Scripture that the time of trouble at the end will be so severe that "unless those days were shortened, no flesh would be saved; but for the elect's sake those days will be shortened." (Matthew 24:22) In addition, Paul, quoting the gospel prophet Isaiah, says, "For He will finish the work and cut it short in righteousness, because the Lord will make a short work upon the earth." (Romans 9:28) And of course, as we saw earlier in the outline of Biblical chronology we cannot know with precision the actual number of years that have elapsed since the Creation. However, there is evidence enough to convince us that we are very near the end of the sixth millennium.

Adventists have been so concerned to avoid the appearance of date setting that some of our authors have downplayed the significance of what has been called "the 6,000-year theory." Of course it's no theory if you understand biblical principles and accept the evidence from Ellen White and other Adventist pioneers. As a minister and an attorney, I am convinced that the weight of evidence falls clearly on the general validity of this so-called theory and that we are in danger of throwing out the proverbial baby with the bathwater when we downplay this material. We have the biblical evidence and the affirmation of the Spirit of Prophecy. And we have the constant shout of last-day events that we are truly at the end of time.

We cannot, dare not, ignore the fact of Christ's <u>imminent</u> return. "Though no man knoweth the *day* and *hour* of His coming, <u>we are instructed and required to know when it is near.</u>" *(The Great Controversy,* p. 371)

It's hard for human beings to comprehend large blocks of time. Hundreds of years seem forever, and thousands are almost mythical. But we have the ability to measure time against our own short lifespan. And we do understand the basic proportion inherent in the face of a clock. Let's see if we can put the time question into meaningful visual form.

Let's take the face of a clock to portray the scope of history at a glance. We can start at Creation and end at the second coming of Christ. For the sake of illustration we will observe only the hour hand as it makes a full sweep around the clock from noon to midnight. The twelve hours from noon to midnight will equal 6,000 years. Accordingly, each hour represents 500 years of time and each minute represents 100 years. This will give us an everyday perspective of overall historical time and just where we might be.

Let's place some major events of Bible history on the clock. During the first 1,500 years time seems to move rather slowly. Remember that many of the men before the flood lived nearly 1,000 years. It's nearly 2:00 before the death of Adam at 930 years of age. And it's approximately 3:00 by the time of Noah and the flood. By 4:00 we come to the time of Abraham, and 5:00 is the approximate time for the Exodus. One hour later, 6:00, we are at the time of king David. At 7:00 we have advanced to the time of the prophet Daniel.

Ellen White makes an interesting statement regarding the first coming of Christ in regard to "the clock of time." "The prophecy of Daniel revealed the time of His advent, but not all rightly interpreted the message. Century after century passed away; the voices of the prophets ceased. The hand of the oppressor was heavy upon Israel, and many were ready to exclaim, 'The days are prolonged, and every vision faileth.' Ezekiel 12:22.

"But like the stars in the vast circuit of their appointed path, God's purposes know no haste and no delay. Through the symbols of the great darkness and the smoking furnace, God had revealed to Abraham the bondage of Israel in Egypt, and had declared that the time of their sojourning should be four hundred years. 'Afterward,' He said, 'shall they come out with great substance.' Gen. 15:14. Against that word, all the power of Pharaoh's proud empire battled in vain. On 'the selfsame day' appointed in the divine promise, 'it came to pass, that all the hosts of the Lord went out from the land of Egypt.' Exodus 12:41. <u>So in heaven's council the hour for the coming of Christ had been determined. When the great clock of time pointed to that hour, Jesus was born in Bethlehem.</u>" *(The Desire of Ages, p. 32)*

Everything Jesus did was right on time as we saw earlier in the book. But let's go back to our clock. Time is hurrying on. Christ's first advent has taken us to 8:00! By 9:00 we've come to the fall of Rome and the rise of the papal power. At 10:00—the equivalent of 1000 A.D.—we are at the mid-point in the Dark Ages. Eleven o'clock (1500 A.D.) is the beginning of the great Protestant Reformation. The beginning of "the time of the end," a date-point in prophecy, is approximately 11:58 p.m. The year is 1798 and we're two minutes till midnight. Then at 11:58:44 p.m. is the beginning of the Antitypical Day of Atonement—the Judgment (1844). Today this figurative clock is pointing at 11:59 plus! We are only seconds from midnight!

When you look at this clock chart, all of earth's history from the Creation to the second coming of Christ seems to fall into place. And yes, every one of the Bible's time prophecies fits on the clock as well.

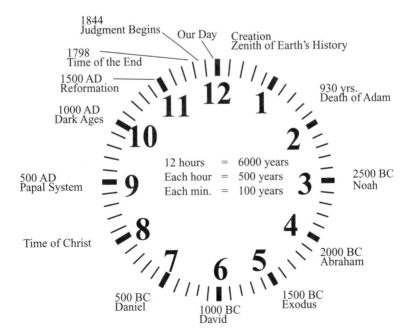

Now let's look on a linear scale to get a view of the whole picture from Creation to the beginning of "the Millennium." For this illustration let's assign seven inches of a ruler for 7,000 years. Each inch equals 1,000 years and each half inch equals 500 years.

A Parallel Between the Weekly Cycle and the Overall History of the Earth

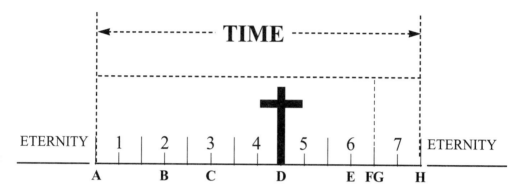

Events

  A. Creation and Fall of Man

  B. The Flood

  C. Exodus From Egypt

  D. Christ's Ministry

  E. Reformation

  F. Present day: You are here! The Friday Night of Earth's History

  G. Second Coming of Christ

  H. The Wicked Destroyed/The Earth Re-created

The Seven Millennial Periods

1–6. The working out of the plan of salvation.

  7. The Millennium–The earth rests, saints are in heaven with God. The earth is desolate.

Perhaps the significance of these illustrations can be summed up with the following statement. "By a thorough investigation of the prophecies we understand where we are in this world's history; and we know for a certainty that the second coming of Christ is near." *(Testimonies for the Church,* vol. 4, p. 592)

And from *Education,* page 178: "The history which the great I AM has marked out in His word, uniting link after link in the prophetic chain, from eternity in the past to eternity in the future, tells us where we are today in the procession of the ages, and what may be expected in the time to come."

The great clock of time continues to tick off the seconds on earth's final countdown. Our clock and our ruler are, of course, only devices to visualize where we are relative to known points. The "proof" is in the earlier chapters. They simply illustrate what has been discussed at some length in this book. We do not follow cunningly devised fables if we look to the more sure word of prophecy. Indications are clear that "time" is running out. Let's not be taken unawares by current or coming events.

CHAPTER 21

High Time

The focus of this book is to underscore the nearness of Christ's second coming. We are not date setting, but simply pointing out where we are in time. And for that we have clear instructions from the Spirit of Prophecy. "One saying of the Saviour must not be made to destroy another. Though no man knoweth the *day* nor the *hour* of His coming, we are instructed and required to know when it is near. We are further taught that to disregard His warning, and refuse or neglect to know when His advent is near, will be as fatal for us as it was for those who lived in the days of Noah not to know when the flood was coming." *(The Great Controversy,* p. 371)

The Lord's messenger to our day went on to say, "Thus it was shown that Scripture gives no warrant for men to remain in ignorance concerning the nearness of Christ's coming. But those who desired only an excuse to reject the truth closed their ears to this explanation, and the words, 'No man knoweth the day nor the hour' continued to be echoed by the bold scoffer and even by the professed minister of Christ." *(Ibid.,* p. 372)

"By a thorough investigation of the prophecies we understand where we are in this world's history; and we know for a certainty that the second coming of Christ is near." *(Testimonies,* vol. 4, p. 592) These words are certainly underscored by what we have reviewed in this book.

We know that the Lord's coming is near. What should we be doing about this knowledge? The apostle Paul has the answer. "And do this, knowing the time, that now it is high time to awake out of sleep; for now our salvation is nearer than when we first believed. The night is far spent, the day is at hand. Therefore let us cast off the works of darkness, and let us put on the armor of light. Let us walk properly, as in the day, not in revelry and drunkenness, not in licentiousness and lewdness, not in strife and envy. But put on the Lord Jesus Christ, and make no provision for the flesh, to fulfill its lusts." (Romans 13:11-14.)

It's high time we wake up and recognize that God is sending us warnings of His soon coming in the natural disasters occurring around us on a frequent basis. "The Lord is soon to come. In fire and flood and earthquake He is warning the inhabitants of this earth of His soon approach." *(Review and Herald,* May 24, 1906)

We have ignored the multiplying disasters around the world. Now they are striking here in the United States. The disasters are so common that we hardly recognize them for what they are. Hurricane Andrew, for example, was the worst natural disaster in U.S. history. It caused an estimated $30 billion in damage, destroyed or severely damaged more than 63,000 south-Florida homes, left nearly 300,000 people homeless, and bankrupted at least five insurance companies. Yet very few people lost their lives. The same thing could be said of the awesome Midwest floods in the Summer of 1993. Tremendous loss of material things but very little loss of life. It was repeated in the fires that destroyed so many expensive homes in southern California. *Newsweek,* Nov. 8, 1993, reported it this way, "The Santa Ana winds fanned more than a dozen fires, charring 720 buildings, 152,000 acres and causing at least $500 million in damage. Remarkably, no one was killed." Evidently, God, in His mercy, is sending warnings while at the same time sparing life. Need I say more? What about the Los Angeles earthquake in January of 1994? The list could go on and on.

When Jesus was asked by His disciples what it would be like at the end of time He answered, "And there will be signs in the sun, in the moon, and in the stars; and on the earth distress of nations, with perplexity, the sea and the waves roaring; men's hearts failing them from fear and the expectation of those things which are coming on the earth, for the powers of heaven will be shaken. Then they will see the Son of Man coming in a cloud with power and great glory." (Luke 21:25-27) Jesus speaks here not only of distress of nations, but also of perplexity. A closer look at this word, *perplexity,* will point out more clearly that He was describing our day. *Perplexity* appears nowhere else in the New Testament. The Greek word is *aporia.* Lexicographers state that it literally means "without a passage out." Or as we would say today, "No way out." In every direction there appears to be a dead end.

In economic matters nations face a very bleak picture indeed.

Apparently things will get a lot worse in the months ahead. Any number of NAFTA and GATT agreements can't disguise the national debt still hanging over our head, wish away rampant unemployment, salvage the trade wars, and prop up total economic collapse in much of the old Soviet bloc.

The AIDS scourge continues with no hope for those infected. Estimates are that 10,000,000 have died or are doomed worldwide. In addition, millions more are probably carrying the HIV virus which can be carried for up to three years before tests can detect it. The National Committee for the Prevention of AIDS reports that 70% of today's teenagers are sexually active with very little being done to prevent infection. Condom distribution not only doesn't work; it encourages the moral decline.

The so-called "war on poverty" that began in the sixties has made very little progress. Homelessness is on the increase. There is only one person working for every one who is drawing some form of welfare benefits. And over 20,000 American families declare bankruptcy every week.

Crime is quite literally out of control. As I write, it tops national polls as public concern number one. People are killed, kidnapped, and raped in broad daylight. In the Washington, D.C., area where I live, crime is so rampant that hundreds are killed every year. The mayor has petitioned the federal government for permission to use the National Guard to patrol the streets to keep some kind of order. Students are killing teachers. Crazed men are killing little children. Children are killing their parents.

With the much discussed breakdown of the family, Christian morality is being neither taught nor practiced by a large percentage of the population. Simple adultery, as bad as it is, is mild compared to what is practiced today. Immorality way beyond description is practiced— sadistic hedonism where victims are tortured and killed, open homosexuality in every level of society and even in religious organizations. The problem is compounded by the fact that this type of activity is photographed for distribution in movies and magazines. *U.S. News* reported (Nov. 22, 1993) that there could be up to 2,000,000 prostitutes in the U.S. with estimated *daily* expenditures on prostitution of $40,000,000.

The list of this type of thing could go on and on. Surely enough has been said.

"The conditions prevailing in society, and especially in the great cities of the nations, proclaim in thunder tones that the hour of God's judgment is come and that the end of all things earthly is at hand. We are standing on the threshold of the crisis of the ages." *(Prophets and Kings,* p. 278)

And now we see another most interesting phenomenon. Mystics, astrologers, and Eastern religions talk of the coming of a "messiah" by the year 2000. The New Agers say that we are now in the age of Pisces, and the year 2000 will usher in the age of Aquarius—the age of enlightenment and illumination. In addition, many Christians believe that Christ will return to earth to usher in the millennium of peace. Surely with much of the world in this frame of mind, the impersonation of Christ by the antichrist may well come in this decade.

So what time is it? It's high time to wake out of spiritual sleep—both ministers and laity—all of us. "Ministers should become Bible students. Are the truths which they handle mighty? Then they should seek to handle them skillfully. Their ideas should be clear and strong, and their spirits fervent, or they will weaken the force of the truth which they handle. By tamely presenting truth, merely repeating the theory without being stirred by it themselves, they can never convert men. If they should live as long as did Noah, their efforts would be without effect. Their love for souls must be intense and their zeal fervent. A listless, unfeeling manner of presenting the truth will never arouse men and women from their deathlike slumber. They must show by their manners, by their acts and words, and by their preaching and praying, that they believe Christ is at the door. Men and women are in the last hours of probation, and yet are careless and stupid, and ministers have no power to arouse them; they are asleep themselves. Sleeping preachers preaching to a sleeping people!" *(Testimonies for the Church,* vol. 2, p. 337)

Ellen White made this statement in an appeal to ministers. She later urged, "The return of Christ to our world will not be long delayed. Let this be the keynote of every message." *(Testimonies for the Church,* vol. 6, p. 406)

It seems that we have all been waiting a long time, and now it's the sleepiest part of the night. We are all in this together, so let's help to keep each other awake. I encourage you to pray for your pastors. Ask them to study and share with you. And I encourage pastors to study and preach the Word. It is an awesome responsibility to stand before people as a leader. May God help us all.

The Bible prophecies demand our attention. "We should dig deep and obtain the precious jewels that can be found in God's word. Christ says that 'the kingdom of heaven is like unto treasure hid in a field: the which when a man hath found, he hideth, and for joy thereof goeth and selleth all that he hath, and buyeth that field.' Matt. 13:44. Everything should be secondary compared with the Holy Writ." *(Manuscript Releases,* vol. 3, p. 92)

Jesus' longest recorded prayer, the entire chapter of John 17, is to His Father on behalf of the disciples and the believers right down to our day. Jesus' repeated plea was that His followers be "one." Unity is vital to success. Some well intended folks have felt that near the end it would be "every man for himself." But the counsel came back, "draw together." And it's the counsel for today, for us in the last moments of history.

"Some have advanced the thought that, as we near the close of time, every child of God will act independently of any religious organization. But I have been instructed by the Lord that in this work there is no such thing as every man's being independent. The stars of heaven are all under law, each influencing the other to do the will of God, yielding their common obedience to the law that controls their action. And, in order that the Lord's work may advance healthfully and solidly, His people must draw together." *(Testimonies for the Church,* vol. 9, p. 258)

So many things vie for our attention—worldly business, sports, fashion, amusements, television. Unfortunately, the primary focus of these areas is this world. God's Word counsels that we should set our affections on things above. "Do not love the world or the things in the world. If anyone loves the world, the love of the Father is not in him. For all that is in the world—the lust of the flesh, the lust of the eyes, and the pride of life—is not of the Father but is of the world. And the world is passing away, and the lust of it; but he who does the will of God abides forever." (1 John 2:15-17)

We are only pilgrims and strangers here. Those who seek God as their refuge and strength through the difficult times ahead will meet Him face-to-face very soon.

CHAPTER 22

Profile of the Saved

W e've looked again at the grand prophecies of the Bible. We've compared them with evidence in our day, and they hold true. I know, like me, you have a firm belief that the end of all things is at hand—that our Lord and Master, Jesus Christ, is coming very soon.

Even with this conviction one question remains. From such a world of sin and wickedness, who will be saved? Jesus, in His sermon on the mountain, tells us clearly such a thing will not happen naturally. He advised mankind, "Enter by the narrow gate; for wide is the gate and broad is the way that leads to destruction, and there are many who go in by it. Because narrow is the gate and difficult is the way which leads to life and there are few who find it." (Matthew 7:13, 14)

This passage clearly says that most people, unfortunately, will go with the crowd, follow the course of least resistance, and walk in the broad way—eventually to be lost—eternally. But there is also a group who search for the right way and walk in it, even though the way at times is difficult, and traveling companions few. They realize that this narrow, difficult way leads to life—eternal life. They do this for love of the Jesus they will meet at the end of the road. They see by faith that God has prepared a home for them the likes of which "Eye has not seen, nor ear heard, nor have entered into the heart of man the things which God has prepared for those who love Him." (I Corinthians 2:9)

I plan to be a part of that small "remnant" group, don't you? And I think it is important to identify the characteristics of that group.

It is clear from Scripture that many who claim to be looking forward to the Second Coming are, in fact, unprepared for it and will themselves be lost. These are described as those who are "at ease" in Zion and "put far off the day of doom." (Amos 6:1, 3) It is sad that any of us should be described that way. Unless we are prepared, the Lord's coming will not be a day of joy. "Woe to you who desire the day of the Lord! For what good is the day of the Lord to you? It will be darkness, and not light. It will be as though a man fled from a lion, and a bear met him; Or as though he went into the house, leaned his hand on the wall, and a serpent bit him. Is not the day of the Lord darkness, and not light? Is it not very dark, with no brightness in it?" (Amos 5:18-20)

The New Testament repeats the warning that many of those who profess to be waiting for the Second Coming will not be ready and will themselves be lost. Jesus' disciples, knowing that He would soon be leaving them, asked about signs of His coming. His answer covers two whole chapters in the Bible—Matthew 24 and 25. Matthew 24 deals with signs we will see in the world around us—wars, earthquakes, crime, etc. Very importantly, Matthew 25 deals with signs that we will see in the church! This chapter should always be included in our eschatological studies. Knowing the signs of the end as outlined in Matthew 24 and other places is one thing, but it is quite another to be ready—to be on the winning side of the parables of Matthew 25.

The parables of Matthew 25 are given for our generation. They contain the most awesome counsel and warning for us today. Each parable depicts God's people. Each ends with the judgment and the second coming of Jesus. Each involves service. Each shows the final rewards. And a most interesting fact is that in each case, those who are lost thought they would or should be saved.

The Ten Virgins parable emphasizes personal preparation for the Second Coming. The chapter in *Christ's Object Lessons* covering this parable is a must-read. There is much in it for us today.

The parable of the Talents lets us know what God expects us to do with the talents with which He has endowed us.

The third end-time parable, the Sheep and the Goats, tells us the basis upon which the judgment is meted out.

The time is late. Perhaps these messages from Jesus will speak to us in a positive way. We need to study them as never before.

"We are living in the most solemn period of this world's history. The destiny of earth's teeming multitudes is about to be decided. Our own future well-being and also the salvation of other souls depend upon the course which we now pursue. We need to be guided by the Spirit of truth. Every follower of Christ should earnestly inquire: 'Lord, what wilt Thou have me to do?' We need to humble ourselves before the Lord, with fasting and prayer, and to meditate much upon His word, especially upon the scenes of the judgment. We should now seek a deep and living experience in the things of God. We have not a moment to lose. Events of vital importance are taking place around us; we are on Satan's enchanted ground." *(The Great Controversy,* p. 601)

So what can we do to prepare? A study of God's Word reveals a number of basic characteristics of those who will be saved:

- They will know Jesus and trust Him fully.
- They will be filled with and transformed by the Holy Spirit.
- They will be sharing the gospel—the good news of grace and the glory of God.
- They will be liberal with God's cause in a self-sacrificing manner.
- Their lives will testify that this earth is not their home. They are watching and longing for the second coming of Jesus.

They will know Jesus and trust Him fully.

Remember, those who are lost—those left standing on the outside—hear the words, "Depart from Me, I don't know you." (Matt. 7:23; 25:12) Those that are saved know Him. They are fully surrendered to Jesus. They have internalized the words of I Corinthians 10:31, "Whether you eat or drink, or whatever you do, do all to the glory of God." Instead of selfishly saying, "I'll watch whatever I want to watch; I'll wear what I want to wear; I'll eat what I want to eat;" they will say, "Whatever brings glory to Your name, that's what I want to do." Their simple motto is, "If Jesus said it, I believe it, and that's good enough for me."

Daniel 11:32 tells us why knowing God is so important. "The people who know their God shall be strong, and carry out great exploits." And Paul adds in his letter to the Philippians, "I can do all things through Christ who strengthens me." (Phil. 4:19)

When Jesus returns, those who have developed a love relationship with Him will be thrilled. With excitement they will shout, "Behold, this is our God; We have waited for Him, and He will save us. This is the Lord; We have waited for Him; We will be glad and rejoice in His salvation." (Isaiah 25:9)

They will be filled and transformed by the Holy Spirit.

Many books have been written on this subject. I would especially recommend Leroy Froom's *The Coming of the Comforter.* All who study the work of the Holy Spirit quickly see two purposes for His work—

character development and equipping for service. This work is called by various terms such as pardon and power, transformation and empowerment, Calvary and Pentecost.

The bottom line is unless our lives are being transformed by the power of the Spirit and we are working for others with His power, we have not received the Spirit. Jesus was very direct in His statement to Nicodemus. "Most assuredly, I say to you unless one is born of water and the Spirit, he cannot enter the kingdom of God." (John 3:5) The Spirit's power is to do a work within us and through us. Both of these areas are gifts of Jesus. He gave His life for us at Calvary, and He promised the power of the Spirit, the Comforter, at Pentecost.

We have been told, "Time is very short, and all that is to be done must be done quickly. The angels are holding the four winds, and Satan is taking advantage of everyone who is not fully established in the truth. Every soul is to be tested. Every defect in the character, unless it is overcome by the help of God's Spirit, will become a sure means of destruction. I feel as never before the necessity for our people to be energized by the spirit of truth, for Satan's devices will ensnare every soul who has not made God his strength. The Lord has much work to be done; and if we do what He has appointed for us to do, He will work with our efforts." *(Testimonies for the Church, vol. 5, p. 573)*

A study of the final outpouring of God's Spirit quickly reveals that the greatest days for the church and its advancement of the gospel commission are just ahead. "The time has come when we must expect the Lord to do great things for us. Our efforts must not flag or weaken. We are to grow in grace and the knowledge of the Lord. Before the work is closed up and the sealing of God's people is finished, we shall receive the outpouring of the Spirit of God. Angels from heaven will be in our midst. The present is a fitting-up time for heaven when we must walk in full obedience to all the commands of God." *(Selected Messages, vol. 1, p. 111)*

The story of the ten virgins underscores the critical need of the Holy Spirit in the life. There is apparently no visible difference between those categorized as wise and foolish virgins. The class represented by the foolish virgins are not hypocrites. They believe the truth. They have even taught the truth! And they like to be with other believers. But they have not yielded themselves to the Holy Spirit's working in their own lives. In commenting on this story Ellen White states, "Without the Spirit of God a knowledge of His word is of no avail. The theory of truth, unaccompanied by the Holy Spirit, cannot quicken the soul or sanctify the heart. One may be familiar with the commands and promises of the Bible; but unless the Spirit of God sets the truth home, the character will not be transformed. <u>Without the enlightenment of the Spirit, men will not be able to distinguish truth from error, and they will fall under the masterful temptations of Satan.</u>" *(Christ's Object Lessons,* p. 408)

Perilous times are upon us. Times that will, if possible, deceive "the very elect" of God. Only by the power of God through His Holy Spirit can we discern the right way to go. It is therefore imperative that we be filled with and guided by His Spirit.

They will be sharing the gospel—the good news of grace and the glory of God.

A number of years ago while visiting in the home of a dear Christian lady she said to me, "I sure will be glad when they get the work finished so that we can all go to heaven." Her longing for heaven was admirable, but ignored the clear fact that God has ordained that each of us has a part in sharing the gospel with others. In fact, it is the exercise of witnessing that strengthens our spiritual muscles. "Those who reject the privilege of fellowship with Christ in service, reject the only training that imparts a fitness for participation with Him in His glory." *(Education,* p. 264)

After quoting Matthew 24:14 and the gospel commission from Mark, Chapter 16, Ellen White then asks, "In view of the command, can we educate our sons and daughters for a life of respectable conventionality, a life professedly Christian, but lacking His self-sacrifice, a life on which the verdict of Him who is truth must be, 'I know you not'?" *(Ibid.)*

Have you ever attended a banquet where your name is posted at the place you are to be seated? There is a slight sense of relief when you find your name and realize that you haven't been forgotten. On the other hand, it is quite embarrassing if you don't find your name. God has a place for us in heaven. He died to assure that. However, we are told that we also have a place here where we must use our God-given talents to His glory. "Not more surely is the place prepared for us in the heavenly mansions than is the special place designated on earth where we are to work for God." *(Christ's Object Lessons,* p. 327)

Someone has said, "There comes a time in the life of each individual Christian when he or she must assume some responsibility to actively evangelize the teeming millions of eternally lost souls or devise some means of justifying his lack of involvement to the Lord Jesus Christ."

You see, what is lacking in the church is not ability but availability. Ability is God's to supply; availability is ours to determine. Making yourself available to the Lord doesn't mean you're going to end up in a foreign land, but it does mean you will become available to such a possibility, and actively involve yourself in reaching the lost, involved in the plan the Lord has for you.

We need to start with the basics. The disciples were men who did what the Lord told them to do. They evangelized—shared the Good News—wherever they went. They knew that they were responsible to be faithful in sharing the gospel, not in winning souls. Not that they weren't interested in winning souls, but their priority was in being faithful to share the gospel. We must remember that only a relatively small group will respond to the gospel call and be saved, but all must hear so that they can make a decision.

The Bible teaches that some plant the seed, some water the seed, some get to harvest, but it's God that gives the increase. It's the Holy Spirit that converts the sinner.

Would you just be faithful at planting the seed? The strategy is so simple that we stumble on it. Some have suggested that since we are so near the end that it is too late for seed sowing and that there is time for harvest only. It is true that the end is very near. It is the purpose of this entire book to convey that message. However, I believe that many who will be saved have yet to hear the true message for the first time. They will of necessity have to ripen quickly. But that is God's problem. Let's at least give them a chance.

As the Lord allows you to bring someone to a commitment to God, get busy and disciple that person. Just share what you know about the Lord. Help that new Christian become a part of your local church. Encourage baptism and church membership, and don't stop working with them until they, too, are reaching out to others. This is the process of both planting and watering the seed.

In this process you may find that you are better at discipling than evangelizing. That is all right. Remember, the Lord gave us different gifts. Put your emphasis where your strengths are, but don't stop witnessing. By making yourself available, you will no doubt discover the Lord opening new doors of opportunity in your immediate neighborhood and even around the world. As you step through the open doors, don't forget to keep on doing the basics. Evangelize, disciple, plant, water, harvest—be faithful and available.

How many Christians do you know who are doing this? Your answer probably helps you see why the world is in such a mess. If every Adventist in the world began to follow the Lord's plan, the world would be evangelized very quickly. A warning would be given and a remnant quickly gathered for the Lord's return! There is nothing wrong with our plans, nothing wrong with the instructions, nothing wrong with our abilities. The problem is our availability.

As I mentioned earlier, there comes a time in the life of every individual Christian when he or she must assume some responsibility to actively evangelize the teeming millions of eternally lost souls or devise some means of justifying his lack of involvement to the Lord Jesus Christ. We have reached the time of decision. Please choose to get involved either by personal involvement or by whatever means you can. Throw away your list of excuses.

Ellen White made an appeal in *Acts of the Apostles* that is so fitting here. "It is a *fatal* mistake to suppose that the work of soul-saving depends alone upon the ministry. . . Hundreds, yea, thousands, who have heard the message of salvation, are still idlers in the market-place, when they might be engaged in some line of active service. To these Christ is saying, 'Why stand ye here all day idle?' and He adds, 'Go ye also into the vineyard.' Why is it that many more do not respond to the call? Is it because they think themselves excused in that they do not stand in the pulpit? Let them understand that there is a large work to be done outside the pulpit, by thousands of consecrated lay members.

"Long has God waited for the spirit of service to take possession of the whole church, so that every one shall be working for Him according to his ability. When the members of the church of God do their appointed work in the needy fields at home and abroad, in fulfillment of the gospel commission, the whole world will soon be warned, and the Lord Jesus will return to this earth with power and great glory." (pp. 110, 111)

What challenges we have been given through the messenger to the remnant. In the last volume of the *Testimonies for the Church* she stated, "Time is short, and our forces must be organized to do a larger work. Laborers are needed who comprehend the greatness of the work and who will engage in it, not for the wages they receive, but from a realization of the nearness of the end. The time demands greater efficiency and deeper consecration." (vol. 9, p. 27)

Each of us can stop and take inventory of our lives and determine whether or not we are currently headed in the right direction. Frankly, I am very optimistic about the future because we know how it will end and who wins! We have even been given a picture of how the work will be finished in one of the last chapters of *The Great Controversy*. We need to ensure that we are in this group described as carrying the final message to the world.

"Servants of God, with their faces lighted up and shining with holy consecration, will hasten from place to place to proclaim the message from heaven. By thousands of voices, all over the earth, the warning will be given. Miracles will be wrought, the sick will be healed, and signs and wonders will follow the believers. Satan also works with lying wonders, even bringing down fire from heaven in the sight of men. Revelation 13:13. Thus the inhabitants of the earth will be brought to take their stand.

"The message will be carried not so much by argument as by the deep conviction of the Spirit of God. The arguments have been presented. The seed has been sown, and now it will spring up and bear fruit. The publications distributed by missionary workers have exerted their influence, yet many whose minds were impressed have been prevented from fully comprehending the truth or from yielding obedience. Now the rays of light penetrate everywhere, the truth is seen in its clearness, and the honest children of God sever the bands which have held them. Family connections, church relations, are powerless to stay them now. Truth is more precious than all besides. Notwithstanding the agencies combined against the truth, a large number take their stand upon the Lord's side." *(The Great Controversy,* p. 612)

Praise the Lord! I want to be in that group of workers, don't you?

They will be liberal with God's cause.

We have already discussed the role of money and finances in the end-time setting. However, we need to emphasize again the importance of true stewardship principles in relation to our eternal well-being. The following few sentences will clearly set the tone for this section.

"The Lord tells every man that in the sight of God he is not the owner of what he possesses, but only a trustee . . . God will call you to account for your stewardship . . . Your accountability to Heaven should cause you to fear and tremble. <u>The decisions of the last day turn upon our practical benevolence.</u> Christ acknowledges every act of beneficence as done to Himself." *(Testimonies to Ministers,* pp. 399, 400)

We hear plenty of stewardship sermons from a text or two in Malachi, Chapter 3. But I recommend reading the entire chapter for yourself sometime. You will easily see that the setting is preparation for the <u>Second Coming.</u> Faithfulness in tithes and offerings will be a characteristic of those who are saved. This faithfulness does not come from a guilt complex or any effort to seek merit. It comes from a right relationship with Jesus.

Many have thought that the talents in the parable of Matthew, Chapter 25, are the gifts or abilities that we are given by God. We have inspired counsel regarding these talents. "I was shown that the parable of talents has not been fully understood. This important lesson was given to the disciples for the <u>benefit of Christians living in the last days.</u> And these talents do not represent merely the ability to preach and instruct from the word of God. <u>The parable applies to the temporal means which God has entrusted to His people</u> . . . God requires those who have possessions here, to put their money out to usury for Him—to put it into the cause to spread the truth." *(Testimonies for the Church,* vol. 1, p. 197)

I often ask myself the question, as I know others do, "What if?" For example, "<u>What</u> would happen <u>if</u> everyone was faithful in tithing?" Or, "<u>What</u> would happen <u>if</u> every family contributed offerings on a systematic basis to support the cause of God?" We know the answer, don't we?

"When all are faithful in giving back to God His own in tithes and offerings, the way will be opened for the world to hear the message for this time. <u>If</u> the hearts of God's people were filled with love for Christ, <u>if</u> every church member were thoroughly imbued with the spirit of self-sacrifice, <u>if</u> all manifested thorough earnestness, there would be no lack of funds for home or foreign missions. Our resources would be multiplied; a thousand doors of usefulness would be opened, and we should be invited to enter. Had the purpose of God been carried out by His people in giving to the world the message of mercy, Christ would, ere this, have come to the earth, and the saints would have received their welcome into the city of God." *(Testimonies for the Church,* vol. 6, p. 450)

If more people recognized how near we are to the end, there would be a lot of changes in lives. "Did they [God's professed people] but realize how near is the end of all work for the salvation of souls, they would sacrifice their possessions as freely as did the members of the early church. They would work for the advancement of God's cause as earnestly as worldly men labor to acquire riches. Tact and skill would be exercised, and earnest and unselfish labor put forth to acquire means, not to hoard, but to pour into the treasury of the Lord." *(Counsels on Stewardship,* p. 41) This statement has always intrigued me. I gather from it that some may even seek extra work in order to bring in more money, not to use on themselves, but rather to put it into the treasury of God.

Again, in this aspect of our lives as Christians we have been given a picture of what it will be like at the end. "In the last extremity before this work shall close, thousands will be cheerfully laid upon the altar. Men and women will feel it a blessed privilege to share in the work of preparing souls to stand in the great day of God, and they will give hundreds as readily as dollars are given now." *(Ibid.,* p. 40)

We are the <u>only</u> generation that have ever been asked of God to give everything for the cause of God. You understand, of course, that we will not be taking any of our money or possessions to heaven. In addition, "There is a time coming when commandment keepers can neither buy nor sell. Make haste to dig out your buried talents. If God has entrusted you with money, show yourselves faithful to your trust; unwrap your napkin, and send your talents to the exchangers, that when Christ shall come, He may receive His own with interest." *(Ibid.)*

Much is at stake in our financial readiness to serve God. "Lay all upon His altar—self, property, and all, a living sacrifice. It will take all to enter glory. Lay up for yourselves treasure in heaven, where no thief can approach or rust corrupt." *(Early Writings,* pp. 66, 67)

This earth is not their home.

We moved a lot when I was a boy. My father was in the logging business, and his work took us to every state in the West except Wyoming. Certain activities help us discern when someone is moving. Usually they begin by collecting a lot of strong boxes and packing material.   Then they begin to pack things. Frequently, they have a "moving sale," so they won't have to transport the things that they no longer use or are too difficult to move. Often when a family accepts a mission appointment where they will be gone from home and friends for as long as six years, it is a very traumatic time. Some have declined such calls just because of the emotional experience of parting with possessions and moving.

The Bible says that the Old Testament patriarchs "all died in faith," but they saw afar off by faith what God had prepared for them and "confessed that they were strangers and pilgrims on the earth." (Hebrews 11:13) In fact, we are told that Abraham lived in a tent to show that he was a foreigner. It has been said that twentieth-century Christians are the best disguised pilgrims in Christian history. In other words, if heaven is as great as we say it is, why are we spending so much time, effort, and money settling in down here?

If we really believe that we are pilgrims and that we are leaving this old world soon, we will live and act in a manner that is quite different than those around us who are not planning on moving to heaven. The world today is materialistic and unrestrained. God's people are giving and self-controlled. "We are pilgrims and strangers who are waiting, hoping, and praying for that blessed hope, the glorious appearing of our Lord and Saviour Jesus Christ. If we believe this and bring it into our practical life, what vigorous action would this faith and hope inspire; what fervent love one for another; what careful holy living for the glory of God; and in our respect for the recompense of the reward, what distinct lines of demarcation would be evidenced between us and the world." *(Evangelism,* p. 220)

There is no better role model for leaving this world than that of Noah. We sometimes speak glibly about Noah, safely insulated as we are by almost 4,500 years from the brutal ridicule he endured, the spending of all his money that preparation demanded, and the seemingly endless decades of work before "the end." To endure that for 120 years simply for the sake of faith is a classic example of true surrender; everything on the line—his whole future, his reputation, even his personal wealth—in exchange for something he couldn't even scientifically prove. There is nothing easy about such an experience. People may have questioned his sanity but never his belief and commitment. But he saved his family! Are we willing to make such a commitment? It will take just such a decision.

Nearly 2,000 years ago the cross of Christ cast a shadow across time. Thousands, yes millions, have joined His army. Now today we face the final showdown. A line is being drawn. Stepping across means total commitment. Years ago we were told that not one in twenty was ready for that commitment. God in His mercy has delayed His coming that more might be saved. But now time is running out.

EATD-8

This book has shown how time is running out and how the forces of evil are building up around us for the last great conflict. It's time for our final decision. Make that decision right now, if you haven't already. Make a decision that says, "Whatever it takes, I want to be on God's side"; a commitment that says, "I want to know Jesus and trust Him fully; I want to be filled with and transformed by His Spirit; I want to be involved in sharing the gospel with others; I want to recognize that all my possessions are God's property, and I want to use them to advance His kingdom; I want my life to testify that this world is not my home."

To sum it all up, I want to hear the words of Jesus when He calls my name, "Well done, good and faithful servant. Enter into the joy of your Lord." I am making my personal commitment again as I write these last lines. If we were together at this moment we could pray, "Lord, please honor our commitment. Strengthen our decision. Equip us to do the job before us. Keep us faithful. Help us to represent the good news of the gospel and Your soon coming to our loved ones, our children, our parents, our spouses, our brothers and sisters, our neighbors, our former church members. We have made a decision today to stand with You through the days ahead. We know this is what we want to do. We want to meet You soon in the clouds of heaven. Even so come, Lord Jesus, and in His holy name, Amen."

APPENDIX

CHAPTER 1

A conceptual model or visual description of the 7,000-year time line looks like this: It depicts seven 1,000-year periods flanked on either end by eternity past and eternity future. I will use this chart as an illustration throughout the balance of the book to show how our more established traditional prophetic interpretations and current events support the 7,000-year time line. Remember this chart is not intended to set a date for the second coming of Christ. Its only purpose is to illustrate the concept and to point out that we are very near the end.

The Great Week of Time
The Antitypical Sabbatical Cycle

-------------------------- 7000 years-------------------------->

------------------- 6000 years --------------------->

---------- 4000 years ------------->----2000 years --->- 1000 yrs -

| Eternity past | | | | B.C. | A.D. | | millennium -earth desolate -saints in heaven | Eternity future |

| 1 | 2 | 3 | 4 | 5 | 6 | 7 |

Due to space limitations in a book of this size, it will not be possible to develop each of the time prophecies and their traditional Adventist interpretations, the integrity of which I personally accept and teach. For this book, then, I will assume that the reader has already studied and accepted the evidence for the establishment of such dates as 457 B.C., 27 A.D., 1798, and 1844.

Today we need wisdom to understand the times in which we live and the answers to the questions that perplex us. I believe God has the answers: "If any of you lack wisdom let him ask of God . . . and it shall be given him." (James 1:5)

It is wisdom that allows us to see that house payments, domestic troubles, car problems, and taxes are really not what life is all about. These things are only incidentals.

Many people just get in a routine and live the same week and year over and over again. They end up planning just for the weekends and when they can retire at age sixty-five, but not really understanding the times. Wisdom allows us to back up and see the big picture—to see life from God's point of view; to weigh our actions and decisions in the light of eternity; to see that God has allotted roughly 6,000 years for the great controversy to run its course—the last two hundred years of which would be called the "time of the end." (See the 1260 day/year prophecy.) Wisdom allows us to see that today we are living in the last days of the time of the end. Time for this earth will not go on for ever and ever.

CHAPTER 2

"There is a class of persons who are not following the example of Christ in keeping God's law, yet they claim to be holy. They are ready to appropriate the promises of God without fulfilling the conditions upon which they are given. But their faith has no foundation; it is like sliding sand. There is another class who see the claims of the law of God, and, although it involves a cross, they choose the path of obedience, coming out and separating themselves from the world. They do not consult convenience, nor shrink from accepting the truth for fear of reproach. They step out from the path of transgression, and place their feet in the way of God's commandments. The promises of God, which are given on condition of obedience, are for those who walk in the light of His holy word. Those who do his will may claim all the benefits the Lord has promised. The obedient do not simply cry, 'Believe, all you have to do is believe Christ;' but their faith is like Noah's and Abraham's, which led them to keep the commandments. They follow the example of Christ, they listen and wait to catch every word of direction from the Captain of their salvation. They respond to the voice that says, 'This is the way, walk ye in it.' Every step that Noah and Abraham took in obedience to God's word was a step of victory. A 'Thus saith the Lord' fortified Noah in doing his work of warning the world. The testimony in regard to Noah is, 'And Noah did according to all that the Lord commanded him.' (Gen. 6:22) The path of obedience is the path in which our safety lies; for it is the willing and obedient that shall eat the good of the land. <u>If we keep the commandments of God, we may claim His recorded promises in all their fullness</u>. Many feel so unworthy that like the poor publican they dare not lift up so much as their eyes to heaven. They should encourage faith. We may have an intelligent faith; we may not only say we believe, but we may in meekness and confidence be able to define what we believe, and why we believe as we do. We should exercise living faith, not a blind credulity. <u>All heaven is at the command of those who keep the commandments of God and have the faith of Jesus</u>." (*Signs of the Times*, March 31, 1890)

CHAPTER 3

"Our ultimate goal is to see government become a friend of the family again. The Coalition favors school choice, lower taxes on families, tougher laws against crime and drugs, a Balanced Budget Amendment, religious liberty, and protection of innocent unborn human life.

"The Christian Coalition also serves as a permanent presence on the American political landscape representing the views of churchgoing families before the U.S. Congress, state legislatures, and local bodies. It maintains a grassroots network of forty-two state affiliates (nineteen with full-time staff) and 872 local chapters in all fifty states, connected by a sophisticated communications network of computers, phone banks, telephone trees, direct mail, and fax machines.

"In just three years, the Coalition's membership has skyrocketed from 57,000 in 1990 to 450,000 today. It has an additional 350,000 grassroots activists on its national mailing list, and 1.6 million households on its pro-family voter database.

"The coalition informs citizens how their elected representatives vote on issues affecting the family. Its Congressional Scorecard will reach 10 million households this year, informing Christians how their senators and members of Congress voted on term limits, taxes, education, abortion, and pork-barrel spending.

"The Christian Coalition conducts nonpartisan voter registration drives and distributes nonpartisan educational voter guides. In 1992 the Coalition distributed 40,000,000 voter guides through 60,000 churches nationwide, and helped generate the largest turnout of evangelical voters in history.

"The results have been remarkable. In 1992 an estimated 500 pro-family candidates ran for school board, city counsel, and state legislatures, and 40% won.

"In May, 1993, the Coalition distributed 500,000 voter guides in cooperation with minority groups and the Catholic Archdiocese in the New York City school board races. An estimated 63% of pro-family candidates won, and conservatives gained majorities in ten of thirty-two school districts.

"Now regarded by friends and critics alike as one of the most effective grassroots citizen organizations in America today, Christian Coalition is not resting on its laurels. It plans to double its dues-paying membership to 1,000,000 by the end of the decade, identify 10,000,000 pro-family voters on computer, and have precinct coordinators in each of America's 175,000 precincts. [If the CC is successful in establishing their precinct coordinator goal they will have achieved a level of political organization greater than either the Republican or Democratic Parties national organizations.]

"Its immediate goals are to oppose job-killing mandates on small business, taxpayer-funding of elective abortion under a national health care plan, and to see a turnout of 30,000,000 evangelical and pro-family Roman Catholic voters in the 1994 elections. For friends of the family, the future is bright and the tide is turning." (*Christian Coalition Road to Victory '93 Official Program*, p. 8)

CHAPTER 4

Attorney Morland's account of the April 1655 massacre by the

Catholic soldiers tends to get too graphic and gruesome for general reading so I have placed just a sample here in the Appendix. "A certain woman of St. Giovanni, whose name was Martha Constantin, the wife of Facopo Barral, after she had seen several others before her most cruelly put to death, was her self first ravisht [raped], and then had her breasts cut off, and likewise part of her privities, by some of the soldiers, who also carried the same to Marcel in Piemont, where they fried them, and fet them before some other of their comrades." (Morland, p. 340) "A certain man of Trassiniere, servant of Facopo Michalino of Bebio, being taken prisoner the 8th of May, received divers stabs with a dagger in the sole of his feet, and in his ears, by the hands of one Gulielmo Roche a famous massacrer of Lucerna, and another called Mandolin, who afterwards cut off his privy members, and then applied a burning candle to the wound, frying it with the flame thereof, that so the bloud might be stopt, and the torments of that miserable creature prolonged; this being done to their mindes, they tore off his nayls with hot pincers, to try if they could by any means force him to renounce his religion. But when nothing would do, they tied one of his legs to the marquess of Lucerna's mule, and so dragg'd him along the streets, till such time as he had almost ended his painful life, and then binding his head about with a cord, they strained and twisted the same with a staff so hard, that it made his eys and brains drop out of his head; in the end, when they had sufficiently satiated their appetites with all the variety of cruelties they could well devise, they cast the dead carkass into the river." *(Ibid.,* p. 341)

Apostolic Succession

"Early Protestant creeds unanimously call the Pope Antichrist—not only because of Rome's heresies but because the lives of many popes exemplified Antichrist's evil. More than one Pope vacated 'Peter's throne' when killed by a furious husband who caught him in bed with his wife. Even Catholic historians admit that many of the popes were among the most inhuman monsters to walk this earth. In *Vicars of Christ,* Jesuit Peter de Rosa reminds us that Pope after Pope engaged habitually on a grand scale in wholesale mayhem and murder, pillage, rape, incest, simony (the buying or selling of a church office), and corruption of the worst sort. Their evil lives are a blot upon the pages of history. It is a travesty to refer to such shameless perverts and master criminals as 'His Holiness' or 'Vicar of Christ,' as they *all* are in official Roman Catholic dogma and documents.

"Even if the popes had all been paragons of virtue, it would still be a mockery to claim that they represent an unbroken chain of 'apostolic succession' back to Peter. Such a concept is unknown in the New Testament. And even if it were, it would have been necessary for each 'Pope,' as the possessor of an authority allegedly passed down from Peter, to have passed it on personally to his successor. Yet the popes did not choose their successors (and still do not to this day), much less lay hands upon and pass on any authority to them. It became the custom for the popes to be voted in by the populace of Rome—a populace which had its own selfish reasons for desiring one candidate above another. Such a majority vote could hardly be called 'apostolic succession' and in fact is not acceptable by Rome today. Some popes were deposed by angry mobs in protest of their unbearable evil. Some were installed and/or deposed by kings and emperors. Political expediency along with the wealth and influence of the candidate as often as not determined who would be Pope. 'Apostolic succession' indeed!" (Dave Hunt, *Global Peace and the Rise of Antichrist*, pp. 108, 109)

CHAPTER 5

"Holy Alliance"

"Only President Ronald Reagan and Pope John Paul II were present in the Vatican Library on Monday, June 7, 1982. It was the first time the two had met, and they talked for 50 minutes. . . In that meeting, Reagan and the Pope agreed to undertake a clandestine campaign to hasten the dissolution of the communist empire. Declares Richard Allen, Reagan's first National Security Adviser, 'This was one of the greatest secret alliances of all time.'

"The operation was focused on Poland. . .

"Until Solidarity's legal status was restored in 1989, it flourished underground, supplied, nurtured, and advised largely by the network established under the auspices of Reagan and John Paul II. Tons of equipment—fax machines (the first in Poland), printing presses, transmitters, telephones, shortwave radios, video cameras, photocopiers, telex machines, computers, word processors—were smuggled into Poland via channels established by priests and American agents and representatives of the AFL-CIO and European labor movements. Money for the banned union came from CIA funds, the National Endowment for Democracy, secret accounts in the Vatican, and Western trade unions."

"According to U.S. intelligence sources, the Pope had already advised Walesa through church channels to keep his movement operating underground, and to pass the word to Solidarity's 10 million members not to go into the streets and risk provoking Warsaw Pact intervention or civil war with Polish security forces. Because the communists had cut the direct phone lines between Poland and the Vatican, John Paul II communicated with Jozef Cardinal Glemp in Warsaw via radio. He also dispatched his envoys to Poland to report on the situation. 'The Vatican's information was absolutely better and quicker than ours in every respect,' says Haig. 'Though we had some excellent sources of our own, our information was taking too long to filter through the intelligence bureaucracy.'

The Catholic Team

"The key Administration players were all devout Roman Catholics—CIA Chief William Casey, [National Security Advisor, Richard] Allen, [Reagan's second National Security Advisor, Judge William] Clark, [Secretary of State, Alexander] Haig, [U.S. Ambassador at large, Vernon] Walters and William Wilson, Reagan's first ambassador to the Vatican. They regarded the U.S.-Vatican relationship as a holy alliance: the moral force of the Pope and the teachings of their church combined with their fierce anticommunism and their notion of American democracy. Yet the mission would have been impossible without the full support of Reagan, who believed fervently in both the benefits and the practical applications of Washington's relationship with the Vatican. One of his earliest goals as President, Reagan says, was to recognize the Vatican as a state 'and make them an ally.'

How the Diplomacy Worked

"Meanwhile, in Washington a close relationship developed between Casey, Clark and Archbishop Laghi (the Pope's ambassador to the U.S.). 'Casey and I dropped into his [Laghi's] residence early mornings during critical times to gather his comments and counsel,' says Clark. 'We'd have breakfast and coffee and discuss what was being done in Poland. I'd speak to him frequently on the phone, and he would be in touch with the Pope.' Says Laghi: 'They liked good cappuccino. Occasionally we might talk about Central America or the church's position on birth control. But usually the subject was Poland.

"'Almost everything having to do with Poland was handled outside of normal State Department channels and would go through Casey and Clark,' says Robert McFarlane, who served as a deputy to both Clark and Haig and later as National Security Adviser to the President. 'I knew that they were meeting with Pio Laghi, and that Pio Laghi had been to see the President, but Clark would never tell me what the substance of the discussions was.'

"On at least six occasions Laghi came to the White House and met with Clark or the President; each time, he entered the White House through the southwest gate in order to avoid reporters. 'By keeping in such close touch, we did not cross lines,' says Laghi. 'My role was primarily to facilitate meetings between Walters and the Holy Father. The Holy Father knew his people. It was a very complex situation—how to insist on human rights, on religious freedom, and keep Solidarity alive without provoking the communist authorities further. But I told Vernon [Walters], "Listen to the Holy Father. We have 2,000 years' experience at this."'"

Strategy and Results

"'The Administration plugged into the church across the board,' observes Derwinski, now Secretary of Veterans Affairs. 'Not just through the church hierarchy but through individual churches and bishops. Monsignor Bronislaw Dabrowski, a deputy to Cardinal Glemp, came to us often to tell us what was needed: he would meet with me, with Casey, the NSC and sometimes with Walters.' John Cardinal Krol of Philadelphia, whose father was born in Poland, was the American churchman closest to the Pope. He frequently met with Casey to discuss support for Solidarity and covert operations, according to CIA sources and Derwinski. 'Krol hit it off very well with President Reagan and was a source of constant advice and contact,' says Derwinski. 'Often he was the one Casey or Clark went to, the one who really understood the situation.'

"By 1985 it was apparent that the Polish government's campaign to suppress Solidarity had failed. According to a report by Adrian Karatnycky, who helped organize the AFL-CIO's assistance to Solidarity, there were more than 400 underground periodicals appearing in Poland, some with a circulation that exceeded 30,000. Books and pamphlets challenging the authority of the communist government were printed by the thousands. Comic books for children recast Polish fables and legends, with Jaruzelski pictured as the villain, communism as the red dragon and Walesa as the heroic knight. In church basements and homes, millions of viewers watched documentary videos produced and screened on the equipment smuggled into the country.

"With clandestine broadcasting equipment supplied by the CIA and the AFL-CIO, Solidarity regularly broke into the government's radio programming, often with a message 'Solidarity lives!' or 'Resist!' Armed with a transmitter supplied by the CIA through church channels, Solidarity interrupted television programming with both audio and visual messages, including calls for strikes and demonstrations. 'There was a great moment at the half time of the national soccer championship,' says a Vatican official. 'Just as the whistle sounded for the half, a "SOLIDARITY LIVES!" banner went up on the screen and a tape came on calling for resistance. What was particularly ingenious was waiting for the half-time break; had the interruption come during actual soccer play, it could have alienated people.' As Brzezinski sums it up, 'This was the first time that communist police suppression didn't succeed.'

" 'Nobody believed the collapse of communism would happen this fast nor on this timetable,' says a cardinal who is one of the Pope's closest aides. 'But in their first meeting, the Holy Father and the President committed themselves and the institutions of the church and America to such a goal. And from that day, the focus was to bring it about in Poland.'

"Step by reluctant step, the Soviets and the communist government of Poland bowed to the moral, economic and political pressure imposed by the Pope and the President. Jails were emptied, Walesa's trial on charges of slandering state officials was abandoned, the Polish communist party turned fratricidal, and the country's economy collapsed in a haze of strikes and demonstrations and sanctions.

"On Feb. 19, 1987, after Warsaw had pledged to open a dialogue with the church, Reagan lifted U.S. sanctions. Four months later, Pope John Paul II was cheered by millions of his countrymen as he traveled across Poland demanding human rights and praising Solidarity. [Read all about it in *Keys of This Blood*.] In July, 1988, Gorbachev visited Warsaw and signaled Moscow's recognition that the government would not rule without Solidarity's cooperation. On April 15, 1989, the two sides signed agreements legalizing Solidarity and calling for open parliamentary elections in June. In December, 1990, nine years after he was arrested and his labor union banned, Lech Walesa became President of Poland." (These excerpts were taken from "The Holy Alliance," *Time*, Feb. 24, 1992—a full eight-page investigative report.)

CHAPTER 6

"Canadian Catholic Bishop Hubert P. O'Connor of Prince George, B. C., was charged by police with six sex-related assaults on females, all over 18 at the time, while he was the head of a native residential school in the mid-1960s. The 62-year-old prelate is the highest-ranking Catholic Church leader to be charged with such offenses in Canada. In an open letter, he denied the charges, saying, never in his life did he 'sexually abuse any child, be it male or female.' [Note, however, that the charge was assault against women over 18.] His lawyer said he would plead not guilty to charges of rape and gross indecency. Priest Harold McIntee, 60, a former superintendent at the now-closed school in Williams Lake, was released on parole in October after serving 16 months of a two-year sentence for a 1988 conviction on charges of repeatedly abusing 17 native boys. Another priest in the order that ran the school, Oblates of Mary Immaculate, is awaiting trial on charges of sexually abusing 5 boys. Canada's bishops recently announced plans to hold a national conference to decide how to respond to calls for a public inquiry into allegations of sexual, emotional, and physical abuse at church residential schools across the country.

". . . In the aftermath of a sex scandal involving priests in Newfoundland, Pope John Paul II appointed Bishop James H. MacDonald of Prince Edward Island to replace Archbishop Alphonsus L. Penney of Newfoundland, who resigned last summer. Penney saw more than 20 of his priests, former priests, and others charged with or convicted of sexually abusing boys over a 30-month period (*NIRR* 7/30/90.) An inquiry led by former Newfoundland Lt. Gov. Gordon Winter, an Anglican, estimated that as many as one out of every three priests in Newfoundland may be homosexual. The panel said church officials had heard rumors, reports, or formal accusations of misconduct but didn't halt the abuse. It said Penney let the problem escalate. In his letter asking to be relieved of his duties, Penney accepted responsibility for the scandal." (*National & International Religion Report*, Feb. 11, 1991)

The Atlanta *Constitution* gave front-page coverage on May 6, 1988, to the installation of Archbishop Eugene A. Marino as Atlanta's new archbishop. "In a two hour ceremony filled with colorful church pageantry, diverse religious music, and joyful expressions of welcome, Atlanta's Roman Catholics met their new archbishop Thursday.

"In accepting the office as head of North Georgia's 156,000 Catholics, Eugene A. Marino became the highest ranking black Roman Catholic in the United States."

"The Atlanta Civic Center, filled to its 4,000 plus capacity, thundered with applause as Marino entered behind a procession of 800 white-robed clergymen, including almost 100 bishops. The Fox theater, also with a 4,000-plus capacity, filled with the overflow crowd who watched the service on closed-circuit television. The service was also carried live on local television and nationally on Catholic cable television.

"As Marino reached the stage, removed his miter, and kissed the altar, the audience applauded again. Archbishop Pio Laghi, personal representative of Pope John Paul II in the United States, who presided over the celebration Mass, remarked on the number of clergy present including 'so many bishops.'

"'That means that the selection made by the Holy Father of Bishop Marino as the new archbishop of Atlanta is the right one,' he said.

"The crowd greeted the remark with a standing ovation.

"As papal representative, Laghi asked Marino, 'Are you willing to accept this archdiocese in the tradition of the apostolic faith of our Holy Mother, the church?'

"In his first words before the crowd, Marino replied in a clear voice bearing the soft Southern tones of his Mississippi roots, 'With faith in our Lord, Jesus Christ, and trusting in His merciful assistance, I do accept the pastoral care of the people of God in the Archdiocese of Atlanta. May God give me the grace to worthily lead His people in worship, faithfully teach them His holy word, and guide them with a shepherd's care.'

"Laghi then presented Marino his crosier, the pastoral staff derived from the shepherd's crook, and led him to the cathedral, the chair that symbolizes his authority as archbishop."

Now why would we be interested in the details of this papal installation in Atlanta? For several reasons: (1) to show the outward pageantry and wonderment displayed by the Roman Catholic Church on such occasions; (2) to show that the Roman Catholic Ambassador to the United States also represents the pope in church matters. Indeed this Ambassador is "diverse from his fellows"; also, (3) to show that despite the outward show, behind the scenes there is within the clergy a tremendous amount of immorality. Two years later Marino was removed from his position, because shortly after he was installed as archbishop, he became involved in an affair with 27-year-old layworker Vicki Long. She now says that Marino seduced her after she came to him seeking counsel for sexual abuse she had suffered (presumably from another Catholic priest, Michael Woods, who confessed to his congregation that he had an 'intimate' relationship with Ms. Long). Apparently, Marino would have continued this illicit affair with Long on a perpetual basis, because he did not confess it until it was disclosed by a third party. The man who took Marino's place said in a news conference, "The church learned of the affair in mid-April from an unnamed source, and the prelate confirmed the allegation."   This report goes on to say that both Woods and Marino have paid Vicki Long money on several occasions for "medical and other needs."

The incidents listed above brought the following comment: " 'Certainly priests are vulnerable from the inside because of their own sexual drives and from the outside because they become very attractive sexual targets,' said A.W. Richard Sipe, a former Benediction monk now practicing psychotherapy in Baltimore. He will publish a 25-year study next month concluding that half of all priests break celibacy vows." (*National & International Religion Report*, Aug. 13, 1990)

This type of activity is not just a list of isolated incidents. We could go on to talk about "Father" Porter who has just been convicted of molesting at least twenty-two young boys who are now adults. He leaves a legacy of a lifetime of violations and abuse. There is Archbishop Robert Sanchez of New Mexico who has just admitted to sexually abusing teenage girls during his "ministry" in the Southwest. (*NIRR*, March 22, 1993)   And now there is even a case of a man claiming he got AIDS from his priest. "After a 20-year relationship, Thomas Perea is suing his former Catholic priest for transmitting HIV to him. Named in the suit are retired priest Delbert Blong, 67, and the Diocese of Pueblo (CO), which Perea says should have known about the abuse. The priest-parishioner relationship began in 1971. Perea said Blong took advantage of his emotional distress as a confused 15-year-old, and sexually molested him. Perea said he broke off his involvement with Blong last year. He said that after seeing a television show featuring members of the Chicago-based Survivors Network for Those Abused by Priests, or SNAP, he came to see himself as a victim. . . Blong, who is also HIV-positive, admitted to the *Denver Post* that his sexual relationship with Perea was 'very wrong.'" (*Ibid.*, Sept. 20, 1993)

"Some published estimates suggest that about 100 of the Catholic Church's 188 U.S. dioceses have had such [sexual abuse] cases, and that the church has had to pay as much as $400 million to settle damage suits arising from them." (*NIRR*, June 29, 1992)

CHAPTER 7

"My brother, my sister, you cannot be a Christian and cherish at the same time a spirit of covetousness. You can not be a Christian and yet not be putting forth effort to win souls for Jesus. When you hear that there are thousands upon thousands who are in the darkness of error and superstition, knowing not the things that are coming upon the earth, how can you enjoy the truth and remain at ease? Do you feel that the little you can do will be so inadequate to the demand that you might as well do nothing? If each one will do what he can, God will bless the effort, and the treasury will be supplied with funds. If you were perishing from cold and hunger, would you call one your friend who refused even to attempt to relieve you? Think of the multitudes in foreign lands who are perishing for want of the bread of life; and remember that Christ identifies His interests with the interests of these needy ones. 'Inasmuch,' He says, 'as ye did it not to one of the least of these, ye did it not to me.'" (*Review and Herald*, Oct. 5, 1886)

CHAPTER 10

The series of six *Review and Herald* articles authored by Andrews carried the title "**THE GREAT WEEK OF TIME or THE PERIOD OF SEVEN THOUSAND YEARS DEVOTED TO THE PROBATION AND THE JUDGMENT OF MANKIND.**" We are not talking here about a casual mention in passing while addressing another subject. Andrews' study consisted of six full articles directly on this topic. I have reproduced below the entire copy of the first article from the *Review and Herald*, July 17, 1883, which was printed under the title listed above.

"The day of Judgment was appointed before the creation of our world. It was appointed before the rebellion of Satan and his angels; for when they had sinned, they were not immediately judged and consigned to punishment, but were reserved to the day of judgment to be punished. Jude 6; II Pet. 2:4.

"It is evident, therefore, that when God created the angels, He appointed a day of Judgment. It was necessary that such a day should be appointed when God first created intelligent beings; for the angels though innocent, were placed upon probation, and when that probation should end, the case must be decided whether they had been faithful or unfaithful in the trial through which they had passed. A day of Judgment must therefore have been appointed to mark the close of their period of probation; and it is evidently for this reason that they were not punished as soon as they had sinned, but have been allowed to go on in sin, and will be allowed thus to go on during all the period which must elapse before the day of Judgment.

"That day of Judgment must therefore have been appointed as early as the creation of the angels, for they were made amenable to it; otherwise they could not have been reserved to its decision before being punished. But the angels were in existence when God created our earth (Job 38:4-7), and therefore the day of Judgment was appointed before the creation of our earth and of the human race. And so the day of Judgment, being fixed before the sin of man, comes neither earlier nor later in consequence of that sin.

"When God created man, He placed him upon probation as He had previously placed the angels. After a brief period, man sinned against God, and brought upon himself the sentence of death. But because there were some mitigating circumstances in the case of Adam, for he did not sin against so great light as did the angels, God saw fit to give to man a second probation,—a mercy which was not extended to the angels.

"We know that this second probation of the human race will end at the day of Judgment, so that man will be judged at the time originally appointed for the judgment of the angels. And we have reason to believe that if the human race had not sinned against God, the probation under which man was first placed would have terminated at the same time that his second probation will terminate; namely, at the day of Judgment. His first probation was to determine the question whether he would be faithful to God in persevering his innocence; his second probation is under circumstances much more difficult, for he must recover his lost innocence, and in the same trial must prove his fidelity.

"When God created our earth, He indicated the period of time which must elapse before the day of Judgment. He employed six days in the work of creation; on the seventh day He rested from all His work. He sanctified the seventh day to be an everlasting memorial of the work of creation. But it appears that God designed by the first seven days of time to indicate the period assigned to the probation and judgment of mankind.

"St. Peter says that one day is with the Lord as a thousand years, and a thousand years as one day. II Pet. 3:8. By this we think he meant, not simply that the day of Judgment will occupy the period of 1,000 years, though this fact seems to be revealed in Rev. 20, in what is said of the two resurrections, but we think St. Peter also signified by it that the period devoted to the history of man before the day of Judgment, was also indicated by the days that God employed in the work of creation. We think, therefore, that at the end of 6,000 years from creation, the day of Judgment will commence, and that that day will last for the period of 1,000 years.

"Thus we have for the probation and judgment of mankind a great week of time,—the period of 7,000 years. This period commenced at creation, when God spake the word which called the elements into existence, and it will end with the destruction of the wicked in the lake of fire. Then God will create new heavens and new earth, which will remain through endless ages the eternal abode of those who have passed the period of their probation, and have been approved in the day of Judgment. Before the commencement of this great week of time, infinite ages had elapsed during all of which God had existed. And after the expiration of this great week, the righteous will enter with Christ upon a kingdom that cannot be moved and that shall never end. Thus the period of 7,000 years is cut off from the eternity of the past and from the eternity of the future, and assigned to the probation and the judgment of mankind.

"It has been the faith of the most eminent servants of God, not only during the entire gospel dispensation but also during some hundred years previous to Christ's first advent, that the period of 6,000 years from the creation would extend to the day of Judgment. And we think that the most careful study of the chronology of the Bible and of the prophetic periods will strongly confirm this view. Though the two great prophetic periods of Daniel 8 and 12 do not mark the exact time of Christ's coming, they evidently terminate not far from that event, and we shall find on examination that if the age of the world at the dates of the commencement of these two periods be added to the periods themselves, we shall have in each case very nearly the sum of 6,000 years.

"We shall have occasion to speak at some length on this point hereafter, and we shall also have occasion to speak of the sabbatical year and the year of jubilee, in Lev. 25, as typifying the great week of 7,000 years. We propose to trace the history of the world during each of the periods of 1,000 years down to the great day of Judgment, or final thousand years, which elapses between the resurrection of the righteous and that of the wicked. We invite all of our readers to carefully study this series of articles on this subject which the present article is designed to introduce"

(Signed) J. N. A.

So there you have it—the full text of the first article. The emphasis was added by this author, but the text is word for word. Articles two-five in the Andrews' series simply trace the events down through time during each of the successive 1,000-year periods. Those articles make for interesting reading, but the last article, number six, gives the most convincing evidence of the validity of this prophetic interpretation. Therefore, the text of the sixth article is printed below, so that we can have Andrews' reasoning behind his stated belief. Here then is the sixth and final article in the series entitled "THE GREAT WEEK OF TIME," subtitled "Events of the Seventh Thousand Years" and printed in the *Review and Herald* on August 21, 1883:

"In the first article of this series concerning the great week of human history, we showed that the day of Judgment was appointed as early as the creation of the angels, and that the creation of intelligent, accountable beings made such a day necessary even though neither angels nor men had ever sinned. God has seen it necessary that the fidelity of all intelligent beings should be tested during a certain period, and He has therefore appointed a day of examination and decision to arrive at the end of this period, in order that the result in the case of angels and of men may be declared, and after that decision, those who are found overcomers will never be in danger of falling into sin.

"It was not therefore inconsistent that the day of Judgment should be appointed for innocent beings; and it was highly proper that the time of that event should be indicated to our first parents in their innocence. We think that God chose the period of six days such as are known to man for the work of creation in order to represent to man that in six days of 1,000 years each, days such as are known to God, He would accomplish the period assigned to man before the Judgment. II Pet. 3:7, 8. That the great week of 7,000 years was indicated by the first week of time has been the judgment of many of the wisest and best of men for the period of more than two thousand years.

"The law of Moses was designed to represent the good things to come through Christ in the same manner that a shadow represents the tree by which it is cast. Heb. 10:1. This was true in a special sense of the three festivals, the passover, the pentecost, and the feast of tabernacles, and of the seven annual sabbaths connected with these feasts, and of the twelve or thirteen new moons of each year, and of the sabbath of the seventh year. These are enumerated in Col. 2:14-17, where the Greek word for sabbath is plural, and all the things mentioned are said to be the shadow of things to come. They are ordained in Lev. 23:4-8, 15-21, 24, 27-43; 25:1-5; Num. 10:10. They are distinguished from the Sabbath of the Lord in Lev. 23:38; for the Sabbath of the Lord only belongs to the moral law (Ex. 20:8-11), and it points backward to the creation and not forward to the renewing of the earth, and it will be an eternal memorial of the Creator in the new earth. Isa. 66:22, 23.

"The week of years in which, after the land had been cultivated six years, it was to remain without cultivation the seventh (Lev. 25:1-7), is certainly a type of the great week of 7,000 years, in which after the earth has been cultivated by its inhabitants during 6,000 years, it will remain uncultivated and desolate during the seventh period of 1,000 years while the Judgment takes place. But this is not all. After seven of these weeks of years came the year of jubilee. Lev. 25:8-10. In this year liberty was proclaimed throughout all the land to all its inhabitants, and every man returned to his own inheritance. This signifies that after the great

Sabbath, during which the earth will remain uncultivated for 1,000 years, the great week of 7,000 years being finished, the curse will cease, after having consumed the earth with all who are wicked. Then the earth will be created anew by the power of God, and all the just will return to their inheritance in the new earth, and never know sin nor sorrow any more.

"The seventh period of 1,000 years commences with the resurrection of the martyrs, and of all those who have not worshiped the beast nor his image. Rev. 20:4. This period terminates at the resurrection of the unjust. Rev. 20:5. As the dead in Christ are to be raised at the second coming of Christ (I Cor. 15:23, 51, 52; 1 Thess. 4:16, 17), we know that this period of 1,000 years will commence at the sound of the last trumpet. Peter seems to assign the period of 1,000 years to the day of Judgment (II Pet. 3:7, 8), and John expressly assigns this period to that grand event. Rev. 20:4.

"At the commencement of the 1,000 years our Lord will descend from Heaven with power and great glory, with the voice of the archangel, and with the trump of God. Matt. 24:30, 31; I Thess. 4:16, 17. The saints, whether living or dead, will be changed to immortality in a moment and caught up to meet the Lord in the air. I Cor. 15:51-55; Heb. 11:39-40; Phil. 3:20, 21. The Saviour will take them to the New Jerusalem, the house of His Father, where He has prepared a place for each of them. John 14:1-3; Rev. 7:9-17; 19:1-9. Here they will sit down with Christ on thrones of judgment to examine the books with respect to the wicked angels and wicked men. Rev. 20:4; I Cor. 4:5; 6:1-7; Dan. 7:22. The saints will not decide the question whether those whom they judge shall be saved or lost, for this was decided already when Christ separated the just from the unjust at the sound of the trumpet. Their work will be to examine the books, that the measure of every man's guilt may appear, for God will reward all men according to their works. Rom. 2:5-8; Matt. 16:27.

"At the commencement of the 1,000 years will occur the events of the seventh plague. Rev. 16:17-21. In the battle of the great day the slain of the Lord will be from one end of the earth to the other. Jer. 25:30-38; Rev. 19:11-21. The great earthquake will turn the earth upside down, and the great hailstones will complete the destruction of the sinners then living upon the earth. Isa. 24:18-23; Rev. 16:18-21; Isa. 28:17; Job 38:22, 23; Ps. 46:1-3. The earth will become without form and void, as it was at the commencement, when God called it the abyss. Compare Jer.

4:23-25; Gen. 1:1, 2; Rev. 20:1-3. The binding of Satan at the commencement of the 1,000 years is by the destruction of his subjects and he will then be confined to the ruined earth as his prison. When the high priest finished his work for the people of God in the earthly sanctuary he put their sins upon the head of the scapegoat. Lev. 16:7-10, 25-22. This represents the case of Satan when he shall be confined in the desolate earth after Christ has finished His work as High Priest.

"Some time before the 1,000 years terminates, the holy city will descend upon a place prepared for it upon the earth; for at the end of that period the wicked dead come forth from their graves, and Satan, being loosed out of his prison, goes out to deceive them and to induce them to make a final assault upon the city of God. Rev. 20:5, 7-9. When they are thus brought into the presence of Christ, the dreadful sentence, 'Depart from me, ye cursed, into everlasting fire, prepared for the devil and his angels,' will then be pronounced upon them. Matt. 25:41. Then the fire from God out of heaven will fall upon them to devour them, and they will receive their punishment in the presence of the Lamb and the holy angels. Rev. 20:9; 14:10. The earth will become a great lake of fire, and will be wholly melted. Rev. 20:14, 15; II Pet. 3:7-13; Mal. 4:1-3. The second death will consume the wicked, and the new heaven and the new earth will be created, in which the just will dwell eternally, and God will be all and in all. Rev. 21:1, etc; II Cor. 15:28."

(Signed) J. N. A.

CHAPTER 14

SEVEN PRINCIPLES FOR UNDERSTANDING BIBLICAL CHRONOLOGY

"An important first step in seeking to establish a reliable biblical chronology is to formulate some guiding principles or testing standards. The following requirements are suggested and evaluated.

1. "The Bible, as it was originally given, is a completely reliable historical source for the chronological data, that is consistent with itself. Our part is always to ask the Bible what it means and not to tell it what it should have said. Accordingly, we should seek to discover the Bible's own chronological system and not impose upon it our preconceived standards and ideas. This involves due recognition of the different calendars and methods of reckoning time used at different periods, and

the particular system used at any point must be determined by the prevailing history and the workability of the data in the over-all plan. We should never change revealed facts so as to give an appearance of harmony. The Scriptures themselves must furnish the clues that resolve the seeming contradictions we find. And further, the more uniform, the more straightforward, and the more simple our explanations of the Scriptural facts in attempting to reveal their essential harmony, the more likely we will be following a true course.

"This means that a difference should be made between generalized time statements, such as that in Acts 13:20, and specific ones, such as that in I Kings 6:1, with the latter commanding preference. Similarly, a difference must be made between genealogies giving specific time data, such as those given in Genesis 5 and 11, and genealogies with no time data and which have obviously been arranged into a symbolic pattern, such as the 14 plus 14 plus 14 generations of Matthew 1:17. In view of the purpose of Bible Chronology, stated above, we should also be careful not to interpret all data given in round numbers as inexact time statements.

2. "Large periods are more reliable than many small ones in building a chronological sequence. In working on the difficult period of the Kings of Judah and Israel, chronologists usually concentrate on the small steps involving each king's reign—with widely conflicting results. As necessary and as laudable as this approach may be, it has this limitation: with each step being handled the probability of error is increased due to the possibility of incorrectly interpreting the Biblical data. Therefore attempts to establish twenty small steps in a chronological sequence are necessarily frought with twenty times as much possibility of error due to misinterpretation of the data, as could be encountered if the whole period could be resolved in one step. To concentrate, for example, on individual ages between Abram and the Exodus, leads nowhere. But if we are able to fix the commencement of the 400 and 430-year periods with certainty, then, according to Exodus 12:40, 41, we have an exact date for the Exodus in terms of Abram and Creation, the intermediate problems notwithstanding. Moreover, the establishment of a large period of time with reasonable accuracy, should help resolve the problems attending the intermediate steps.

3. "Fulfilled prophecy provides reliable data for chronology. This depends upon a correct interpretation of prophecy, with special attention

given to the period involved and its beginning and end. Involved here are such periods as the 400 years of Genesis 15:13, the 70 years of II Chronicles 36:21, and the 2,300 and 490 years of Daniel 8:14 and 9:24-27. Thus prophecy depends on chronology and chronology draws on prophecy in their interdependent relationship.

4. "The more correct a chronological outline, the more data it should be able to harmonize over the broadest period of time. This naturally refers to time data, but also includes synchronous events, and textual problems. The more correct a scheme, the more likely it will bring to light significant patterns in sacred history, with typological implications. This proviso—over the broadest period of time—is necessary so that the profuse material of a short period, such as that of the Kings, should not exercise a disproportionate influence over the whole outline.

5. "A correct chronology must harmonize with the added light of the Spirit of Prophecy. Ellen White's visions of salvation history give an inspired authority to her chronological statements which cannot be lightly regarded by Adventists. Admittedly, most of these time statements speak in round numbers, and serve only as a general guide in building a chronology. They are qualified by terms such as 'nearly,' 'about,' 'more than,' almost,' etc. These statements are sometimes important, however, since 'more than' a given number of years cannot mean 'less than' that period, and 'nearly' a given number of years cannot mean 'more than' that period of time. Then there are a few seemingly casual and yet very specific statements which have importance far beyond their unpretentious appearance. Instead of closing our eyes to these statements, or wishing they had never been written, or trying to explain them away and follow the dull sparks of man's kindling—as some of us do—we should rather set ourselves to discover light in God's light, and much of the profound scholarly darkness in this area of research would give way to glorious light.

6. "A sound sacred chronology must be linked to an absolute date in secular chronology. Here, of course, we enter contested terrain. So often have so-called 'facts of history that disprove the Bible' been revised, and the Bible's reliability been confirmed, that we all need to be extremely cautious. Notwithstanding claims that Egyptian chronology has been established by eclipses, very recent research has cast serious doubts on its 'absolute' dates. Although most Egyptologists are naturally reticent to

give up a system which they have build up so laboriously over the past 150 years, there is convincing evidence that failure to allow sufficient overlapping of dynasties has, together with a number of other factors, resulted in an erroneously elongated chronology. While Assyrian chronology rests on a firmer foundation than Egyptian chronology, let us take warning and stay on the ultra-safe side. Too often scholars demand the most stringent proof for every Bible statement, while accepting statements from ancient pagan sources without question.

"A cuneiform clay tablet in the Berlin Museum, which records numerous astronomical observations of the sun, moon and planets, made during the 37th year of Nebuchadnezzar's reign, has enabled astronomers to establish to the very day that this is the year of April 22, 568, to April 11, 567 BC. With the help of the thousands of dated cuneiform business records of the time, it is possible to identify 605 BC as the year of Nebuchadnezzar's first conquest of Jerusalem, which was also his accession year, and 'the third year' of Jehoiakim, king of Judah (Dan. 1:1, 2). The following year, 604 BC, ('after' the first captivity, Jer. 24;1), is identified by Jeremiah (25:1, 3) as the fourth of Jehoiakim, and as Nebuchadnezzar's first. This synchronism is the most reliable of all links between biblical and secular chronology. Accordingly, the writer makes no apology for accepting the year 605 BC (when the first Jewish exiles were taken by Nebuchadnezzar) as the earliest date on which complete agreement is reached between sacred and secular chronology. The profuse and exact data from both biblical and secular history for this period, make this a safe point at which to reconcile both systems without compromising either. However, where real differences exist between the facts of sacred and secular chronology, the Bible must be accepted as final authority. It is amazing how ingeniously some scholars will rationalize the biblical information to reconcile it with Assyrian chronology, as if the latter were the absolute standard of truth. If their considerable genius were used as zealously in the reverse direction they might well surprise themselves and others with the discovery that the fallible Assyrian system can be made to agree with God's Word."

7. "A correct sacred chronology need not resolve every last problem attending the biblical data. This is particularly true of the intermediate steps in the periods of the Judges and the Kings of Judah and Israel. Problems may arise and remain because of differing interpretations of the data within these periods, without disrupting the larger chronological

sequence. Having done our best, we should be willing to admit that some chronological problems may be more than we can resolve with our present resources, and will have to be explained by the Master Teacher Himself in the Higher School hereafter." (Lello, pp. 5, 6)

CHAPTER 16

An explicit explanation of type and antitype parallel is given in *Christ's Object Lessons*, p. 34. "Christ's mission was not understood by the people of His time. The manner of His coming was not in accordance with their expectations. The Lord Jesus was the foundation of the whole Jewish economy. Its imposing services were of divine appointment. They were designed to teach the people that at the appointed time One would come to whom those ceremonies pointed. But the Jews had exalted the forms and ceremonies and had lost sight of their object. The traditions, maxims, and enactments of men hid from them the lessons which God intended to convey. These maxims and traditions became an obstacle to their understanding and practice of true religion. And when the Reality came, in the person of Christ, they did not recognize in Him the fulfillment of all their types, the substance of all their shadows. They rejected the antitype, and clung to their types and useless ceremonies."

CHAPTER 18

One of the things that wisdom and knowledge offer succeeding generations is the opportunity to learn from the mistakes of the past. "Upon us is shining the accumulated light of past ages. The record of Israel's forgetfulness has been preserved for our enlightenment. In this age God has set His hand to gather unto Himself a people from every nation, kindred, and tongue. In the advent movement He has wrought for His heritage, even as He wrought for the Israelites in leading them from Egypt. In the great disappointment of 1844 the faith of His people was tested as was that of the Hebrews at the Red Sea. Had the Adventists in the early days still trusted to the guiding Hand that had been with them in their past experience, they would have seen the salvation of God. If all who had labored unitedly in the work of 1844 had received the third angel's message and proclaimed it in the power of the Holy Spirit, the

Lord would have wrought mightily with their efforts. A flood of light would have been shed upon the world. Years ago the inhabitants of the earth would have been warned, the closing work would have been completed, and Christ would have come for the redemption of His people." (*Testimonies for the Church*, vol. 8, p. 115)

To purchase additional copies of
Even at the Door
Call your local ABC at 1-800-765-6955
Or contact the author by writing to:
      Omega Productions
      P.O. Box 600
      Fulton, MD 20759

Or Fax inquiries to: (Fax only) (301) 680-8953

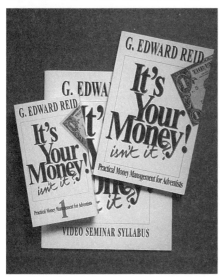